CRITICAL AND CREATIVE THINKING

Third Edition

Edited by Debra L. Welkley and Santos Torres, Jr.

cognella® | ACADEMIC PUBLISHING

Bassim Hamadeh, CEO and Publisher
Kassie Graves, Director of Acquisitions and Sales
Jamie Giganti, Senior Managing Editor
Jess Estrella, Senior Graphic Designer
Carrie Montoya, Manager, Revisions and Author Care
Natalie Lakosil, Licensing Manager
Kaela Martin, Associate Editor
Abbey Hastings, Associate Production Editor
Sue Murray, Interior Designer

Cover art by Santos Torres, Jr.

Printed in the United States of America

ISBN: 978-1-5165-2187-6 (pbk) / 978-1-5165-2188-3 (br)

This is dedicated to my family and friends. You know who you are, and I am glad you are who you are.

~ Santos Torres, Jr.

This is dedicated to the numerous teachers throughout my journey, which include those with that title as well as all of my students throughout the years..

~ Debra L. Welkley

ൠ CONTENTS ☙

SECTION 3: CRITICAL AND CREATIVE THINKING RESOURCES

ᘓ Preface ᘓ

The subject of this book is critical and creative thinking. Its scope is the identification of strategic techniques to enhance one's thinking. Our aim is to share
important ideas about teaching and learning critical and creative thinking.

After review of the second edition of the book, we looked at ways to improve the
quality of its delivery so that it might better align with current topics as well as critical and
creative thinking efforts in the classroom. This approach was informed by our understanding of the Quality Matters (QM) Rubric for Higher Education (Refer to https://www.
qualitymatters.org/). While QM aims to support well-conceived and well-designed online
or hybrid courses, we believe the focus on alignment and clarity was transferable in many
ways to the approach in this text. In this third edition of the book, five articles in the last
edition were omitted and five new articles were added to broaden the scope of topics
covered. Among those added are some specific essays that relate to immigration, Moylan's
(2014) "The One Who Left" and Bowie's (2014) "In Search of Country: How Chasing the
American Dream Can Become a Nightmare." In turn we have updated the introduction
pieces to each topical section. Additionally, we have added some handouts and information
in **Section 3: Critical and Creative Thinking Resources**. Our hope is that these changes
will enhance the reader's learning, exploration, and application of critical and creative
thinking.

We wrote this book to help us teach the subject in our own classes. It is informed by
our experiences and the collective wisdom of our colleagues and students alike. We have
titled the first chapter "Now Begins the Adventure" because we think of the book as an
important intellectual journey. We hope that it serves as a useful resource to others and
would greatly value your thoughts.

Buy the ticket, take the ride.
~ Hunter S. Thompson

❧ Section 1 ❧

Getting Started

NOW BEGINS THE ADVENTURE

Teaching is only demonstrating that it is possible. Learning is making it possible for yourself.

— Paulo Coelho

As authors beginning the initial steps for this book, we kept returning to one central question: When teaching critical and creative thinking in a finite amount of time, such as a single term or semester, what is important to teach? This, then, became the guiding light as we began anew a journey into critical and creative thinking, exploring the primary aspects of what needs to be addressed as we teach (and learn) about *critical and creative thinking*.

One of the first things to explore is what critical and creative thinking is. We ask the reader to consider what you believe is meant by this term. How do you think it should be defined? How, in your opinion, does the

> What an astonishing thing a book is. It's a flat object made from a tree with flexible parts on which are imprinted lots of funny dark squiggles. But one glance at it and you're inside the mind of another person, maybe somebody dead for thousands of years. Across the millennia, an author is speaking clearly and silently inside your head, directly to you. Writing is perhaps the greatest of human inventions, binding together people who never knew each other, citizens of distant epochs. Books break the shackles of time. A book is proof that humans are capable of working magic.
>
> —Carl Sagan

expression *critical thinking* affect common everyday interactions, if at all? We believe, depending on context, i.e., home, work, or school, critical thinking means different things. Then when we add creative to the concept, we move into another dimension of thinking. We believe that starting at this point of exploration, this book will be made more understandable and, hopefully, more accessible to a broader audience.

WHAT IS CRITICAL AND CREATIVE THINKING?

Before we offer what we have developed as the meaning of the expression *critical and creative thinking*, we thought we would share with the reader various ways other scholars and researchers have defined the term *critical thinking*. When the average person is faced with defining critical thinking, they often arrive at the notion that critical thinking is just good, old-fashioned common sense. At times a definition is given that "Critical thinking is to clearly examine the information being considered." A key aspect of this element is "clearly." Therefore, the listener will want to probe the writer/speaker on what they mean by "clearly."

? What does critical thinking mean to you?

Additionally, one might ask if this basic definition is really enough to demonstrate to someone "what does 'critical thinking' mean," especially in light of the fact that we have many different critical thinking courses that are required as a general education requirement in state universities in California. The reader should also ask, why has this been made a requirement? Perhaps because it is held as important. Before reading definitions from the literature, take a moment to write out your ideas on what you think is the meaning of *critical and creative thinking*.

According to Cooper and Patton (2007), the term *critical* needs to be examined when defining critical thinking. They write that:

> the term critical means censorious or faultfinding, but it comes to us from the Greek *kriticos* and Latin *criticus*, meaning able to discern or separate. It is this sense of critical that we have in mind—discerning or discriminating thought characterized by careful analysis and judgment. (p. 5)

The founders of the *Foundation for Critical Thinking*, Dr. Richard Paul and Dr. Linda Elder, believe critical thinking "is a process by which the thinker improves the quality of his or her thinking by skillfully taking charge of the structures inherent in thinking and imposing intellectual standards upon them" (2004, p. 1). Paul and Elder go on to write that as a result of engaging in this process, one will become a "well cultivated thinker." Finally, they state "critical thinking is, in short, self-directed, self-disciplined, self-monitored, and self-corrective thinking" (2004, p. 1). With this in mind, they indicate that there are *standards* and *elements* (see Section 3 for a discussion) of excellence that we can use as we engage ourselves in the process of critical thinking along with the consideration of developing eight *intellectual traits* that will help us master the standards and elements. The following list identifies the traits and what the authors consider central to the characteristics

1. **Intellectual Humility**: recognizing that one should not claim more than one actually knows
2. **Intellectual Courage**: having the courage to be true to our own thinking
3. **Intellectual Empathy**: having the ability to reconstruct accurately the viewpoints and reasoning of others and to reason from premises, assumptions, and ideas other than our own
4. **Intellectual Autonomy**: learning to think for oneself, to question when it is rational to question, to believe when it is rational to believe, and to conform when it is rational to conform
5. **Intellectual Integrity**: holding oneself to the same rigorous standards of evidence and proof to which one holds one's antagonists
6. **Intellectual Perseverance**: sensing the need to struggle with confusion and unsettled questions over an extended period of time to achieve deeper understanding or insight
7. **Confidence in Reason**: encouraging people to come to their own conclusions by developing their own rational faculties
8. **Fair-mindedness**: having a consciousness of the need to treat all viewpoints alike, without reference to one's own feelings or interests (adapted from Paul & Elder, 2014)

Along with Paul and Elder, we believe critical and creative thinkers seek to develop, fine tune, and perfect these traits. Here, we review just three of these traits to make them concrete and doable. For example, when in a meeting with a group of people and you have reached the limits of what you know about the topic under consideration, actively seeking input from the others or helping to create a safe space where opinion seeking is a valued part of the process reflects intellectual humility. To demonstrate intellectual courage, generate a list of talking points and outcomes you think will occur, then notate what does occur and compare the information. Consider what actually transpired. Where they differ, actively challenge the assumption that your expectation(s) is the right point of view. Finally, let's take up the trait of fair-mindedness. What does this look like in terms of action steps? One step is before giving your opinion, you ask the view of another. This involves dialoguing about the merits of the other's view as well as one's own, which is achieved by listening and reflecting what one hears to the speaker versus deciding which one has the most value or persuasiveness. Therefore, we encourage the reader to consider ways they can exercise the other traits as they apply the elements and standards of critical and creative thinking.

Writer and professor Gerald Nosich provides several definitions of critical thinking from his review of the literature. In addition to Paul and Elder's definition provided previously, he reviews two other definitions. First, Robert Ennis's classic definition, "Critical thinking is reasonable, reflective thinking that is focused on deciding what to believe or do" (2005, p. 2). Next, Matthew Lipman's "Critical thinking is skillful, responsible thinking that is conducive to good judgment because it is sensitive to context, relies on criteria, and is self-correcting" (p. 2). Nosich distills from these definitions that "critical thinking is reflective," "critical thinking involves standards," "critical thinking is authentic," and "critical thinking involves being reasonable" (pp. 3–4).

Nosich states critical thinking "involves thinking about your thinking" (p. 3); this encourages us to examine what we already believe we know (to be *reflective*). To further clarify, if the topic of immigration comes up in class, one is likely to have their own ideas and have drawn their own conclusions regarding the issue. This in and of itself is not critical thinking. Rather, we should ask where did these views come from? What evidence do we have to support our views? What are other *points of view*? These questions help us to think about our thinking.

Nosich (2005) offers a set of standards to guide our understanding on what demonstrates critical thinking. He reasons that *accuracy*, *relevance*, and *depth* are standards that illustrate "reasonableness" when stating one's opinion or view.

Being authentic in our reasoning means addressing real problems and questions. While hypothetical problems, brain teasers, and the like help us practice reasoning and logic skills, Nosich (2005) argues that "critical thinking comes into play only when you address real problems and questions rather than artificial ones" (p. 4). He also states there are no "sure-fire rules of reasoning" but rather guidelines. This is because there is nothing to guarantee *how* we have examined and considered a particular problem is right or correct.

Finally, Nosich (2005) states that there are three parts to critical thinking:

1. Asking questions
2. Answering questions through reason
3. Believing the results of the reasoning

Critical thinking ...
- Is reflective
- Involves standards
- Is authentic
- Involves being reasonable

When *asking questions*, we do not just pose questions to pose them, but ponder what needs to be asked in order to better understand and go to the heart of the matter. It is important to think about what is relevant and needs to be examined in order to garner accurate information and provide depth to our understanding. Learning how to cultivate these kinds of questions serves as a central tool in critical and creative thinking.

Using *reason to answer questions* may include reformulating the question. For instance, when a group of students work on developing an argument to support the position "Roe v. Wade should not be overturned," they may want to think about abortion, but they will also need to ask why some people want Roe v. Wade to be overturned. Is the question only about abortion or are there other facets to be considered as the argument is developed? They may also want to ponder what the implications are if it were to be overturned and then move back to the initial question and how they can support it. Figuring out what information or evidence is relevant and accurate versus relying on assumption is one way to "reason it out."

Believing the results of our reasoning is an important aspect of thinking, according to Nosich (2005). He provides some indicators of when people do not believe the results of their reasoning:

1. Strong emotions arise against the result or reasons
2. Believe contradictory things
3. Unable to provide good reasons for a strong belief that is already held
4. Actions do not follow the reasons one provides

We agree that the preceding indicators create barriers to our critical and creative thinking process. Yet the more we are willing to explore our zones of discomfort and accept a new position, when the reasoning warrants it, we are less impacted by these barriers. M. Neil Browne and Stuart M. Keeley (2007), in *Asking the Right Questions: A Guide to Critical Thinking,* indicate "Thinking carefully is always an unfinished project. ... Critical questions provide a stimulus and direction for critical thinking; they move us forward toward a continual, ongoing search for better opinions, decisions, or judgments" (p. 2). These authors also identify:

1. Awareness of a set of interrelated critical questions
2. Ability to ask and answer critical questions at appropriate times
3. Desire to actively use the critical questions

When we ask students what they believe critical thinking is, a common response we receive is "critical thinking is being able to understand all sides of an issue while not being swayed by fallacies or misinformation." Earlier we asked the reader to write an answer to

"What does critical thinking mean to you?" Based on the foregoing discussion, how would you modify that definition?

IDENTIFYING THE ARGUMENT

The next area that is important to this process is to know the parts of an argument and their significance. All too often we jump into an analysis or react to material before first examining the pieces: where they are, what they are, and if they are all present.

It is important to note that when using the term *argument*, we are not referring to a disagreement between two or more people; rather, this refers to how to structure one's position on an issue. Simply put, the elements of an argument as described here are:

1. an **issue** (more specific than a topic),
2. a **conclusion** (sometimes referred to as a *claim* or *position*), and
3. **reasons** (many times referred to as *premises*).

If a speaker/author presents only their stance on an issue yet does not provide any evidence or reasons to support the position, then they have merely made a *statement,* not provided an *argument.* All three elements need to be present to refer to the position as an argument. Identifying these elements helps us lay the foundation for our evaluation and assessment of the information.

First we identify the **issue**, which should not be confused with *topics. Topics* are much more general (ideas or subjects) and *issues* are specific elements or questions relative to the topic. As a means of identifying the issue, when you begin reading an article or book, you may want to identify the overall topic and then ask yourself what specific aspect of the topic the author(s) is addressing (e.g., a **topic** might be health care and the **issue** might be an author who is addressing why the United States should not adopt a universal health care program). Practice this by going to one or two of the articles included in this book and first identify the topic (the general and broad area to be addressed) and then ask yourself what it is about that overall topic that the author seems to be exploring or addressing. You should be able to identify this component of the argument by looking at the article title and reading the first couple of paragraphs.

Structure of Argument

- Issue
- Conclusion
- Reasons

When identifying the second part of an argument, the **conclusion**, there are many "clues" that can be used to help ensure you have found what the author is attempting to state or prove. Remember this is a *statement,* **not** *a section* of the article or book, which gives the reader an indication of the author's position on the issue that is being addressed. It may or may not be clear. You will assess clarity, as well as quality and depth, when you evaluate the components of the argument (this is addressed later in the text). Initially, you must identify the elements of the argument so that we are better able to clearly focus on the author's conclusion and reasoning as opposed to what we *want* or *expect* because of our own biases or preconceived notions.

Sherry Diestler (2009) provides some pointers for identifying the author's conclusion:

1. Find the issue and ask what position the writer/speaker is taking on the issue.
2. Look at the beginning or ending [ending is preferred] of [the passage]; … the conclusion is often found in either of these places.
3. Look for conclusion indicator words: *therefore, so, thus, hence.* Also, look for indicator phrases: *My point is, What I am saying, What I believe is.* Some indicator words and phrases are selected to imply that the conclusion drawn is the right one. These include *obviously, it is evident, there is no doubt* (or *question*) *that, certainly,* and *of course.*
4. Ask yourself, "What is being claimed by this writer/speaker?"
5. Look at the title of an essay; sometimes the conclusion is contained within the title. For example, an essay might be titled "Why I Believe Vitamins Are Good Health." [This may be the author's conclusion, but be sure to look for a specific statement in the article.]

Additionally, Browne and Keeley (2010) offer pointers to help find conclusions. These are not intended to be used in lock-step fashion. Keep in mind these pointers are designed to aid in identifying the author's conclusion and not simply a conclusion arrived at by the reader.

Clue No. 1: Ask what the issue is. The conclusion is usually a response to an issue. Remember, looking at the title and first few paragraphs is a good technique for identifying the issue.

Clue No. 2: Look in likely locations. Conclusions tend to occupy certain locations. The first two places are the beginning and the end. [The authors of this text highly recommend that readers **check the end first** to get yourself out of your normal routine in looking for this information.] One should be able to find the conclusion statement without reading the entire article. What makes it a conclusion statement is not that it *summarizes* the article; although that may end up being true, it is *not a qualifier* for being the conclusion statement.

Clue No. 3: Look for indicator words. The conclusion will frequently be preceded by indicator words that announce a conclusion is coming. A list of such words includes:

but	proves that
consequently	shows that
hence	so
indicates that	suggests that
in fact	the most obvious explanation
in short	the point I'm trying to make is
it follows that	therefore
it is highly probably that	the truth of the matter is
it should be clear that	thus
point to the conclusion that	we may deduce that

Clue No. 4: Remember what a conclusion is not. Conclusions will not be any of the following: examples, statistics, definitions, background information, or evidence.

Clue No. 5: Ask the question, "and therefore?"

(Adapted from Browne & Keeley, 2010, pp. 23–24)

As you can see, Diestler's as well as Browne and Keeley's pointers for locating the conclusion statement are very similar. You may already feel that you have no difficulties identifying the conclusion in an article. Great—once you have identified it, apply these pointers to what you have identified to see how they indeed work and are able to be applied.

The last component of an argument consists of the ***reasons.*** By identifying the reasons, we are able to "reason things out" and understand the extent to which the reasons support the conclusion. An argument can be formed with only one reason in conjunction with the conclusion and issue. When identifying reasons in a discussion, it is important to understand that "reasons provide answers for our human curiosity about why someone makes a particular decision or holds a particular opinion" (Browne & Keeley, 2010, p. 28). They are "beliefs, evidence, metaphors, analogies, and other statements offered to support or justify the conclusion" (p. 28). After identifying the conclusion statement, you can move to finding the ***reasons*** by asking yourself "Why?" relative to that conclusion statement. Therefore, posing the question "Why does this writer/speaker believe their conclusion?" can assist in finding the reasons. "You cannot determine the worth of a conclusion until you identify the reasons" (p. 29).

Any idea that is used to support an author's conclusion is a reason, even when you (as the reader) do not believe it provides good or adequate support. Remember, we are not assessing or evaluating, but identifying. Asking "why does the writer believe the conclusion?" helps identify their reasons.

For many critical thinkers, this part of identification of the argument is the most challenging. Remember to identify the conclusion first, as that will help you find what the author uses to support their claim. Another strategy is to apply the "reason formula" (see below). For example, theThe reader should fill in what they believe the conclusion is where it states "conclusion statement" (such as, *marijuana should be legalized in the United States*), then identify statements that can fill in the blank (such as, *marijuana is no more harmful to our health than cigarettes are*) where it states "because (of)."

_____ because (of) _____.	
Conclusion statement	*Reason(s)*

Additionally, there are some indicators that may assist in locating reason statements. A list of expressions that may serve as indicators follows:

as a result of	for the reason that
because of the fact that	in view of
is supported by	because the evidence is
studies show	

(Adapted from Browne & Keeley, 2010, pp. 31)

These are helpful in locating reason statements and creating one's own reason statements, as well as testing what you believe you have identified as an author's reason(s). Remember these are all tools to add to your critical and creative thinking repertoire. Practice them, try them out, and discover how they can add to what you have already incorporated into your thinking.

IMAGE CREDIT

Fig. 1.1: Copyright © Depositphotos/alphaspirit.

CS two SO

VALUES, LANGUAGE, AND ASSUMPTIONS

Did you ever stop to think, and forget to start again?

— Winnie the Pooh

When we consider an argument, we locate the elements of the argument. Before we move to assessing how well these pieces fit together, how the reasons support the conclusion, the clarity of the information provided, and the quality of the information offered, it is important to consider the **values** and use of **language** and/or *assumptions* presented by the author. As a component of culture, understanding our personal and cultural values is important. Values are defined as those "ideals, standards, and principles [one] believe[s] are important and consider worthy" (Diestler, 2009, p. 32). They operate as standards that we have about what is good/bad, acceptable/unacceptable, and right/wrong. In sociology, the term *culture* is defined as a group of people's way of life. This includes tangible items (e.g., cell phones, automobiles, houses, schools, hospitals, jewelry) as well as intangibles (e.g., patriotism, family, education, health care). Values, gestures/symbols, language, and norms (expected patterns of behavior) are all a part of the intangible (nonmaterial) aspects of a culture. A culture's norms, language, laws, and policies are influenced by the adopted values. Therefore, individuals are also impacted by what they believe is okay or not okay and how this

Why English Is Hard to Learn

We'll begin with box; plural is boxes, but the plural of ox is oxen, not oxes. One fowl is a goose, and two are called geese, yet the plural of moose is never called meese.

You may find a lone mouse or a house full of mice; but the plural of house is houses, not hice. The plural of man is men, but the plural of pan is never pen.

If I speak of a foot, and you show me two feet, and I give you a book, would a pair be a beek? If one is a tooth and whole set are teeth, why shouldn't two booths be called beeth?

If the singular's this and the plural is these, should the plural of kiss be ever called kees?

We speak of a brother and also of brethren, but though we say mother, we never say methren. Then the masculine pronouns are he, his, and him; but imagine the feminine she, shis, and shim!

— ANONYMOUS

influences their overall sense of right and wrong. Many differences of opinion or disagreements occur because of strongly held values. The truth is that those who maintain opposing sides of an argument may hold similar values, but due to the meaning of those values and how they believe one should evidence (or act upon) those values, they will have very different positions on an issue.

Language and words are taken for granted as we communicate in our society. We assume people speaking the same language attribute the same meanings to words or that they construct their ideas in the same way we do. However, many misunderstandings occur precisely due to these assumptions. When we begin to consider what skills and tools are needed when considering information, arguments, and decision making, it becomes very apparent that language matters.

Sociologically speaking, *symbol* is an important cultural concept to understand. Symbol is defined as a sign with meaning. This includes tangible things such as a sign, a red octagon on a post at an intersection with the word STOP, to mean we must stop moving. Another form of symbol would be the intangible concept of family. As Diestler (2009) writes, "The meaning of words lies in people not, magically, in the words themselves. Misunderstandings of words and phrases can be clearly seen when people speak different languages" (p. 282). It is how we individually, and at times collectively, define and understand a word or idea (symbol) that gives it the meaning by which we then interact and act upon that communication. Additionally, language itself shapes our understanding of our reality or worldview. Language is another element of culture and is defined as a system of symbols that has been created for a group of people to transmit information. When we examine ideas or the argument that someone is putting forth, we need to ensure we have clarity relative not only to the ideas that are shared but also to the language used (the meaning of the words chosen to convey the message). "Language plays a crucial role in the development of many of our ideas" (McKay, 2000, p. 54). In light of this, we need to become comfortable with asking questions and developing an awareness and sensitivity to the meaning of words and language used when constructing our own arguments as well as interpreting the words and language of others.

The situation in which a word is being used is very important to understanding its meaning. The context and place in which something is used gives us an indication of its relevance. For instance, what is the difference or similarity between these words: "gum band," "rubber band," and "elastic"? Do you know what each is? For some, one or more of these words may have no meaning, especially because no context is being given. If someone wants to keep a collection of envelopes together and asks you to get them a "gum band," what would you go searching for? If an orthodontist indicates she is going to have you use "rubber bands" on your braces, will that make sense to you? While this is something very basic, one can see how confusion may result. Discerning whether our confusion relative to wording is due to our own frame of reference, or whether it would be useful for the writer to explain something to us, is a skill we can use when looking at the clarity of the information presented in an argument.

Additionally, words can impact "attitudes and emotional responses that may be related or unrelated to their cognitive content" (McKay, 2000, p. 57). Therefore, clarifying the *connotation* (personal, colloquial, or cultural meanings assigned to a word or phrase) and the *denotation* (dictionary definition) of key words/concepts is very important as we critically examine and then evaluate the speaker/author's message. In addition to assessing whether the key concepts are clearly defined, consider that the choice of certain words over others is often used to convey an attitude, which may slant our view on the issue. For instance, if someone is described as a "very trusting person," we get a different image in our head than if the same person is described as a "very gullible person." Eliciting different reactions in a reader can impact their evaluation of the material presented. "When a factual evaluation is important, a critical listener must get past that initial reaction and sort out the factual content from the expression of attitude" (McKay, 2000, p. 58).

Therefore, as you evaluate the information presented in an argument, consider what the words are conveying. What information is factual and presented in that manner? What words might be used to influence the reader? Are the key concepts (words that are very important to the issue, the conclusion, or reasonings, such as *reform* and *immigration* in a conversation about immigration reform) defined for the audience? This assists in the identification of assumptions in the author's information as well as helps to eliminate the readers' biases. Finally, asking ourselves these same questions when we construct an argument can assist in our provision of clarity and removal of bias where it does not belong.

A useful sociologic theory, the Sapir-Whorf Hypothesis, poses that "language both reflects and affects our view of reality" (Diestler, 2009, p. 283). This is not only referring to the meaning of words in a language but also to how the language is constructed (i.e., where nouns and verbs are placed in relationship to one another). The manner in which the language is created and works, as well as the definitions of the words within the context of the system in which they exist, impact how people who speak and write in that language think and interpret their world. "Our frames of reference, our unique windows on the world, are influenced by our culture, our expectations, personalities, values, experiences, ages, genders, and education" (Diestler, 2009, p. 284).

Assumptions may be considered basic truths that have been proved and re-proved so that they are universally accepted with little reservation. However, many assumptions are based on misinformation, obsolete data, or cultural traditions. Assumptions are "ideas we take for granted … [and] are often left out of a written or spoken argument" (Diestler, 2009, p. 29). Like opinions, assumptions should be tested. As a reminder of this, consider a famous 1936 poll, which reported that Alf Landon would beat Franklin Roosevelt in the presidential election. The pollsters called people listed in hundreds upon hundreds of telephone directories. These random calls to men and women, African Americans and whites, young and old, city dwellers and farmers, liberals and conservatives would, they believed, give them an accurate view of the electorate. But, their basic assumption was flawed. In the Depression, millions of people could not afford telephones. Lower-income voters, who tended to support Roosevelt's New Deal, were never called. Despite the pollsters' hard work, their research failed because of a false assumption.

So how do we go about identifying assumptions in an argument? Keep in mind, you are most interested in assumptions that impact the quality of the structure of an argument. Therefore, one should concentrate on the conclusion and reasons presented to ascertain if there are any assumptions in the argument. Assumptions may appear relative to what is taken for granted for you as the reader to see that the reason(s) supports the conclusion or unstated information that is needed in order for the reason to indeed be true.

One way to see if there are any assumptions is to identify the conclusion statement and the reason statements. Then look at each reason statement in relationship to the conclusion and assess if there is any "invisible glue" that is needed to connect that reason to the conclusion. Then as you go through the reading, see if the author addresses the initial assumption and how important that assumption is to the discussion. By doing this you are able to assess the clarity of the argument as well as begin laying a foundation for looking at the quality of the reasoning.

Browne and Keeley (2010) pose that one's task in finding assumptions is "to reconstruct the reasoning by filling in the missing links" (p. 64). Therefore, the critical thinker's task is to locate ideas that help the writer/speaker's reasoning make sense. Understanding the assumptions that may be prevalent in an argument can many times help us, as readers, understand the author's point of view (even when we still may not agree with it). There are two basic types of assumptions: *value assumptions* and *descriptive assumptions*. A value assumption is a "taken-for-granted belief about the relative desirability of certain competing values" (Browne & Keeley, 2010, p. 56). Some typical value conflicts include loyalty vs. honesty, competition vs. cooperation, freedom of press/speech vs. national security, equality vs. individualism, and rationality vs. spontaneity. Many times, this includes beliefs about how the world should be, not necessarily how it is. Can you think of any current value conflicts that are evident in social issues in the media today?

On the other hand, descriptive assumptions are beliefs one has about how the world is. Sometimes these are also referred to as "reality assumptions." For instance, many believe that the "normal family" in the 1950s looked similar to the Cleaver family on *Leave It to Beaver*: a man and a woman who were married with a couple of children, the father worked outside the home, the family owned a home, and everyone operated together to maintain the happiness of the family. Further, the belief was that this family constellation contributed to family happiness and overall well-being. Therefore, many assume that if our society were to return to family configurations that existed in the 1950s, we would not have the degree of family and child problems that exists today (domestic violence, behavioral problems in schools, gang violence, etc.).

Browne and Keeley (2010) offer a set of strategies to assist in locating both value and descriptive assumptions:

Clues for Identifying Value Assumptions

- Investigate the author's background.
- Ask, "Why do the consequences of the author's position seem so important to the author?"
- Search for similar controversies to see if there are some analogous assumptions.
- Use reverse role-playing (take a position opposite to the author's position and identify which values are important).
- Look for common value conflicts, such as individual responsibility versus community responsibility.

Clues for Identifying Descriptive Assumptions

- Think about the gap between the conclusion and reasons.
- Look for ideas that support the reasons (a reason may be presented with no explicit support).
- Identify with the writer/speaker (how you can defend the conclusion).

- Identify with the opposition (by doing so you may see what is left unstated).
- Recognize the potential existence of other means of attaining the advantages referred to in the reasons.

(Adapted from Browne & Keeley, pp. 60 & 67)

Locating hidden and debatable missing connections will be of assistance as you evaluate the reasoning of the argument. Acknowledging assumptions where possible to provide clarity for the consumer of information helps provide logic while giving supportive evidence and information for the conclusion and for the audience to accept the argument.

As we move beyond reflecting on the values, language, and assumptions in an argument, attempting to assess and evaluate the reasoning of an argument entails the application of several modes of reasoning as well as the consideration of any fallacies that might be included in the argument. A central aspect of this is our attempt to discern the "truth" of the information presented. There are many ideas that are enveloped into this attempt to discover truth, such as the logic of the argument and the factualness of the information.

Creative and critical thinking requires that one does not simply identify and declare that a problem exists, but it also requires identifying potential solutions and strategies for achieving them. In other words, if we can think ourselves into a problem, then we should be able to think our way out of it.

What happens when an individual decides or expresses the view that their opinion/observation constitutes the correct interpretation or understanding on a given problem or issue? Quite often we present information or facts, or an assemblage of data, on a given topic—let us say, on *rates of welfare dependency across the last three generations in the United States*—in a course we are teaching. Invariably someone in the class will, after reflecting on these data, comment on how a family member of a friend of theirs has always lived on welfare and does so a quality of life the rest of us are left to envy.

We often find that we must refrain from redirecting the conversation into the exploration of concepts such as stereotyping, assumptive thinking, putting personal observation before accumulated wisdom, and so forth. Typically, if we push our way into such a diversion, we feel that we are creating a sense of chastisement and negative judgment toward the student and not availing ourselves of the chance to use what the student thinks to enrich the situation or teachable moment. Instead, we reframe the situation so that we can experience such comments as an indication of at least a passing interest in the topic under consideration.

Then, usually, something interesting happens. The speaker will share a generalization based on their personal observation or experience, such as, "most people on welfare are cheats and lay-abouts." The student has just opened the door to talk about some aspect of critical and creative thinking framed by something they thought and said. The ensuing dialogue can devolve quickly into a volley of rapid-fire superlatives and even expletives on the general decay of morals and personal accountability in America and in the world as a whole. It is usually at this point we begin to wonder in what distant valley our little wagon train of facts and data has put down stakes and is now holed up, since it has clearly stopped while the class has headed for taller timbers.

We would not want to appear as if we do not deeply appreciate students being engaged and participatory; no, actually, we are always grateful when such is the case. So how can we take advantage of the aforementioned classroom dynamics? We believe these events lend themselves to exploring inductive and deductive reasoning. The reader will note that we did not pit these two reasoning categories into the traditional one-versus-the-other phrasing. We like to teach about them as a means of conducting a conceptual proof analogous to the simple mathematical checking we all learned in elementary school where one uses addition to verify subtraction or multiplication to verify division. We can use an inductive approach to test premises and arrive at a conclusion that allows us to move from the specific to the general and then use deductive reasoning to move in the other direction of the general to the specific.

Deductive reasoning follows forms of logic to relate one fact to another. These include forms referred to as syllogism, modus tollens, modus ponens, chain argument, and disjunctive syllogism.

When considering the statements in the box provided here, they may have a logical relationship, which demonstrates validity. However, the discussion does not demonstrate truth; therefore, we cannot say the argument is sound.

As stated earlier, inductive reasoning allows us to take specific information and move to a general conclusion. This approach is central to research conducted in the social sciences through the use of the scientific method. According to Bassham et al. (2011, p.77), the following conditions apply in a strong inductive argument:

- If the premises are true, the conclusion is probably true.
- The premises provide probable, but not logically conclusive, grounds for the truth of the conclusion.
- The premises, if true, make the conclusion likely.

Valid but Not Sound

"Because they have eight wheels and four people on them, and four plus eight is twelve, and there twelve inches in a foot, and one foot is a ruler, and Queen Elizabeth was a ruler, and Queen Elizabeth was also a ship, and the ship sailed the seas, and in the seas are fish, and fish have fins, and the Finns fought the Russians, and the Russians are red, and fire trucks are always 'russian' around."

(According to the Monty Pythonesque application of the principles of logic and etymology, Chapman et al., 1975)

Central here is not that the premise is "proved" but that the information has been collected and presented in such a way that the conclusion is "likely" and that the degree of likeliness is very strong. When assessing the inductive reasoning of an argument and its strength, an understanding of how research is done is helpful, as this provides a way to make decisions about the quality of the data or statistical evidence provided.

 Here is a helpful website for understanding deductive and inductive reasoning.

https://www.socialresearchmethods.net/kb/dedind.php

Three basic questions to ask when conducting a research study:

- What do I want to know about or know more about?
- What subjects do I want to investigate to give me insight about what I want to know?
- Can I study a segment of the subjects I am investigating to get accurate answers regarding my research question?

The first question helps to determine the *research question*, whereas the second and third questions identify the *population* and *sample* of the research study, respectively. To conduct systematic studies or to solve problems we can use these steps:

- Identify of a research question
- Review of the literature
- Develop a hypothesis or set of hypotheses
- Select a research method(s)
- Select sample
- Collect of the data
- Analysis of the data
- Generate conclusions and share findings

When evaluating the data and statistical generalizations made from a study, there are several things to keep in mind. When quantified information is included, the critical thinker needs to consider several conditions. First, consideration of the **sample** and how it relates to the **population** is very important. **Population** is defined as the group of people the researcher is seeking knowledge about. Therefore, if I want to understand more about the interests of high school seniors in the United States, my population (or target population) is classified as "high school seniors residing in the United States." The number for this population is quite high. As a researcher, I do not have to survey all of them to gain reliable information that can be accurately generalized to this group of people. Rather, a sample can be used. A **sample** is defined as a segment of the population, implying, therefore, that not every high school senior, but rather a portion of all high school seniors residing in the United States be included in the sample.

> **Research question** – area of inquiry
> **Population** – the group one seeks knowledge about
> **Sample** – a segment of the population

In quantitative research studies, there are some general principles to keep in mind regarding the data used for analysis. Data collected from a sample are considered more reliable when they are both **random** and **representative**. A random sample means that every individual in the population had the same level of chance of being selected for the **sample**. For the sample to be a representative sample, the demographic breakdown must represent the target population (i.e., the proportion of males and females in the population must be the same proportion in the sample). Finally, the *size* of the sample must be considered, as the size must be adequate. A general principle for national polls or large population groups is that at least 1,000 people should be in the random representative sample. However, this is generally when the population size is around 8,000 or more. With smaller population sizes, the sample can then be smaller (generally at least 10%). The reason we do not need to look for a 10% sample for a national poll is we have found that responses reach a saturation point once they get to 1,000 (however, some statisticians say that it is closer to 1,500). These guidelines are used when considering quantitative data/research (survey research, secondary analysis, etc.). However, when conducting qualitative research, the size guideline shifts to a smaller number due to the type of research that is being executed.

So what does this mean for the critical and creative thinker? When reviewing information from a quantitative research study, ask what seems to be the relationship between the population and the sample relative to size, random selection, and representation. This will provide information on how reliable and generalizable the information reported is relative to any conclusions or reasons being offered.

When evaluating reports that provide statistical data, it is important to consider all of the following questions:

- What is the sample size?
- Is the sample representative relative to all significant characteristics in this population and research question?

- Have all significant characteristics been considered?
- Are the questions biased (if the study was a survey)?
- What is the credibility of the researcher or research organization?
- Is the survey biased due to any vested interests of the company or individual who may have financially supported the research?
- Can the results be duplicated or have they been?
- Are the results statistically significant?

A *fallacy* is many times defined as a misleading notion, an erroneous belief, a myth; it could also be a mistake in logic or a deceptive form of reasoning or a reasoning trick. Such tricks might be used to persuade you, the reader, to accept a conclusion without providing quality (accurate and clear) information or valid and rational construction of the argument (use of deductive or inductive reasoning).

There is a plethora of different fallacies that has been labeled to help in their identification in a presented argument. Some will identify as many as 44 different fallacies and others around a dozen. Regardless of how many are labeled and given specific names, two things are important to keep in mind: (1) fallacies may be reasons that seem logical and make sense, but when looked at more closely, do not really support the conclusion; and (2) fallacies are statements that distract readers/listeners from the topic at hand. We are able to examine the presence of fallacies by identifying the argument: the issue, conclusion statement, and reasons. Then, since fallacies are demonstrated in the reasons, ask what would need to be true for the reason to be true and support the conclusion. Ask yourself if the assumptions that are uncovered make sense. If there is an obvious false assumption, you have found a fallacy in the reasoning and then should reject or discount that particular reason. Be careful of distractions created by related but irrelevant information as well as strong appeals to your emotions; this is a trick to solicit your buy-in to the author's conclusion.

The following is a list for locating and assessing fallacies in an argument adapted from Browne and Keeley (2010):

1. **Ad Hominem:** Attacks a person or person's background instead of the person's ideas/reasons.
2. **Slippery slope:** Makes assumptions that a proposed step will set off an uncontrollable chain of undesirable events, yet there are procedures in place to prevent such a chain of events and/or there is not any evidence to suggest that chain will indeed occur.

3. **Ad Populum:** Appeals to popularity or majority. Justifies a claim by appealing to sentiments of large groups of people. This falsely assumes that anything favored by a large group is desirable. Also referred to as "jumping on the bandwagon."

4. **Appeals to questionable authority:** Supports a conclusion by citing an authority that lacks special expertise on that particular issue. This may be an individual or an organization.

5. **Confuses "what should be" with "what is":** Reasons need to deal with what is, not how things could, would, or might be. Think back to the discussion on assumptions. When we attempt to build a premise on evidence that might exist, we are attempting to build our house on a foundation that may or may not exist (so to speak).

6. **Confuses naming with explaining:** Falsely assumes that because you have provided a name for some event or behavior, you have also adequately explained the event/situation/evidence. This could be an instrumental concept not defined, or name-dropping someone as an expert but not explaining how that person is an expert on that issue.

7. **Reflects a search for perfect solutions:** Falsely assumes that because part of a problem would remain after a solution is tried, the whole solution should not be adopted.

8. **Begs the question:** An argument in which the conclusion is assumed in the reasoning. The reasons may simply repeat the conclusion but not offer support, or the reasons may just pose questions relative to the issue but not offer support to the claim, thereby beating around the bush.

9. **Equivocation:** A word or phrase is used that has two or more meanings in an argument so that the argument then fails to make sense once the meaning is shifted.

10. **Appeals to Emotions/Appeal to Pity:** Use of emotionally charged language to distract readers and listeners from relevant reasons and evidence. Common emotions appealed to are fear, hope, patriotism, pity, and sympathy.

11. **Attacks a straw person:** Distorts an opponent's point of view so that it is easy to attack, thus we attack a point of view that does not actually exist and/or was not stated.

12. **Presents a faulty/false, either–or dilemma:** Assumes only two alternatives when there are more than two.

13. **Overgeneralizing:** Use of vague, emotionally appealing words that predispose us to approve something without closely examining the reasons.

14. **Red Herring:** An irrelevant topic is presented to divert attention from the original issue and help to "win" an argument by shifting attention away from the argument and to another issue.

Identification of fallacies can be used as a tool for analyzing the quality of reasoning provided to support a particular stance on an issue. If a fallacy is used, you should ask yourself how distracting it was and how strong the other reasons offered are. Then make an assessment of the quality and strength of the evidence and overall argument.

IMAGE CREDIT

Fig. 2.1: Copyright © Depositphotos/Fourleaflovers.

∞ three ∞

APPROACHES TO CRITICAL AND CREATIVE THINKING

I saw the angel in the marble and carved until I set him free.

— Michelangelo

Next we have compiled and synthesized many resources to construct our critical and creative thinking matrix. Paul and Elder (2004) introduced the idea of there being **elements** and **standards** of critical thinking. The elements are pieces that are included to be examined in any argument, while the standards assist with the assessment of the quality of the elements. They should not be thought of in simple linear fashion but rather as being dynamically interrelated. Critical and creative thinkers are encouraged to incorporate these as they inspect arguments.

While many experts in critical thinking circles prescribe specific steps one must employ to demonstrate critical thinking, Notar and Padgett (2010)

Elements and Standards of Critical Thinking-Reasoning-Reading

Elements	Standards
• Purpose	• Clarity
• Questions	• Accuracy
• Information	• Relevance
• Inferences/Conclusions	• Depth
• Concepts (Key Concepts)	• Logic
• Assumptions	• Breadth
• Implications/Consequences	
• Points of View	*(Paul & Elder, 2004)*

propose that critical thinking involves creativity and innovation, which may be referred to as "thinking outside the box." They examined what was meant by the phrase *thinking outside the box* and definitions offered in the literature by others and conclude that the "box does not exist." Furthermore, Notar and Padgett indicate that in order to think outside the box, we will need to stop thinking in a fixed manner but open our minds to unlimited possibilities, which entails having an open mind. Therefore, "if we are not in a 'box,' we can creatively design instruction and assessments that meet all the diverse needs of our students within the context of rules and regulations" (2010, p. 295). They propose that there is no box "other than what we create for ourselves" (p. 297) and so the question becomes what box(es) we have constructed. To think outside of it may require embracing attributes offered by Bernacki (2002):

- Willingness to take new perspectives to day-to-day work.
- Openness to do different things and to do things differently.
- Focusing on the value of finding new ideas and acting on them.
- Striving to create value in new ways.
- Listening to others.
- Supporting and respecting others when they come up with new ideas.

We believe that incorporating these attributes along with what Paul and Elder propose is important to teaching and learning critical and creative thinking.

Sweet, Blythe, and Carpenter (2013) contributed a very useful, albeit brief, discussion on teaching and creative thinking in *Higher Education Advocate*, the publication of the National Education Association. In a mere four pages, these authors familiarize the reader with what they believe are some of the core elements and tenets essential in facilitating creative thinking. What is considered in their article "is a new teaching-learning paradigm that goes beyond active learning." These authors discuss three teaching/mentoring para-digmatic streams: *sage on the stage*, *guide on the side*, and finally, *mentoring from the middle*.

The first of these, the sage on the stage approach posits that educators function to deliver didactic inputs reflecting the collective wisdom of the age and students are there only to ingest these conceptual pearls. The guide from the side paradigm, perhaps emerging as a challenge to the aforementioned traditional strategic approach, advances a more egalitarian prescription where power, wisdom, and learning are shared and attained most effectively through a more democratic ideological lens. However, the authors write, "both paradigms produced pronounced weaknesses. The former required nothing more than students memorize mountains of information (almost all of which they would shortly forget) to regurgitate to the sage during test times. The latter often resulted in the almost

Essential Roles for Mentoring from the Middle

- FACILITATOR: The mentor is responsible for creating the course, aligning it to proper outcomes, and running all classroom sessions, managing both the big-picture learning experience, and responding to individual student needs.

- COACH: The mentor breaks skills into skill points, motivates students to develop the necessary knowledge, determines the roles of various students, and acts as damage controller when things go awry.

- ARTIST: The mentor promotes risk-taking to find solutions as well as the traditional "right" answers, adapts to changing situations, shifts perspective so as to view things from other points of view (including students'), and synthesizes the ideas, processes, and products of the learning experience.

- CRITICAL REFLECTOR: The mentor displays metacognition of class proceedings, exhibits fair-mindedness, and shows students how to properly evaluate arguments.

- MODEL: In all that is done, the mentor acts as a model leader and learner.

- SCHOLAR: Effective mentors not only know the discipline and its pedagogy, but also constantly demonstrate the scholar-researcher frame of mind by keeping current in the field, and by publishing in it and with students when possible. The goal is to get students to join the scholarly conversation. (Sweet, Blythe, & Carpenter, 2003, p. 8)

total abdication of instructor power and knowledge and too much dependence upon alpha students to guide the lost tribes through the wilderness of group work."

The latest paradigm moving us along the teaching-learning continuum is commonly referred to as mentoring from the middle (founded by Erica McWilliams in application with college students). The six essential roles taken by the teacher are facilitator, coach, artist, critical reflector, model, and scholar and are defined here.

Sweet, Blythe, and Carpenter (2013) also suggest that these roles are enacted through six phases of the mentoring process.

- Information gathering: The mentor uses the web, print resources, and other forms of knowledge to develop both breadth and depth outside of and during class.
- Crystallizing: The mentor leads students in analyzing, assessing, and synthesizing information into powerful and guiding concepts.
- Creating the project: The mentor leads the class in deciding what project/product can be accomplished employing these concepts.

- COMPLETING THE PROJECT: The mentor helps students actively make something.
- SKILL MAKING: The mentor determines what additional activities are necessary to transform abstract vocabulary and concepts into deeply learned skills.
- EVALUATING THE LEARNING UNIT: The mentor figures out whether or not the total project and class have achieved the desired outcomes. (pp. 8–9)

So, mentors are seen as harvesting, distilling, guiding, executing, refining, and finally assessing with the student learner. In our opinion, these roles and tasks in tandem contribute to a useful instructional framework.

> These roles and phases are what make the Mentor-from-the-Middle model distinct and more effective than the traditional lecture method of teaching. The method also emphasizes skills such as shifting perception, piggybacking, brainstorming, glimmer-catching, collaborating, playing, recognizing pattern, using metaphor, and going with the flow. (Office of Student Learning, Outcomes Assessment & Accreditation. <http://web.uri.edu/assessment/mentor-from-the-middle/>)

By utilizing the nine teaching-learning specific skills of creative thinking presented here, the teacher-mentor can aid students in becoming strong critical and creative thinkers.

- Shifting perception: learning to regard a person, idea, or situation from multiple angles.
- Piggybacking: learning to borrow old ideas from others in order to form new ideas.
- Brainstorming: learning how to come up with many potential solutions to a problem.
- Glimmer-catching: learning to capture that out-of-focus idea or barely perceptible sight or sound.
- Collaborating: learning to work with others.
- Playing: learning to develop a total openness to the world around us and have fun with it.
- Recognizing pattern: learning to discern the figure in the carpet by weaving together separate strands into a coherent whole.
- Using metaphor: learning to use the known to help you understand the unknown.
- Going with the flow: learning how to let the creative process overwhelm you and take you with it.

(Adapted from the NEA Higher Education Advocate)

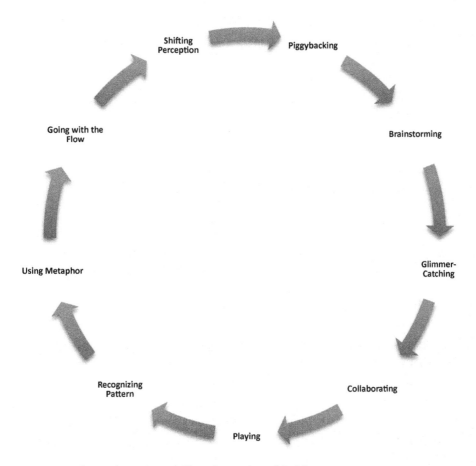

Figure 3.1: Teaching-learning skills of creative thinking.

We would like to encourage the reader to view the preceding discussion on types of mentoring, essential roles, phases, skills, elements, and standards as contributing to the construction of a critical and creative teaching-learning matrix. We now endeavor to render this complex array of ideas more reader-friendly and practical-action-step oriented. In addition to the information that follows, we have also provided handouts and resources in Section 3 of this book for teachers-learners to incorporate into their matrix.

It is our hope that these different approaches will encourage you to think productively when considering information, evaluating issues, or arriving at solutions to problems. "These strategies are common to the thinking styles of creative geniuses in science, art, and industry throughout history" (Study Guides and Strategies, 2014).

NINE APPROACHES TO CREATIVE PROBLEM SOLVING:

1. Rethink! Look at problems in many different ways.
2. Visualize! Utilize diagrams and imagery to analyze your dilemma.
3. Produce! Genius is productive.
4. Combine! Make novel combinations.
5. Form! Form relationships.
6. Opposite! Think in opposites.
7. Metaphor/simile! Think metaphorically.
8. Failure! Learning from your mistakes is one example of using failure.
9. Patience! Don't confuse inspiration with ideas.

(Study Guides and Strategies. http://www.studygs.net/genius.htm)

As you read through these nine strategies, you probably see that quite often you have used one or more of them. Please keep in mind that in order to effectively incorporate critical and creative thinking into daily living, one should follow a routine. The routine we recommend is that one *identify*, *apply*, *evaluate*, and *integrate* when considering information.

We engage in *identifying* behavior from the moment our day begins. We almost immediately consider who we are going to communicate with and tasks we need to accomplish and problems left unresolved from the day before. This was also addressed earlier in this book where we encourage students to first identify the form of the argument before moving into any of the other aspects. If you have not established what you are examining or what may need closer inspection, the explanations and assessments generated will not be grounded.

> "Everybody is a genius. But if you judge a fish by its ability to climb a tree, it will live its whole life believing that it is stupid."
>
> —Albert Einstein

Application is doing what you thought; turning your thoughts into action. Bottom line: steps have to be taken for something to happen. We are not suggesting randomly throwing at a target, but strategically applying what you have identified as important and then deliberately and with a plan moving toward a goal.

Evaluation is often an assessment you make at a given moment in time or it can be new insights drawn from accumulated knowledge and experience. Systematic evaluation acts to inform the next steps in the analytical or problem-solving process. When you effectively evaluate, you will arrive at drawing connections between what was previously viewed as unrelated events or outcomes.

Finally, *integrating* critical and creative thinking into your everyday life will not only strengthen your ability to identify, apply, and evaluate, but will likely also increase your success and productivity. One of the most prolific inventors in world history, Thomas Edison, is estimated to have held at least 1,093 patents. In order to encourage productivity, he established *idea quotas* for himself and his assistants. Additionally, Dean K. Simonton, Distinguished Professor Emeritus of Psychology at the University of California, Davis, reported that the most respected scientists produced important successes and failures. Part of arriving at excellence is a willingness to take risks and fail.

Paul Cézanne (1839–1906) is recognized as one of the 19th century's greatest painters, and is often called the father of modern art, an *avant garde* bridge between the Impressionists and the Cubists. During his life he had only a few exhibitions, though his influence on subsequent artists was great as an innovator with shape and form. His genius, however, was not evident until late in life. He was refused admission to the Ecole des Beaux-Arts at age 22 and his first solo exhibition was at age 56.

Over the course of our academic careers, we have incorporated critical and creative thinking into the courses we teach. We have found that students are often resistant in these courses because they think critical and creative thinking requires something completely new and different compared to what they are accustomed to, when in actuality they have the requisite capacity and are already exercising many aspects of critical and creative thinking. An assignment we use to provide students a means to enhance and demonstrate their critical and creative thinking skills is the *Critical and Creative Thinking Journal Entry* (see Critical and Creative Thinking Resources). This is used in application to the readings in the next section. This assignment allows students to not merely respond to the questions but to include their reflection of their critical and creative thinking process. Here we offer a means to organize and build upon these skills and tools by drawing from various approaches.

In our opinion, to effectively engage in critical and creative thinking one must make oneself ready. To this end we offer the following strategy: checking-in; practicing presentness; trusting in the process; and accepting the wisdom of uncertainty.

Checking-in: How ready and prepared have I made myself for the work of critical and creative thinking? Have I let go of my frustration of the lousy taste of my morning coffee, the unholy traffic, or the argument with my best friend?

Practicing Presentness: For example, am I in the moment? Is my focus the task before me? Is my attention directed to the here and now?

Trusting the process: Take stock. Ask and answer for yourself, do I believe that problem solving and critical and creative thinking are doable and worth my time and energy?

Accepting the wisdom of uncertainty: I have to accept that I don't know everything, nor that everything is predictable or manageable. If I have actually checked in, and I am present oriented, and I trust in the process, even the unexpected becomes understandable.

Despite what you just read, preparing yourself for critical and creative thinking are not a discreet set of steps; it is more an attitude and approach.

Approaches to Thinking

Linear thinking, and by extension problem solving and decision making, typically offer a sequential A precedes B, B precedes C, and so on perspective. Linearity has many strengths and at least one important limitation, and that is how it creates a bounded-ness that relies on cause preceding effect and action having to always result in consequence. However, a countervailing strength of linearity is how it lends predictability to our lives. If we can depend on A preceding B and B preceding C in a predictable fashion, it allows for highly structured interactions.

> Leonardo da Vinci forged a relationship between the sound of a bell and a stone hitting water. This enabled him to make the connection that sound travels in waves.

Likewise, *cyclical thinking* has the potential for incredible insights into the relatedness of phenomena. Many times, people express negative views about cyclical thinking, arguing what they may believe is the intrinsic flow of a beginning point through processes and reemergence at the starting point. Embedded in the cyclical perspective is a sort of yin yang, atomistic versus gestalt and no matter the point of entry, the thinker passes through predictable stages and ends up at the beginning once again.

A third and final approach to be considered is helical (spiral) thinking. *Helical thinking* is defined here as thinking in many directions simultaneously (as in a multidimensional game of chess). Through this approach, insight, solutions, even the way one conceptualizes a problem may be incremental and operate as disjointed leaps not dependent on linear or cyclical strategies. Critical and creative thinking is not separate and apart from linear, cyclical, or even helical thinking; rather, they serve to enhance it.

In the next section, we have included a limited number of important articles for examination and practice of the different critical and creative thinking tools surveyed in this book. It is our hope these readings spark discussion of the issues, as well as assist in the application and refinement of one's critical and creative thinking skills.

ℰ Section 2 ℰ

Readings for Application

Research

Thinking About the Hard Stuff

Research, statistics, and careful analysis in general are often cited as the "hard stuff." The three articles included here are intended to serve as a resource when attempting to apply critical and creative thinking to research. To assess the reasoning in research articles, an important step is being able to interpret the research and how it was conducted. The application of deductive and inductive reasoning can be considered when assessing data and evidence presented in an argument. As presented in Chapter 2, deductive reasoning is most applicable when moving from the general to the specific and inductive moves from a specific observation to the general. Often, when statistics or numerical data that have been collected from quantitative research are provided as evidence, they are seen as "better" when that is not necessarily the case. Qualitative research is also credible and valid. This should not be a conversation about which type of research is better. Rather, both can be used to examine any research topic. Combining the two methods (use of a "mixed methods" approach) can yield greater understanding than either approach on its own.

Here is a useful website that addresses the utility of quantitative and qualitative research approaches and their related assumptions.

https://www.socialresearchmethods.net/kb/qualval.php

The first two articles in this section provide important points for consideration when presented with statistics and when considering the results from data obtained through survey methods. Some important questions to consider when reflecting on research data or results include:

1. Who collected the data?
2. For what purpose were the data collected?
3. What type of data collection method(s) was used?
4. What was the sample size?
5. Was the sample representative of the population from which it was drawn?

The articles that follow were selected to provide a quick overview (or review) of survey data, the use of statistics, and the relevance of both quantitative and qualitative research. Hence, an article on the efficacy of qualitative research is included that also highlights what to consider when evaluating the data gleaned from qualitative interviews. Students are encouraged to think about the different ways that data are collected and reported and how this influences the *quality of evidence* provided in an article, argument, lecture, etc.

Questions for Consideration:

1. Have you ever found that you have fallen into "statistical traps"?
2. In what ways do you believe your critical and creative thinking skills were strengthened by exposure to the information contained in these articles?
3. How can critical and creative thinking help you when considering the quality and value from quantitative and qualitative research?

cs four so

SENSE AND NONSENSE
ABOUT SURVEYS

By Howard Schuman

S urveys draw on two human propensities that have served us well from ancient times. One is to gather information by asking questions. The first use of language around 100,000 years ago may have been to utter commands such as "Come here!" or "Wait!" Questions must have followed soon after: "Why?" or "What for?" From that point, it would have been only a short step to the use of interrogatives to learn where a fellow hominid had seen potential food, a dangerous animal, or something else of importance. Asking questions continues to be an effective way of acquiring information of all kinds, assuming of course that the person answering is able and willing to respond accurately.

The other inclination, learning about one's environment by examining a small part of it, is the sampling aspect of surveys. A taste of something may or may not point to appetizing food. A first inquiry to a stranger, a first glance around a room, a first date—each is a sample of sorts, often used to decide whether it is wise to proceed further. As with questions, however, one must always be aware of the possibility that the sample may not prove adequate to the task.

Schuman, H. (2002). Sense and nonsense about surveys. *Contexts, 1*(2), 40-47.

SAMPLING: HOW GALLUP ACHIEVED FAME

Only within the past century—and especially in the 1930s and 1940s—were major improvements made in the sampling process that allowed the modern survey to develop and flourish. A crucial change involved recognition that the value of a sample comes not simply from its size but also from the way it is obtained. Every serious pursuit likes to have a morality tale that supports its basic beliefs: witness Eve and the apple in the Bible or Newton and his apple in legends about scientific discovery. Representative sampling has a marvelous morality tale also, with the additional advantage of its being true.

The story concerns the infamous Literary Digest poll prediction—based on 10 million questionnaires sent out and more than two million received back—that Roosevelt would lose decisively in the 1936 presidential election. At the same time, George Gallup, using many fewer cases but a much better method, made the more accurate prediction that FDR would win. Gallup used quotas in choosing respondents in order to represent different economic strata, whereas the Literary Digest had worked mainly from telephone and automobile ownership lists, which in 1936 were biased toward wealthy people apt to be opposed to Roosevelt. (There were other sources of bias as well.) As a result, the Literary Digest poll disappeared from the scene, and Gallup was on his way to becoming a household name.

> The percentage of people who refuse to take part in a survey is particularly important. In some federal surveys, the percentage is small, within the range of 5 to 10 percent. For even the best non-government surveys, the refusal rate can reach 25 percent or more, and it can be far larger in the case of poorly executed surveys.

Yet despite their intuitive grasp of the importance of representing the electorate accurately, Gallup and other commercial pollsters did not use the probability sampling methods that were being developed in the same decades and that are fundamental to social science surveys today. Probability sampling in its simplest form calls for each person in the population to have an equal chance of being selected. It can also be used in more complex applications where the chances are deliberately made to be unequal, for example, when oversampling a minority group in order to study it more closely; however, the chances of being selected must still be known so that they can later be equalized when considering the entire population.

INTUITIONS AND COUNTERINTUITIONS ABOUT SAMPLE SIZE

Probability sampling theory reveals a crucial but counterintuitive point about sample size: the size of a sample needed to accurately estimate a value for a population depends very little on the size of the population. For example, almost the same size sample is needed to estimate, with a given degree of precision, the proportion of left-handed people in the United States as is needed to make the same estimate for, say, Peoria, Illinois. In both cases a reasonably accurate estimate can be obtained with a sample size of around 1,000. (More cases are needed when extraordinary precision is called for, for example, in calculating unemployment rates, where even a tenth of a percent change may be regarded as important.)

The link between population size and sample size cuts both ways. Although huge samples are not needed for huge populations like those of the United States or China, a handful of cases is not sufficient simply because one's interest is limited to Peoria. This implication is often missed by those trying to save time and money when sampling a small community.

Moreover, all of these statements depend on restricting your interest to overall population values. If you are concerned about, say, left-handedness among African Americans, then African Americans become your population, and you need much the same sample size as for Peoria or the United States.

WHO IS MISSING?

A good sample depends on more than probability sampling theory. Surveys vary greatly in their quality of implementation, and this variation is not captured by the "margin of error" plus/minus percentage figures that accompany most media reports of polls. Such percentages reflect the size of the final sample, but they do not reveal the sampling method or the extent to which the targeted individuals or households were actually included in the final sample. These details are at least as important as the sample size.

When targeted members of a population are not interviewed or do not respond to particular questions, the omissions are a serious problem if they are numerous and if those missed differ from those who are interviewed on the matters being studied. The latter difference can seldom be known with great confidence, so it is usually desirable to keep omissions to a minimum. For example, sampling from telephone directories is undesirable because it leaves out those with unlisted telephones, as well as those with no telephones at all. Many survey reports are based on such poor sampling procedures

CALLING SPIRITS FROM THE VASTY DEEP

Two characters in Shakespeare's Henry IV illustrate a pressing problem facing surveys today:

> **Glendower:** I can call spirits from the vasty deep.
>
> **Hotspur:** Why, so can I, or so can any man; But will they come when you do call for them?

New impediments such as answering machines make contacting people more difficult, and annoyance with tele-marketing and other intrusions discourages people from becoming respondents. The major academic survey organizations invest significant resources in repeatedly calling people and also in trying to persuade people to be interviewed. Thus far response rates for leading surveys have suffered only a little, but other organizations more limited by time and costs have seen rates plummet.

Fortunately, research about the effect of nonresponse on findings has increased. Two recent articles in *Public Opinion Quarterly* report surprisingly small differences in results from surveys with substantial differences in response rates. One study focuses on the University of Michigan's Survey of Consumers and finds that the number of calls required to complete a single interview doubled from 1979 to 1996. However, controlling for major social background characteristics, the authors also report that stopping calls earlier and making fewer attempts to convert refusals would have had little effect on a key measure, the Index of Consumer Sentiments. In a second study researchers conducted two basically similar surveys: one accepted a 36 percent response rate to conserve time and money; the other invested additional time and resources to obtain a 61 percent response rate. On a wide range of attitude items, the researchers found few noteworthy differences in outcomes due to the large difference in response rates.

It is important to keep in mind that bias due to nonresponse will occur only if non-respondents differ from respondents on the measures of interest and in ways that cannot be controlled statistically. Thus, while high response rates are always desirable in principle, the actual effects of nonresponse call for careful empirical research, not dogmatic pronouncements.

that they may not deserve to be taken seriously. This is especially true of reports based on "focus groups," which offer lots of human interest but are subject to vast amounts of error. Internet surveys also cannot represent the general population adequately at present, though this is an area where some serious attempts are being made to compensate for the inherent difficulties.

The percentage of people who refuse to take part in a survey is particularly important. In some federal surveys, the percentage is small, within the range of 5 to 10 percent. For even the best non-government surveys, the refusal rate can reach 25 percent or more, and it can be far larger in the case of poorly executed surveys. Refusals have risen substantially from earlier days, becoming a major cause for concern among serious survey practitioners. Fortunately, in recent years research has shown that moderate amounts of nonresponse in an otherwise careful survey seem in most cases not to have a major effect on results. Indeed, even the *Literary Digest,* with its abysmal sampling and massive nonresponse rate, did well predicting elections before the dramatic realignment of the electorate in 1936. The problem is that one can never be certain as to the effects of refusals and other forms of nonresponse, so obtaining a high response rate remains an important goal.

QUESTIONS ABOUT QUESTIONS

Since survey questions resemble the questions we ask in ordinary social interaction, they may seem less problematic than the counterintuitive and technical aspects of sampling. Yet survey results are every bit as dependent on the form, wording and context of the questions asked as they are on the sample of people who answer them.

No classic morality tale like the *Literary Digest* fiasco highlights the question-answer process, but an example from the early days of surveys illustrates both the potential challenges of question writing and the practical solutions.

In 1940 Donald Rugg asked two slightly different questions to equivalent national samples about the general issue of freedom of speech:

- Do you think the United States should forbid public speeches against democracy?
- Do you think the United States should allow public speeches against democracy?

Taken literally, forbidding something and not allowing something have the same effect, but clearly the public did not view the questions as identical. Whereas 75 percent of the public would not allow such speeches, only 54 percent would forbid them, a difference of 21 percentage points. This finding was replicated several times in later years, not only in the United States but also (with appropriate translations) in Germany and the Netherlands. Such "survey-based experiments" call for administering different versions of a question to random subsamples of a larger sample. If the results between the subsamples differ by more than can be easily explained by chance, we infer that the difference is due to the variation in wording.

In addition, answers to survey questions always depend on the form in which a question is asked. If the interviewer presents a limited set of alternatives, most respondents will choose one, rather than offering a different alternative of their own. In one survey-based experiment, for example, we asked a national sample of Americans to name the most important problem facing the country. Then we asked a comparable sample a parallel question that provided a list of four problems from which to choose the most important; this list

Table 4.1 Experimental Variation Between Open and Closed Questions

A. OPEN QUESTION	B. CLOSED QUESTION
"What do you think is the most important problem facing this country today [1986]?"	"Which of the following do you think is the most important problem facing this country today [1986]—the energy shortage, the quality of public schools, legalized abortion, or pollution—or, if you prefer, you may name a different problem as most important."
	1. Energy shortage. 2. Quality of public schools. 3. Legalized abortion. 4. Pollution.

"Adapted from: H. Schuman and J. Scott, "Problems in the Use of Survey Questions to Measure Public Opinion," *Science* v. 236, pp. 957–959, May 22, 1987.

In a survey experiment, less than 3% of the 171 respondents asked the question on the left volunteered one of the four problems listed on the right. Yet, 60% of the 178 respondents asked the question on the right picked one of those four answers.

included none of the four problems mentioned most often by the first sample but instead provided four problems that had been mentioned by fewer than 3 percent of the earlier respondents. The list question also invited respondents to substitute a different problem if they wished (see Table 4.1). Despite the invitation, the majority of respondents (60 percent) chose one of the rare problems offered, reflecting their reluctance to go outside the frame of reference provided by the question. The form of a question provides the "rules of the game" for respondents, and this must always be kept in mind when interpreting results.

Other difficulties occur with survey questions when issues are discussed quite generally, as though there is a single way of framing them and just two sides to the debate. For example, what is called "the abortion issue" really consists of different issues: the reasons for an abortion, the trimester involved and so forth. In a recent General Social Survey, nearly 80 percent of the national sample supported legal abortion in the case of "a serious defect in the baby," but only 44 percent supported it "if the family has a low income and cannot afford any more children." Often what is thought to be a conflict in findings between two surveys is actually a difference in the aspects of the general issue that they queried. In still other cases an inconsistency reflects a type of illogical wish fulfillment in the public itself, as when majorities favor both a decrease in taxes and an increase in government services if the questions are asked separately.

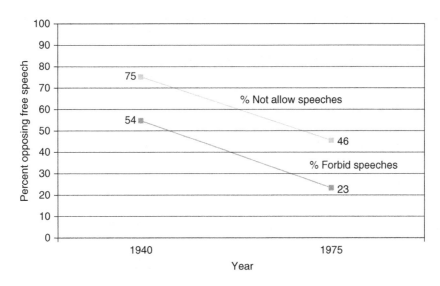

Figure 4.1 Attitudes Toward Free Speech Against Democracy

SOLUTIONS TO THE QUESTION WORDING PROBLEM

All these and still other difficulties (including the order in which questions are asked) suggest that responses to single survey questions on complex issues should be viewed with considerable skepticism. What to do then, other than to reject all survey data as unusable for serious purposes? One answer can be found from the replications of the forbid/allow experiment above: Although there was a 21 percentage points difference based on question wording in 1940 and a slightly larger difference (24 percentage points) when the experiment was repeated some 35 years later, both the forbid and the allow wordings registered similar declines in Americans' intolerance of speeches against democracy (see Figure 4.1). No matter which question was used—as long as it was the same one at both times—the conclusion about the increase in civil libertarian sentiments was the same.

More generally, what has been called the "principle of form-resistant correlations" holds in most cases: if question wording (and meaning) is kept constant, differences over time, differences across educational levels, and most other careful comparisons are not seriously affected by specific question wording. Indeed, the distinction between results for single questions and results based on comparisons or associations holds even for simple factual inquiries. Consider, for example, a study of the number of rooms in American houses. No God-given rule states what to include when counting the rooms in a house (bathrooms? basements? hallways?); hence the average number reported for a particular place and time

4. Do teachers give you a rubric? (Circle One) |always| frequently sometimes never

5. If you receive a rubric, when do you usually receive it? (Circle One) Before |During| After the assignment is given

6. If a teacher gives you a rubric/scoring guide does it help you? Explain

   Yes because it tells what the teacher expects of exemplary work and my goal is to exemplify my work

7. Do you understand how your work is evaluated? (Circle One) always |frequently| sometimes never

8. Describe some of the criteria your English or Social Science teacher uses to evaluate your work. Give specific examples of how your work is evaluated:

   Has to be based on how the student put work into project. Neatness; understanding of what is taught   Over

Page from completed, self-administered questionnaire used to study high school students' views of grading.

should not be treated as an absolute truth. What we can do, however, is try to apply the same definitions over time, across social divisions, even across nations. That way, we gain confidence in the comparisons we make—who has more rooms than who, for example.

We still face the task of interpreting the meaning of questions and of associations among questions, but that is true in all types of research. Even an index constructed from a large number of questions on the basis of a sophisticated statistical calculation called factor analysis inevitably requires the investigator to interpret what it is that he or she has measured. There is no escaping this theoretical challenge, fundamental to all research, whether using surveys or other methods such as field observations.

Survey researchers should also ask several different questions about any important issue. In addition to combining questions to increase reliability, the different answers can be synthesized rather than depending on the angle of vision provided by any single question. A further safeguard is to carry out frequent experiments like that on the forbid/allow wordings. By varying the form, wording, and context of questions, researchers can gain insight into both the questions and the relevant issues. Sometimes variations turn out to make no difference, and that is also useful to learn. For example, I once expected support for legalized abortion to increase when a question substituted *end pregnancy* for the word *abortion* in the phrasing. Yet no difference was found. Today, more and more researchers include survey-based experiments as part of their investigations, and readers should look for these sorts of safeguards when evaluating survey results.

THE NEED FOR COMPARISONS

To interpret surveys accurately, it's important to use a framework of comparative data in evaluating the results. For example, teachers know that course evaluations can be interpreted best against the backdrop of evaluations from other similar courses: a 75 percent rating of lectures as "excellent" takes on a quite different meaning depending on whether the average for other lecture courses is 50 percent or 90 percent. Such comparisons are fundamental for all survey results, yet they are easily overlooked when one feels the urge to speak definitively about public reactions to a unique event.

Comparative analysis over time, along with survey-based experiments, can also help us understand responses to questions about socially sensitive subjects. Experiments have shown that expressions of racial attitudes can change substantially for both black and white Americans depending on the interviewer's race. White respondents, for instance, are more likely to support racial intermarriage when speaking to a black than to a white interviewer. Such self-censoring mirrors variations in cross-race conversations outside of surveys, reflecting not a methodological artifact of surveys but rather a fact of life about

Table 4.2 Percent of White Americans Approving or Disapproving of Racial Intermarriage, 1958–1997

"Do you approve or disapprove of marriage between blacks and whites?"

Year	Approve	Disapprove
1958	4	96
1978	34	66
1997	67	33

Source: Gallup Poll

race relations in America. Still, if we consider time trends, with the race of interviewer kept constant, we can also see that white responses supporting intermarriage have clearly increased over the past half century (see Table 4.2), that actual intermarriage rates have also risen (though from a much lower level) over recent years, and that the public visibility of cross-race marriage and dating has also increased. It would be foolish to assume that the survey data on racial attitudes reflect actions in any literal sense, but they do capture important *trends* in both norms and behavior.

Surveys remain our best tool for learning about large populations. One remarkable advantage surveys have over some other methods is the ability to identify their own limitations, as illustrated by the development of both probability theory in sampling and experiments in questioning. In the end, however, with surveys as with all research methods, there is no substitute for both care and intelligence in the way evidence is gathered and interpreted. What we learn about society is always mediated by the instruments we use, including our own eyes and ears. As Isaac Newton wrote long ago, error is not in the art but in the artificers.

RECOMMENDED RESOURCES

Converse, Philip E. "The Nature of Belief Systems in Mass Publics." In *Ideology and Discontent,* ed. D. E. Apter. New York: The Free Press, 1964. A profound and skeptical exploration of the nature of public attitudes.

Groves, Robert M. *Survey Errors and Survey Costs.* New York: Wiley, 1989. A sophisticated consideration of the sources of error in surveys.

Kalton, Graham. *Introduction to Survey Sampling.* Thousand Oaks, Calif.: Sage Publications (Quantitative Applications in the Social Sciences), 1983. A brief and lucid introduction to sampling.

Page, Benjamin I., and Robert Y. Shapiro. *The Rational Public: Fifty Years of Trends in Americans' Policy Preferences.* Chicago: University of Chicago Press, 1992. In part, a persuasive reply to Converse's skepticism.

Schuman, Howard, and Stanley Presser. *Questions and Answers in Attitude Surveys: Experiments on Question Form, Wording, and Context.* San Diego, Calif.: Academic Press, 1981 (Reprint edition with new preface, Thousand Oaks, Calif.: Sage Publications, 1996). Several experiments discussed in the present article are drawn from this volume.

Stouffer, Samuel A. *Communism, Conformity, and Civil Liberties,* with introduction by James A. Davis. New York: Doubleday, 1955; New Brunswick, N.J.: Transaction Publishers, 1992. Stouffer's keen awareness of both the possibilities and the limitations of survey data is reflected in this classic investigation. Also relevant to today's political climate.

Sudman, Seymour, Norman M. Bradburn, and Norbert Schwarz. *Thinking About Answers: The Application of Cognitive Process to Survey Methodology*. San Francisco: Jossey-Bass, 1996. A clear discussion of survey questioning by three well-known researchers.

Tourangeau, Roger, Lance J. Rips, and Kenneth Rasinski. *The Psychology of Survey Response*. Cambridge: Cambridge University Press, 2000. A comprehensive account of response effects, drawing especially on ideas from cognitive psychology.

HOW TO AVOID STATISTICAL TRAPS

By Gerald W. Bracey

Education statistics are rarely neutral. These principles can help educators interpret what the research really says.

— *Gerald W. Bracey*

There are three kinds of lies: lies, damned lies, and statistics." This quote from Benjamin Disraeli, Prime Minister of England under Queen Victoria, demonstrates that the field of statistics has needed to defend its honor since its inception in Europe centuries ago.

The original term for statistics, *political arithmetic* (Best, 2001), might be more accurate. Statistics are rarely neutral. Those who collect them have a purpose—sometimes benign, sometimes not—and translate the information to serve that purpose. For example, some people, including representatives of the pharmaceutical industry, say that statistics reveal an "obesity crisis" in the United States. Other people, including some financed by the food industry, allege that the "obesity crisis" is a false alarm spread by drug companies that want the standards for diseases constantly made stricter so that they can define more people as patients and sell them expensive drugs. Its true that the numbers accepted as indications of high cholesterol, high blood pressure, and high blood sugar have all become much lower in the last decade.

Bracey, G. W. (2006). How to avoid statistical traps. *Educational Leadership, 63*(8), 78-82.

Contradictory claims like these may be one reason why people say that you can prove anything with statistics. You can't, but people will certainly try to prove their particular viewpoints by using only those numbers that serve their purposes.

MORE THAN ONE NUMBER

You need more than one statistic to get a full picture of just about anything. Educators whose performance is being judged solely by annual standardized test scores will appreciate this point.

As I was writing this, an article in *The New York Times* gave three statistics for various nations' greenhouse gas emissions: total emissions, per capita emissions, and emissions per industrial output (Barringer, 2006). Using total emissions, the United States is number one by far, with China second and Russia third. Using per capita emissions, the United States is still number one and Russia is still third, but Canada is second. (China has lots of people and is still largely a rural nation despite its rapid urbanization.) Using industrial output, Russia is first, China second, and the United States fifth. (Russian and Chinese industries are not as clean as U.S. industries.)

Which statistic is best? All of them together. Using only one would be like evaluating a center fielder only on his batting average or a quarterback only on yards gained per pass. You need more than one statistic to paint a complete picture.

Similarly, a recent e-mailer asked me whether a preschool program, which produced a four-month gain in vocabulary and math and cost $6,000 per kid per year, was worth it. I said that I couldn't tell. For one thing, the program likely produced health, socialization, and other outcomes besides the two mentioned. In addition, the real value of the program might not be clear for years: It took long-term evaluations of the outcomes of the Perry Preschool Project and the Chicago Family Centers project to establish that society gained about $7 for every dollar invested in these programs (Berrueta-Clement, Schweinhart, Bamett, Epstein, & Weikart, 1984; Reynolds, 2001).

When comparing groups, it's important
to make sure the groups are comparable.

PRINCIPLES OF DATA INTERPRETATION

Despite the limitations of individual statistics and public cynicism about being able to prove anything, people remain remarkably trusting when it comes to statistics. Best (2001) observes that "Most of the time, most people simply accept statistics without question" (p. 4). This acceptance would be dangerous at any time, but given todays polarized pohticization of education (and virtually everything else), it is particularly hazardous now. Educators can avoid this danger by following some basic principles of data interpretation.

Go Back to the Data

Many people call the National Commission on Excellence in Education's 1983 report *A Nation at Risk* "the paper Spumifc" because it focused attention on education in the same way *Sputnik* did in 1954. Some still refer to it today as a "landmark" study. It's a landmark, all right: a golden treasury of selected, spun, distorted, and even manufactured statistics.

After opening with a blast of Cold-Warrior rhetoric, the good commissioners listed 13 indicators of the "risk," all referring to test scores. For example, "Over half the population of gifted students do not match their tested ability with comparable achievement in school." Given that achievement tests at the time were the principal means of selecting kids for gifted and talented programs, how could this possibly be true? When 1 sought an answer from some commissioners and their staff members, no one could remember where this statistic came from. How convenient.

Another statistic was, "Average tested achievement of students graduating from college is also lower." The United States has no program to test students graduating from college that would yield a statistic showing their "average tested achievement." What on earth could this mean? These examples illustrate a vital principle of data interpretation: If you find a statement the least bit suspect, ask to see the raw data.

Beware of Selectivity

Some of the other indicators in A *Nation at Risk* illustrate perhaps the most common misuse of statistics: selecting a statistic that, although accurate in itself, paints an incomplete and misleading picture. For instance, the repon claimed that "there was a steady decline in science achievement scores of U.S. 17-year-olds as measured by national assessments in 1969, 1973, and 1977." This was true.

But the statement refers only to science, and only to 17-year-olds. What about the 9- and 13-year-olds also tested in national assessments? No "steady decline" in science for them. What about math? What about reading? No hint of any decline in either subject for any of the three age groups (National Center for Education Statistics [NCES], 2000).

The commissioners had nine trend lines available from NCES data (three ages times three subjects). Only one could be used to support crisis rhetoric, and that was the only one the commissioners mentioned.

Those who collect statistics have a purpose— sometimes benign, sometimes not

---

Compare Rhetoric with the Numbers

Perhaps the most dangerous statistic is the one that Joel Best calls the *mutant* statistic. This statistic begins life as a legitimate datum, but mutates into something new and wrong. Best (2001) gives the example of the claim, widely circulated, that 150,000 women die in the United States each year from anorexia. The U.S. Census Bureau's Statistical Abstract of the United States shows that 55,000 women ages 15–44 die each year of all causes. Even if anorexia had killed all 55,000, given that anorexia mostly affects young women, it is unlikely that we can find another 95,000 anorexia victims younger than 15 and older than 44. In fact, the proper statistic is that 150,000 women *suffer* from anorexia—and even this number is probably a bit inflated because it was produced by an activist group attempting to call attention to the problem.

Mutant statistics afflict education data as well. *Washington Post* pundit George Will wrote in one column that almost half of Chicago's public school teachers sent their own children to private schools (Will, 1993a). This was true. The figure was 43 percent at the time, and that was the highest proportion in the United States. (Religion figured strongly in the Chicago teachers' decisions.) But over a period of six months. Will's neurons replaced "Chicago" with "the nation"; in another column, he wrote, "Nationally about half of urban public school teachers with school-age children send their children to private schools" (Will, 1993b). This was not true. According to data from the 2000 Census, 17.5 percent of all urban families and 21.5 percent of urban public school teachers send their children to private schools. The rate ranges from 43.8 percent of teachers in the Philadelphia/Camden metro area down to 1.7 percent in Oklahoma City. In 21 of these top 50 cities, teachers use private schools less than urban families do (Doyle, DeSchryver, & Diepold, 2004).

Figure 5.1. Pass Rates and Average Score Tell a Different Story

Pass Rate—Gap closed by 10 points		
	2004	2005
Black Students	60%	70%
White Students	100%	100%
Gap	40	30

Average Scores—Gap increased by 8 points		
	2004	2005
Black Students	62	68
White Students	78	92
Gap	16	24

These are hypothetical data. Scored needed to pass = 60.

Will's brain might have been addled by the work of Denis Doyle, whose reports using data from the 1980, 1990, and 2000 censuses have promoted the idea that public school teachers do send their kids to private schools in larger numbers than the general public does (Doyle, 1995; Doyle, DeSchryver, & Diepold, 2004; Doyle & Hartle, 1986). Doyle refers to teachers as "connoisseurs" of education, implying that if they send their kids to private schools, they must know something that the rest of us don't. He writes,

> With teachers choosing private schools, the truth is self-evident: While they work in public schools, they choose private schools lor their own children because they believe they are better. (1995)

This statement creates the impression that all public school teachers in all types of communities use private schools. But if we look beyond the rhetoric to the actual statistics, we find these figures for the United States as a whole (Doyle, 1995; Doyle, DeSchryver, & Diepold, 2004):

	TEACHERS	GENERAL PUBLIC
1990	12.1 percent	13.1 percent
2000	10.6 percent	12.1 percent

The numbers show that teachers made less use of private schools than the general public did. What's more, despite all the lionization of private schools and the demonization of public schools during the 1990s, a smaller proportion of both teachers and the general public had children in private schools in 2000 than in 1990.

Make Sure That Groups Are Comparable

The statistics on the percentages of children sent to private schools point to another principle of data interpretation: When comparing groups, make sure the groups are comparable. Teachers and the general public are not comparable. Teachers are more likely to have at least a bachelors degree and less likely to live below the poverty line. We need to consider the implications of these and similar factors before we draw conclusions about the two groups' public school–private school choices.

This principle often comes into play in figuring out the impact of high-stakes graduation tests. In 2004, Massachusetts announced that 96 percent of its seniors had passed the state test and would graduate. This was true, but it was true only for people who had begun the 2003–2004 school year as seniors and who were still in school. Many in the class of 2004 were no longer present and accounted for. When that cohort of students started 9th grade, it contained 78,000 students; by the time it reached 12th grade, there were only 60,000. Eighteen thousand students had decamped (Wheelock, 2004).

We don't know what happened to these students. Some, of course, left the state and might well have passed the test and graduated if they had remained. But others were retained in grade and were no longer in the class of 2004. Some failed and dropped out or sought a General Equivalency Diploma. If we look at how many who started as 9th graders in the class of 2004 eventually graduated, we find rates ranging from 54 percent for Latino students to 80 percent for white students (Wheelock, 2004). We can't draw an accurate conclusion about the effects of high school graduation exams unless we consider all the groups, including those that did not graduate on time.

Know the Difference Between Rates and Scores

The Massachusetts example also illustrates another principle of data interpretation: Be aware of whether you are dealing with rates or scores. The two metrics can paint very different pictures of a situation. These days, most states are reporting some kind of rate: percent passing, percent proficient, or percent meeting state standards. But if we focus only on the proficiency cutoff, it doesn't matter whether the student exceeds it by one question or 40. We're looking at how many kids can jump over the barrier, not at how high they jump.

Moreover, using passing rates instead of scores can obscure the fact that the white-minority achievement gap may be increasing. Consider the theoretical data in Figure 5.1. If we look only at passing rates, black students have reduced the gap from 40 percent to 30 percent. But if we look at scores, the gap has actually increased from 16 points to 24 points.

This discrepancy might not be so important if the passing score actually meant something in terms of performance in the real world. But it doesn't. These passing scores are totally arbitrary. Some readers might recall that in my recent report on the condition of public education (Bracey, 2005), I awarded a Golden Apple to a student in Ohio because he refused to take the Ohio Proficiency Tests. It was not his act of defiance that garnered him a prize; it was the reasons he gave:

In 13 years of testing, Ohio has failed to conduct any studies linking scores on the proficiency test to college acceptance rates, dropout rates, college grades, income levels, incarceration rates, scores on military recruiting tests, or any other similar statistic. [The student was admitted to several colleges! (p. 140)

Do the Arithmetic

Here's a final principle of data interpretation to examine on your own: Do the arithmetic. In 1995, an article in an education periodical (not *Educational* Leadership) stated that "Every year since 1950, the number of American children gunned down has doubled." Sit down with a calculator and a sheet of paper on which you write in one column the years from 1950 to 1994. Then assume that one child was "gunned down" in 1950 and let the figure double for each successive year. Have fun.

REFERENCES

Barringer, F. (2006, Jan. 26). United States ranks 28th on environment, a new study says. *The New York Times,* p. A3.

Berrueta-Clement, J. R., Schweinhan, L. J., Bameu, W. S., Epstein, A. S,, & Weikart, D. P. (1984). *Changed lives: The effects of the Perry* Preschool *Program on youths through age 19.* Ypsilanti, MI: High/Scope Press.

Best, J. (2001). *Damned lies and statistics: Untangling numbers from the media, politicians, and activists.* Berkeley, CA: University of California Press.

Bracey, G. W. (2005). The fifteenth Bracey report on the condition of public education. *Phi Delta Kappan,* 87(2), 138–153.

Doyle, D. P. (1995). Where connoisseurs send their children to school. Washington, DC: Center for Education Reform.

Doyle, D. P., DeSchryver, D. A., & Diepold, B. (2004, Sept. 7). *Where do public school teachers send their kids to school?* Washington, DC: Thomas B. Fordham Institute. Available: www.edexcellence.net /foundation/ publication/publication.cfm ?id=333

Doyle, D. P., & Hartle, T. W. (1986). *Where public school teachers send their children to school: A preliminary* analysis. Washington, DC: American Enterprise Institute.

National Center for Education Statistics. (2000). *NAEP1999 trends in academic progress.* Report No. NCES-2000-469. Washington, DC: Author.

National Commission on Excellence in Education. (1983). *A nation at risk.* Washington, DC: Author. Available: www.ed.gov /pubs/NatAtRisk

Reynolds, A. J. (2001, May 21-June 2). *Age 21 benefit cost* analysis *of the* Chicago Child-Parent *Center program*. Paper presented to the Society for Prevention Research, Madison, Wisconsin.

Wheelock, A. (2004, June 8). *Massachusetts Department of Education "progress report" inflates "pass rates"for the class of 2004* [Online]. Available: www.massparents.org /news/2004/passrate_2004 htm

Will, G. F. (1993a, March 7). When the state fails its citizens. *The Washington Post,* p. C7.

———. (1993b, Aug. 26). Taking back education. *The Washington Post,* p. A27.

IN THEIR OWN WORDS: MAKING THE MOST OF QUALITATIVE INTERVIEWS

By Robert S. Weiss

In the 1840s, British sociologist-journalist Henry Mayhew sought to learn about the lives of London's seamstresses—how they did their work and managed to survive on so little income. He found his answers by asking the women themselves and his interviews made vivid the dismal conditions of their lives. One young woman, after describing how little she was paid for long hours of work, said: "I was single. ... I had a child, and he used to cry for food. So, as I could not get a living for him myself by my needle, I went into the streets and made out a living that way." The novels of Charles Dickens captured readers' sympathies, but they were only fiction. Mayhew presented the experiences of real people.

Such "qualitative interviews" are now so common that it is easy to forget how radical Henry Mayhew's procedure—which assumes that ordinary people can provide valid accounts of their own lives—was in his day. Indeed, qualitative interviewing was considered by many researchers so simple that it required no special techniques; listening attentively and respectfully was enough. More recently, practitioners have recognized that training is needed to make the most of interviewing and to avoid its pitfalls.

Studies based on in-depth interviews illuminate the social world. They describe the survival struggles of families on welfare, the ups and downs of physicists' careers and the tendency of two-job couples to assign homemaking to the wives. They reveal the emotional and social implications of organizational charts, from prisons to medical schools. Diane Vaughan's interview study of the bureaucratic processes that led to the disastrous 1986

Weiss, R. S. (2008). In their own words: Making the most of qualitative interviews. In J. Goodwin & J. M. Jasper (Eds.), *The Contexts Reader* (pp. 498–506). W. W. Norton & Company, Inc.

Challenger launch has become an important reference for institutions—medical schools as well as NASA—trying to reduce catastrophic errors.

The type of interview used in these studies is often called "qualitative" to distinguish it from an interview done for a survey. Qualitative interviews ask about the details of what happened: what was done and said, what the respondent thought and felt. The aim is to come as close as possible to capturing in full the processes that led to an event or experience. The researchers' report will likely be a densely detailed description of what happened, but it may also provide a basis for a theory of why it happened. In contrast, surveys ask well-crafted questions that elicit brief answers. The answers are then added up and expressed as numbers or percentages. Surveys are quantitative; they report the distribution of people's actions or opinions in tables or statistics (see "Sense and Nonsense about Surveys," page 472). In-depth interviews yield descriptions of experiences, processes, and events.

More than any other technique social scientists use, in-depth interviewing can shed light on events that would otherwise remain unknown because they happened in the past or out of public sight. In-depth interviews can provide vivid descriptions of personal experience—for example, what it feels like to succeed or to fail at an undertaking, or the emotional consequences of a new child or a death in the family. They are the best source of information about people's thoughts and feelings and the motives and emotions that lead them to act as they do.

BUT CAN WE TRUST WHAT WE ARE TOLD?

For her study of religiously inspired terrorism, national security expert Jessica Stern interviewed leaders of terrorist groups. They seemed entirely truthful when they told her about their commitment to producing a better world, but when she asked about the sources of their funds, they exaggerated the importance of small gifts and minimized contributions from wealthy donors. Most of those who were widely known to have received funds from governments simply lied. The adequacy and accuracy of interview data depends on what respondents are willing to report.

Lies or evasions such as these are not the only way interview findings can be compromised. Even respondents who want to be accurate may distort. Memory of an event is never simply a replay of a mental videotape. It is a reconstruction, an integration of fragments of stored knowledge, perceptions, and emotions. From these elements people build a coherent story, perhaps accompanied by visualized scenes of the event. The account and its accompanying images may be close to what happened, but inevitably there will be omissions, distortions, and additions.

Psychologist Elizabeth Loftus and her students have repeatedly demonstrated that memory is vulnerable to false associations. In one study, they showed subjects who lived in the Disneyland area advertisements in which Bugs Bunny appeared as a member of the Disneyland staff. Actually, Bugs Bunny has never entered Disneyland; he is a Warner Brothers property. But nearly a quarter of the subjects who read the false advertisements later reported meeting Bugs Bunny at Disneyland. They seemed to have put together memories of an actual visit to Disneyland with awareness of a link between Disneyland and Bugs Bunny, forgetting that the awareness stemmed from the advertisements. How can sociologists depend on data that are so fallible? And how can readers assess the trustworthiness of their reports?

To begin with, things are not so bad; it is easy to exaggerate the unreliability of interview data. Loftus and her students found that when her subjects reported a false memory, they tended to be less confident than when they reported something that had actually happened. Other indicators of the trustworthiness of a report include the density of detail the respondent provides, the apparent vividness of recall, and the extent to which the respondent's description makes sense in the context of his or her life.

Reports based mainly on interviews are often strengthened by the inclusion of other kinds of information. Jessica Stern, in her report on terrorism, provided a context for her interviews by describing the settings in which the interviews were held: homes, hotel rooms, restaurants, house trailers, and isolated terrorist camps. She also described the dress, manner, and facial features of the terror group members she interviewed and her own reactions of sympathy, repugnance, and fear. In her *Challenger* report, Diane Vaughan relied on interviews to explain what could not be understood from NASA's internal memos, but she reported the memos as well. Often a survey can strengthen arguments based primarily on qualitative interviews, by showing how one person's story or opinion fits into larger patterns.

The interviewer's direct observations can also help readers judge whether skepticism is appropriate. Did a respondent seem to be straightforward or evasive? The interviewer's observations of settings can corroborate what respondents say, as when a view of spacious grounds supports a respondent's claim that an organization is successful, but it can also contradict their claims, as when someone professing asceticism is interviewed in an opulent setting.

DOING IT RIGHT

The cooperation of the respondent is of paramount importance to the success of an interview. While full cooperation cannot always be achieved, cooperation is likely to be maximized by an interviewer who is respectful and friendly, yet task-focused. In my own research, I bring two copies of consent forms describing the study to my interviewees, both copies bearing

FROM INTERVIEW TO REPORT

The following excerpts are from a study of retirement. The first part illustrates the sort of specific interview material a researcher might obtain. It is drawn from one of about a dozen interviews that address "puttering." The second part illustrates how such data are integrated into a general report.

Excerpts

Interviewer: What are your days like?

Respondent: Very quiet and uneventful.

Interviewer: Like yesterday, what, how did yesterday work? Maybe start in the morning.

Respondent: Well, I, I got up, had some breakfast I went out, ah, went out for about three or four hours and did a little bit of window shopping, a little Christmas shopping. I got back around noontime or so. Ah, I had lunch, watched the news … then just puttered around the house. Then I usually go to bed around 9 or 10 o'clock. Last night it was 10 o'clock. I had supper and watched television for a while and then I usually go to bed. But, like I said, very unexciting, very uneventful.

Interviewer: If you wanted to describe a really boring hour and get across what it felt like and what was going on. …

Respondent: Well I don't have a problem with that. I, ah, I can sit down and do absolutely nothing for an hour. And it doesn't bother me. I enjoy a chance to relax and not have the pressure of having to do something.

Report

Puttering is a relaxed way of moving through a day, engaging in activities as they attract one's attention, undertaking nothing that demands energy and concentration. The dishes need doing, so why not do them now? It's nice out, and a bit of gardening might be enjoyable. It's noontime, time for a sandwich and the news on television. Later, magazines need to be picked up and a room straightened. There is time for a bit of reading. E-mail may be checked, or an hour taken to organize the attic. Nothing has special urgency.

Retirees seem not to be bored by puttering. There is always something to fill time with, and the puttering is regularly interrupted by an activity to attend to, a hobby to pursue, a walk, or a bit of shopping or coffee with a friend. Mr. Oldsten was among the many respondents who liked taking it easy. He had been the purchasing director for a high-tech company, a job that was frequently stressful. His wife was still employed and so he spent most of the day alone.

Yesterday, I got up, had some breakfast, I went out for about three or four hours and did a little bit of window shopping. I got back around noontime or so. I had lunch, watched the news, then just puttered around the house. I had supper and watched television for a while. I usually go to bed around 9 or 10 o'clock, last night it was 10 o'clock. Very unexciting, very uneventful. I can sit down and do absolutely nothing for an hour. And it doesn't bother me. I enjoy a chance to relax and not have the pressure of having to do something.

my signature. After briefly explaining the study, I give both forms to the respondent, ask him or her to read one and, if comfortable with it, to sign one of the copies and keep the other. I usually have a tape recorder and ask if it is all right to turn it on. My aim is to establish that the respondent and I are coworkers in producing information the study requires.

A good research partnership is more important to the quality of the interview than the phrasing of specific questions. If the respondent and I get along well, he or she will accept that the detailed accounts I request are important for the study and will tolerate any fumbling or uncertainty in my questions.

In qualitative interviewing, questions are usually formulated during the interview rather than written out beforehand. There are no magic phrasings which will reliably elicit illuminating responses. However, there are several principles that are helpful. Concrete observations are almost always more useful than a respondent's generalizations. It is hard to guess from generalizations what underlying events the respondent is drawing on, or even whether the generalizations are based on specific events at all. So if a respondent says, "We got along fine," the interviewer should ask something like, "When you say that, what are you thinking of?" or "Can you tell me the last time that happened?" or "Can you think of a time that really showed that happening?" It can sometimes help for an interviewer to add, "The more concrete you can be, the better."

Respondents can provide fuller and more accurate reports if they are asked about events that happened recently. To know about the respondent's use of time, it makes sense to ask about yesterday; to learn about an event that occurs frequently, it makes sense to ask about the last time it happened. Should the respondent object that yesterday or the most recent event was not typical, it is then possible to ask what made it unusual, and then to ask for a description of an earlier day or event that was more nearly typical.

When a respondent is describing an important sequence of events, the interviewer might mentally check that the description contains adequate detail. In a study of work stress in an organization, a respondent might say, "I knew I was in trouble so I looked up this vice president and asked him for help." The interviewer might then have the respondent fill in what happened between when he recognized that he had a problem and when he asked for help from a particular executive. So, the interviewer might ask, "Could you start with when you realized you were in trouble and walk me through what happened next? How did the thought of going to the vice president come to you and what happened then?"

Although qualitative interviews are sometimes called conversational, they are not. Imagine a conversation in which a retiree, asked by a friend whether he had gone back to the office to see the people he had worked with, had replied, "People who come back after they've retired, the people who're there are nice, but there's nothing to talk about." The friend would hardly press the retiree for details he had not volunteered by asking, "Is there a specific time you're thinking of? Can you walk me through what happened?" But those are the questions an interviewer would ask.

SHAPING THE STUDY

Good interviews are windows into people's lives. Researchers can often edit the transcripts to cut out the questions and rearrange respondents' answers into engrossing first-person stories. Anthropologist Oscar Lewis, in his book *Children of Sanchez*, painted a compelling portrait of the lives of people in an impoverished Mexican family by presenting edited transcripts of qualitative interviews with the family's father and his four adult children. Journalist Studs Terkel has used excerpts from qualitative interviews as the entire content of books such as *Working*, in which his respondents discuss their jobs.

Both Lewis and Terkel focused on the stories of particular individuals, but many social scientists want to generalize about people's experiences and so want the breadth of information that multiple cases can provide. They want to be able to report not only about one particular retiree's experience, but about the experience of a population of retirees. That requires a sample of cases that includes the full range of important differences in the population. For example, an investigator studying the experience of retiring would want to talk with retirees from a range of occupations, both men and women, the married and unmarried, and people who liked their work and those who hated it.

Sometimes the topic makes it difficult to obtain a good sample. For example, in a study of active drug users an investigator may be restricted to a small group within which he or she finds acceptance. Investigators in such situations must make do, but they must also be aware of the limitations of their sample. They may learn how their respondents are distinct, but in any case, generalizations from unsystematic "convenience samples" have to be treated with caution.

Several factors must be taken into account when determining how many people should be interviewed. The more varied the population, the larger the sample needs to be to cover an adequate range. A study of retired executives requires a broader sample than one of retired bankers. Also important is the extent to which the investigator wants more than one respondent from the same category—for example, how many retired bankers? Redundancy can compensate for omissions and distortions, and can also uncover important variations among people who are apparently similar.

If there seem to be between a half dozen and a dozen important types of respondents, and if the investigator would like five instances of each variation, a sample size of between 30 and 60 is a rough ideal. The larger the sample, the more confidence the investigator will have that there is adequate range and enough redundancy to make other important, perhaps unsuspected, differences apparent.

Most investigators find that the amount of data produced by qualitative interviewing sets an upper limit on the number of respondents. One and a half hours of interviewing can produce 40 single-spaced pages of typescript. A study with 80 respondents might come close to filling a file drawer. Follow-up interviews with each respondent can double the volume. In my experience, 100 respondents are the most that can be dealt with comfortably, and so large a sample will almost surely provide enough material to yield an adequate basis for trustworthy generalization.

WHAT TO DO WITH THE DATA

Analyzing interview data can be daunting. There is likely to be a great deal of it, and no obvious place to start. Researchers may read through a few transcripts and feel excited by what is there, yet wonder how they can ever extract the essential message of those few transcripts, let alone the entire set. But there are fairly systematic ways of proceeding.

Just as in solving a jigsaw puzzle, the analysis of qualitative interview material requires sorting and integrating. For a study on retirement, one might begin by separating out the materials that deal with the decision to retire, with retirement parties, with the immediate reaction to being retired and so on. Within each of the sorted sets of materials, the investigator will identify "meaning units"—passages that deal with the same issue. A respondent's description of being urged to retire by a boss can be a single meaning unit, whether it was a brief comment or a full story. The investigator then summarizes all the meaning units dealing with an issue. That summary, perhaps augmented by interpretations or explanations, constitutes a report on the particular sector. The final study is then produced by integrating all of the sector reports into a single coherent story.

Before computers, researchers made marginal notes on interview transcripts, cut out passages with scissors, and sorted the resulting slips of paper into physical file folders. Computers have changed all this into virtual cutting and sorting. Some investigators use one of several computer programs designed specifically to assist in analyzing interview materials.

Investigators sometimes want to do more than use responses to narrate a subject, they want to explain what they have found. Developing an explanatory theory is a task that inevitably challenges the investigator's knowledge, insight, and creativity. But researchers have the ability to return to their interview transcripts to assess the validity of their conclusions in light of everything they were told.

ROOTING OUT BIAS

In recent years, social scientists who do qualitative interview studies have questioned some of the assumptions that underlie this method. Two lines of critique have been especially important. The feminist critique focuses primarily on the relationship of interviewer and respondent, while the constructivist approach is more concerned with interpretation of interview materials.

The feminist critique arose from the experiences female investigators had while interviewing other women. The researchers were struck by the difference between their relationships with respondents and the sort of relationships that had been taken for granted in earlier studies. Previously, rapport was recognized as important, but respondents were largely related to only as providers of data, people whose words would be taken down, analyzed, and interpreted. Feminist scholars feel that this approach dehumanizes respondents and requires researchers to deny any identification with the interviewees. They feel it is essential to acknowledge their kinship with respondents. After all, the researchers were themselves insiders in their respondents' worlds: they too have families and family problems, work to which they are committed and priorities to juggle. It is more in keeping with this reality to replace inquiring with sharing.

Feminist investigators, among whom Ann Oakley has been a leading figure, also dislike the idea that after extracting information from respondents, they have nothing further to do with them. They want to acknowledge that interviewing establishes a relationship and that gaining access to someone's private life brings with it responsibilities. They feel it important to be of help to those respondents who are doing badly or, at the least, to accurately represent their plight. They also dislike the idea of owning the data drawn from respondents' lives. Some discuss their reports with their respondents and modify statements with which respondents disagree.

Constructivist investigators, such as Kathy Charmaz, were worried by investigators' insufficiently reflective leap from the reports of respondents to more general conclusions. They recognize that interpretations are not implicit in the data, but rather are influenced by the ideas and concerns that investigators bring to the data. In their view, investigators should acknowledge explicitly that their conclusions do not capture reality in the way that one might capture a butterfly. Instead, investigators shape respondents' reports in many possible ways. For example, a respondent's description of a problem with a boss may be classified as an instance of organizational friction rather than as a cause of work stress.

The constructivist perspective recasts the question of how close to reality an investigator can really get by talking to people. It argues that there is no single clear-cut reality to be located by means of interviews. Rather, what an investigator makes of interview information depends on his or her preconceptions and concerns. The interviews themselves may provide a basis for a number of interpretations, each of them consistent with the interview information.

The feminist and constructivist critiques draw attention to problems of ethics and interpretation that are implicit in the conduct of qualitative interview studies. When judging the credibility of a report these issues should be considered alongside other possible challenges, such as respondent credibility and the potential for investigator bias.

Perhaps the major threat to the validity of qualitative interviewing studies, more than distortions during the interview, is investigator bias. An investigator who is determined, consciously or unconsciously, to have a particular theme emerge from his or her study can choose respondents whose interviews are likely to produce that picture, encourage the respondents to give answers consistent with it, and write a report that neglects whatever might disconfirm it. Only a small minority of qualitative interview studies are significantly biased and these can usually be recognized easily.

READING INTERVIEW STUDIES

How can a reader evaluate a qualitative interview study? A good place to begin is with the sample. If the study was of people in a similar situation, did the sample have adequate range and redundancy? Did the interviews take place in a setting that encouraged respondents to provide full and accurate reports? If an event was witnessed by a number of people, are all relevant perspectives represented? And did the interview guide cover the full range of relevant issues? (Reports will often include an "interview guide," a list of the topics covered in the interviews, in an appendix.)

The trustworthiness of the data interpretation also can be judged by how closely it seems to be linked to the interviews, whether it appears to take all the interviews into consideration and the extent to which key points are buttressed by convincing quotations. Also worth considering is the investigator's use of supporting data from quantitative studies or from interviewers' observations. Finally, the investigator's conclusions could be matched against the conclusions of other studies and evaluated for their consistency with everything else the reader knows.

More than 150 years after Mayhew's groundbreaking work, qualitative interviewing is and will remain a fundamental method of social science. Even if other sources of information exist in archives or are accessible to observation, only qualitative interviewing can provide firsthand access to the experience of others. An oft-repeated joke describes a drunk searching for a lost wallet under a streetlight. "Did you drop it here?" someone asks. "Nope," he replies. "Dropped it in the alley. But the light's better here."

Qualitative interviewing is looking in the dark alley, whatever might be the problems of doing so. If we want to learn from the experiences of other people, we must ask them to inform us. Although we are much more knowledgeable about how to conduct an interview than was Mayhew, and more aware of the difficulties that can arise as we try to achieve understanding from the information we obtain, fundamentally our approach remains the same.

RECOMMENDED RESOURCES

Kathy Charmaz. "Grounded Theory: Objectivist and Constructivist Methods." In *Handbook of Qualitative Research*, eds. Norman Denzin and Yvonna Lincoln (Sage Publications, 2000). This is both a brief exposition of how to do a qualitative study and a discussion of constructivist ideas.

Joseph C. Hermanowicz. *The Stars Are Not Enough: Scientists—Their Passions and Professions* (University of Chicago Press, 1998). Describes the interplay of ambition, career, and self-appraisal among physicists.

Arlie Russell Hochschild, with Anne Machung. *The Second Shift: Working Parents and the Revolution at Home* (Viking, 1989). Describes the unequal distribution of familial responsibilities in two-job families.

Oscar Lewis. *The Children of Sanchez, Autobiography of a Mexican Family* (Random House, 1961). In this classic study, Lewis recounts the life stories of a Mexican worker and his children.

Ann Oakley. "Interviewing Women: A Contradiction in Terms." in *The American Tradition in Qualitative Research* Vol. Ill, eds. Norman Denzin and Yvonna S. Lincoln (Sage Publications, 2001). An influential feminist critique of traditional approaches to interviewing.

Jessica Stern. *Terror in the Name of God: Why Religious Militants Kill* (HarperCollins, 2003). Uncovers the aims, strategies, and motives of terrorists who believe they are doing God's work.

Diane Vaughan. *The Challenger Launch Decision: Risky Technology Culture, and Deviance at NASA* (University of Chicago Press, 1996). Describes the rational decision making that led to the tragically mistaken Challenger launch.

Robert S. Weiss. *Learning from Strangers: The Art and Method of Qualitative Interview Studies* (Free Press, 1994). A text on qualitative interview methods.

REVIEW QUESTIONS

1. What are some reasons for being careful about trusting interviewees? How can such problems be minimized?
2. Why is cooperation important in qualitative interviews?
3. What are the feminist and "constructivist" critiques of qualitative interviews? How do these critiques recast the relationship between interviewer and respondent?

Gender

Women and Children First

The first article provided in the following set is used to focus the reader's thinking about gender and sexism, as well as how "words are tools of thought." For many, one's gender is the same as sex, yet in the social sciences we see these as distinct concepts. Regardless, they are both important to our understanding and treatment of women as well as the messages we directly and indirectly give to children as they learn the value placed on people who possess an XX or XY chromosome configuration. Think back to the discussion of language in Chapter 2; the use of words and their meaning are often taken for granted. As you read each article, try identifying the structure of argument presented before drawing your own conclusions.

The reader is encouraged to explore their personal reaction to Kleinman's (2002) discussion of sexist language and think about societal values, norms, and viewpoints about gender that inform people's views and how their behavior has a reciprocal effect on society. How are your preconceived ideas and assumptions influencing your view of the information in the article? As is referenced in Chapter 3, can you shift the perception?

In the second article, Courture and Johnson (2011) address how gender biases impact women in the workplace and at home. The competence of women and their job success are explored along with how the request of parental leave impacts both of these variables. The authors seem to propose that society's definition of the "ideal worker" is lagging behind the reality of today's societal needs. This article may serve as a useful springboard regarding how values, language, laws, and policies intersect (as was introduced in Chapter 2 of this text).

Kleinman (2002) argues that language is important when considering current gender issues, and that it is especially important for our children through the socialization agent of education. Nichols (2011) in "Girls and Boys, Work and Play: Gendered Meanings and Participation in Early Childhood Education" explores messages given to girls and boys during their early education. How do messages received during play impact girls and boys as they are prepared for "work" later in life? While this article focuses on gender, it also brings up some important points regarding the focus of curricula in our educational system, such as raising the question of the merits of a teacher-centered or child-centered curriculum and what the impact of either might be for boys and girls.

Finally, we have included "The Heterosexual Questionnaire" to encourage readers to critically and creatively explore heterosexual norms and their prevalence in our society. This questionnaire was first created in 1972 and attempts to shed light on assumptions we make relative to human sexuality. Review of the different questions posed can spark conversations not only about sexual orientation, but also gender and other group categorizations in society and how our questions, use of language, and behavioral norms continue to perpetuate unquestioned assumptions.

These articles needn't be read in any particular order. They have been selected to aid in the discussion of gender in our society and how the current societal milieu impacts the efforts of women and children. We encourage readers to identify some of the critical and creative thinking skills from Chapters 1–3 as they make their way through.

Questions for Consideration:

1. What critical and creative thinking techniques do you believe are helpful in assessing Nichols's (2011) statement that "disrupting the work-play binary [will] open up new ways of orienting to education and social participation"?
2. What is "inclusive language"? What might our society be like if we were to embrace inclusive language?
3. What is your reaction to the idea that the objectification of women is associated with using language to make women a subset of men?

✧ seven ✧

WHY SEXIST LANGUAGE MATTERS

By Sherryl Kleinman

For eleven years I've been teaching a sociology course at the University of North Carolina on gender inequality. I cover such topics as the wage gap, the "second shift" (the disproportionate amount of housework and child care that heterosexual women do at home), the equation of women's worth with physical attractiveness, the sexualizing of women in the media, lack of reproductive rights for women (especially poor women), sexual harassment, and men's violence against women. But the Issue that both female and male students have the most trouble understanding—or, as I see it, share a strong unwillingness to understand—is sexist language.

I'm not referring to such words as "bitch," "whore," and "slut." What I focus on instead are words that most people consider just fine: male (so-called) generics. Some of these words refer to persons occupying a position: postman, chairman, freshman, congressman, fireman. Other words refer to the entire universe of human beings: "mankind" or "he." Then we've got manpower, man-made lakes, and "Oh, man, where did I leave my keys?" There's "manning" the tables in a country where we learn that "all men are created equal."

The most insidious, from my observations, is the popular expression "you guys." People like to tell me it's a regional term. But I've heard it In Chapel Hill, New York, Chicago, San Francisco, and Montreal. I've seen it in print in national magazines, newsletters, and books. I've heard it on television and in films. And even if it were regional, that doesn't make it right. I bet we can all think of a lot of practices in our home regions we'd like to get rid of.

Kleinman, S. (2002). Why sexist language matters. *Qualitative Sociology, 25*(2), 299-304.

Try making up a female-based generic, such as "freshwoman" and using it with a group of male students, or calling your male boss "chairwoman." Then again, don't. There could be serious consequences for referring to a man as a woman—a term that still means "lesser" In our society. If not, why do men get so upset at the idea of being called women?

What's the big deal? Why does all this "man-ning" and "guys-ing" deserve a place on my list of items of gender inequality?

The answer is because male-based generics are another indicator—and, more importantly, a *reinforcer*—of a system in which "man" in the abstract and men in the flesh are privileged over women. Some say that language merely reflects reality and so we should ignore our words and work on changing the unequal gender arrangements that are reflected in our language. Well, yes, in part.

It's no accident that "man" is the anchor in our language and "woman" is not. And of course we should make social change all over the place. But the words we use can also reinforce current realities when they are sexist (or racist or heterosexist). Words are the tools of thought. We can use words to maintain the status quo or to think in new ways—which in turn creates the possibility of a new *reality*. It makes a difference if I think of myself as a "girl" or a "woman"; it makes a difference if we talk about "Negroes" or "African Americans." Do we want a truly inclusive language or one that just pretends?

For a moment, imagine a world—as the philosopher Douglas R. Hofstadter did in his 1986 satire on sexist language—where people used generics based on race rather than gender. In that world, people would use "freshwhite," "chairwhite," and, yes, "you whiteys." People of color would hear "all whites are created equal"—and be expected to feel included. In an addendum to his article, Hofstadter says that he wrote "A Person Paper on Purity in Language" to shock readers: Only by substituting "white" for "man" does it become easy to see the pervasiveness of male-based generics and to recognize that using "man" for all human beings is wrong. Yet, women are expected to feel flattered by "freshman," "chairman," and "you guys."

And why do so many women cling to "freshman," "chairman," and "you guys?"

I think it's because women want to be included in the term that refers to the higher-status group: men. But while being labeled "one of the guys" might make women *feel* included, it's only a guise of inclusion, not the reality. If women were really included we wouldn't have to disappear into the word "guys "

At the same time that women in my classes throw around "you guys"—even here in the southern United States, where "y'all" is an alternative—they call themselves "girls." I'm not sure if this has gotten worse over the years or I've just noticed it more. When I was an undergraduate in the early to mid 1970s, we wanted to be women. Who would take us seriously at college or at work if we were "girls?" To many of my students today, "woman" is old enough to be "over the hill." A "girl" is youthful and thus more attractive to men than a "woman." Since they like the term so much, I suggest, that we rename Women's Studies "Girls' Studies." And since the Women's Center on campus provides services for them, why not call it "The Girls' Center." They laugh. "Girls" sounds ridiculous, they say. The students begin to see that "girl"—as a label for twenty-one-year-olds—is infantilizing, not flattering.

"Girl" and "you guys" aren't the only linguistic problems on campus. A few years ago Bob, a student in my class, said that his fraternity is now open to women as well as men and that a controversy had erupted over whether to continue to use the term "brother" to refer to all fraternity members, or to use "sister" for female members. Almost all the women in his fraternity, he said, voted to be called brother rather than sister. As with "you guys," the women wanted to take on the word that has more value. Yet the practice of using "brother" reinforces the idea that a real member of the group is a brother (i.e., a man). I asked what would happen if he had suggested that all fraternity members be called sisters rather than brothers, or that they rename the fraternity a sorority. Everyone laughed at the absurdity of this suggestion. Exactly. Yet it is not absurd, but acceptable, to call women by the term "guys" or "brothers."

Since the "fraternity" Bob referred to is no longer exclusively male, and since gender is no longer a criterion for membership, I asked him how he thought others might react if he suggested they substitute "association" or "society" for "fraternity." Perhaps they could call both men and women "members," or, if students preferred a more informal term, "friends?"

"Yes, that makes sense," Bob told us. "But, I just don't think they'll go for it." He paused. "I'm not sure why."

We talked as a class about why this simple solution might meet with resistance. We concluded that many men would resist losing these linguistic signifiers of male superiority, and many women would resist losing the valued maleness implied by "brother" and "fraternity." "Member" would feel like a drop in status for both women and men!

The students, like most people who use male "generics," don't have bad intentions. But as sociologists, we know that it's important to look at the *consequences*. All those "man" words— said many times a day by millions of people every day—cumulatively reinforce the message that men are the standard and that women should be subsumed by the male category.

I worry about what people with the best of intentions are teaching our children. A colleague's five-year-old daughter recently left her classroom crying after a teacher said, "What do you guys think?" She thought the teacher didn't care about what *she* thought. When the teacher told her that of course she was included, her tears stopped. But what was the lesson? She learned that her opinion as a girl mattered only when she's a guy. She learned that men are the norm.

A friend's six-year-old son refused to believe that the female firefighter who came to his school to talk to the class—dressed in uniform—actually fought fires. The firefighter repeatedly referred to herself as a "fireman." Despite the protests of the teacher and the fire-fighter, the boy would not be convinced. "A fireman can't be a woman," he said. His mother, who is fastidious in her use of nonsexist language, had a tough time doing damage control.

So, is it any surprise that the worst insult a boy can hurl at another boy is "girl?"

We know from history that making a group invisible makes it easier for the powerful to do what they want with members of that group. Perhaps that's why linguists use the strong language of "symbolic annihilation" to refer to the disappearance of women into male-based terms. And we know, from too many past and current studies, that far too many men are doing "what they want" with women. Most of us can see a link between calling women "sluts" and "whores" and men's sexual violence against women. We need to recognize that making women linguistically a subset of man/men through terms like "mankind" and "guys" also makes women into objects. If we, as women, aren't worthy of such true generics as "first-year," "chair," or "you all," then how can we expect to be paid a "man's wage," be respected as people rather than objects (sexual or otherwise) on the job and at home, be treated as equals rather than servers or caretakers of others, be considered responsible enough to make our own decisions about reproduction, and define who and what we want as sexual beings? If we aren't even deserving of our place in humanity in language, why should we expect to be treated as decent human beings otherwise?

Some people tell me that making English nonsexist is a slippery slope. As one colleague said to me, "Soon we'll have to say 'waitperson,' which sounds awful. We won't be able to 'man' the table at Orientation. And we'll become 'fellowpersons' at the Institute!" I told him that "server" works well. We can "staff" the table. And why not use "scholars" instead of "fellows?" We've got a big language to roam in. Let's have fun figuring out how to speak and write without making "man" the center. If sliding down that slope takes us to a place where we speak nonsexist English, I'm ready for the ride.

And this doesn't mean that every word with "m-e-n" in it is a problem. Menstruation and mending are fine. Making amends is good, too. There's only a problem when "men," as part of a word, is meant to refer to everyone (freshmen, chairmen, and so on).

Now and then someone says that I should work on more important issues—like men's violence against women—rather than on "trivial" issues like language. Well, I work on lots of issues. But that's not the point. Working against sexist language *is* working against men's violence against women. It's one step. If we cringe at "freshwhite" and "you whiteys" and would protest such terms with loud voices, then why don't we work as hard at changing "freshman" and "you guys?" Don't women deserve it? That women primarily exist in language as "girls" (children), "sluts" (sex objects) and "guys" (a subset of men) makes it less of a surprise that we still have a long list of gendered inequalities to fix.

We've got to work on *every* item on the list. Language is one we can work on right now, if we're willing. It's easier to start saying "you all," "y'all" or "you folks" instead of "you guys" than to change the wage gap tomorrow.

And what might help us make changes in our language? About a year ago I was complaining, as usual, about the "you guys" problem. "What we need is a card that explains why we don't want to be called guys!" Smita Varia, a veteran of my gender course, said. "Let's write one."

"Hey. You Guys!"

Imagine someone walking up to a group of guys and saying, "Hey, girls, how're ya doing?" We doubt they'd be amused! So isn't it weird that women are supposed to accept—even like—being called "one of the guys?" We're also supposed to like "freshman," "chairman" and "mankind."

Get over it, some people say. Those words are generic. They apply to everyone. But then how come so-called generics are always male?

What if generics ended in "white"? Freshwhite, chairwhite, and "hey, you whiteys!" Would people of color like being called "one of the whites?" We don't think so.

The terms "guys" makes women invisible by lumping them in with men. Let's quit doing that. When you're talking to a group of customers, gender doesn't really matter, so why not replace "you guys" with "you all," 'folks," or yall" Or simply say "what can I get you?" That would take care of us all.

Thanks for your help.

And so we did. Smita enlisted T. Christian Helms, another former student, to design a graphic for the card. You can access the layout of this business-sized card from our website: www.youall.freeservers.com. Make lots of copies. Give the cards to friends and ask them to think about sexist language. Leave one with a big tip after you've been "you guysed" during a meal. The card explains the problem and offers alternatives.

And institutional change is also possible. Some universities have adopted "first-year student" (instead of "freshman") because some students and faculty got angry about the male-based generics embedded in university documents. The American Psychological Association has a policy of using only inclusive language in their publications. Wherever you work or play, get together with other progressive people and suggest that your organization use "chair" instead of "chairman," "Ms." instead of "Mrs." or "Miss," "humankind" instead of "mankind," and "she or he" instead of "he." In my experience, members of some activist groups think sexist language is less important than other issues. But if we're going to work on social change, shouldn't we start by practicing nonsexist English among ourselves? Let's begin creating *now* the kind of society we want to live in later.

Nonsexist English is a resource we have at the tip of our tongues. Let's start using it.

REFERENCE

Hofstadter, D. R. (1986). A person paper on purity in language. In D. R. Hofstadter, *Metamagical themas: A questing for the essence of mind and pattern* (pp. 159–167). New York: Bantam.

THE PERSISTENT DISADVANTAGE FACING MOTHERS WORKING IN GENDER-NEUTRAL OCCUPATIONS

By Karen A. Couture and Kathleen R. Johnson

EXECUTIVE SUMMARY

Numerous studies have found that feminine characteristics of the mother stereotype interact with masculine characteristics of the ideal worker stereotype with the result that mothers are perceived more negatively than are fathers and nonparents when the job is male-typed. Our research investigated potential biases in evaluations of mothers performing a gender-neutral job. Our choice of a gender-neutral job was intended to reduce lack of fit perceptions between "mother" and "ideal worker." We assigned participants to one of four experimental conditions crossing target gender (male, female) and parental status (nonparent, prospective parent requesting parental leave). After reviewing performance information, participants evaluated the targets on job-related traits and predicted future behavior. Results indicated that mothers were judged significantly more negatively than were fathers, while male and female nonparents were judged similarly. We argue that sex-based stereotypes persist in the context of gender-neutral jobs and serve to disadvantage working mothers.

Couture, K. A., & Johnson, K. R. (2011). The persistent disadvantage facing mothers working in gender- neutral occupations. *Journal of Applied Management and Entrepreneurship, 16*(1), 53-65.

Despite legislation such as the Civil Rights Act of 1964, women today continue to experience workplace disadvantages and impediments to promotion. Women account for half of those working in management, in the professions, and related occupations but comprise just 15% of all Fortune 500 corporate officers, less than 7% of Fortune 500 top earners, and only 2% of Fortune 500 CEOs (Gunclius, 2009).

One avenue of research that attempts to explain workplace gender inequality focuses on the unconscious biases that continue to interfere with women's advancement. According to this work, traditional ideology promotes the notion that men exhibit such "masculine" characteristics as independence, autonomy, competitiveness, and a success orientation. Because we tend to associate these characteristics with the ideal worker, men have a distinct advantage in the workplace. In contrast, this ideology associates women to a greater extent with such "feminine" attributes as dependency, passivity, and other-orientation—characteristics that often conflict with the model of the ideal worker. Women, in short, do not "fit" the traditional model as well as men and, consequently, experience disadvantages in terms of pay, promotion, and other work rewards (Pelton, 2004; Heilman and Okimoto, 2008).

Women, of course, are a diverse group. How does society look upon working mothers? Traditionally speaking, motherhood epitomizes the ideals of femininity and exaggerates the gender role prescriptions for women. Consequently, mothers face disadvantages in the workplace that include but go beyond those simply related to their gender. In contrast to the iconic male worker who dedicates himself to work and career, society extols mothers for prioritizing family responsibilities (Cook, 1994). Indeed, not only does the working mom violate society's expectations of the ideal worker (because she is not a man) but also because she violates our expectations of motherhood (because she is not completely devoting herself to motherhood). In this context, it is likely that working mothers experience workplace disadvantages more than men and more than women without children (Heilman, 2001; Ridgeway and Correll, 2008).

A number of studies have sought evidence for the disadvantages associated with what has become known as the "motherhood penalty." Fuegan, Biernat, Haines, and Deaux (2004) investigated the impact of parental status on perceptions of worker attributes, hiring standards, as well as hiring and promotion decisions among a sample of undergraduates students and found that participants generally regarded parents as less "committed, less agentic, and as less available on the job than non-parents... [and] "mothers were disadvantaged relative to fathers" (p. 748). In a study conducted by Heilman and Okimoto (2008), participants rated mothers less competent and less likely to be recommended for promotion compared to fathers and non-parent women. Similarly, Cuddy, Fiske, and Glick (2004) found that participants rated consultants who were described as mothers lower in terms of competence than when the consultants were described as not having children. A study by Correll, Bernard, and Paik (2007), which required that participants evaluate applications for a marketing position, found mothers penalized in relation to competence ratings as well as recommended starting salary. Gungor and Biernat's study (2009) provides somewhat of a contrast in that they found no parent or motherhood penalty per se, although their participants exhibited a bias against female job applicants in general, finding them "less self-confident, less committed…and less likely than men to be hired" (p. 232).

While it is unclear whether Cuddy, Fiske, and Glick (2004) or Correll, Bernard, and Paik (2007) provided an important pre-test for gender neutrality in selecting a job category, Fuegan, Biernat, Haines, and Deaux (2004), Heilman and Okimoto (2008), and Gungor and Biernat (2009) specifically applied a male-typed job in their stimulus materials. The selection of a male-typed job highlights conditions under which individuals are more likely to assume that men, rather than women—especially mothers—are more qualified or suitable employees. As Heilman and Okimoto (2008) explain:

> *If mothers are viewed as prototypes of the general stereotype of women, there are likely to be particularly deleterious consequences for mothers who pursue traditionally male careers. They are likely to be seen as being less competent to perform these jobs successfully than are working nonmothers* (p 189).

Much of the previous work that examines the influence of stereotypes on working parents fails to compare perceptions of men and women who work in specifically gender-neutral jobs. Our project examined the extent to which mothers in a gender-neutral job are disadvantaged relative to fathers and non-parents (men and women). Our choice of a gender-neutral job, rather than a male gender-typed job, was intended to reduce lack of fit perceptions between "mother" and "ideal worker." We predicted that, due to the persistence of the mother stereo-type, mothers would continue to be disadvantaged with regard to perceptions of their job-related behaviors. We further predicted that non-parent women and men would be perceived similarly on the dependent measures as there would be a greater overlap between non-parent and successful employee stereotypes when the job is gender neutral.

Rather than simply identifying our experimental employee as a non-parent/parent, we noted that our employee was either (a) married with no children or (b) married, expecting a child, and requesting a 12-week parental leave. We believe that using the term "request for leave" will not only emphasize the parental status of the employee but also intensify any latent biases toward employees with children. Indeed, research suggests that managers find work-life policies, including requests for parental leave, to be disruptive and to get in the way of work goals (den Dulk & de Ruijter, 2008) and negatively to affect employment outcomes (Schneer and Reitman, 1994). Swanberg's (2004) in-depth personal interviews of public employees indicate that from the workers' perspective "women taking leave experienced lower job evaluations, infringement on their leave time, and resistance to planning for their time away from the office" (p. 14). In light of these findings, we believe our study will contribute to a better understanding of the way mothers working in gender-neutral jobs are perceived.

HYPOTHESES

Hypothesis 1: Participants will view the competence of women more negatively than that of men for those workers who request a leave, but not for those workers who do not make such a request.

Hypothesis 2: Participants will view the future job behavior and success of women more negatively than that of men for those workers who request a leave, but not for those who do not make such a request.

Hypothesis 3: Females requesting parental leave will be perceived as significantly less competent than females not requesting parental leave.

Hypothesis 4: The job behavior and success of females requesting parental leave will be perceived as significantly more negative than that of females not requesting parental leave.

Our hypotheses predicted a target gender x parental request interaction in which a significant difference would be obtained between females and males in the parental request condition (parents) but not in the non-request condition (non-parents). Additionally, women who do not request leave will be evaluated significantly more positively than women who do request a leave. These predictions follow from our assumption that women who request a leave will be viewed most negatively due to the motherhood penalty. As discussed in the introduction, society's traditional ideology suggests a greater incongruence between the stereotypical views of the "working mom" and "ideal employee" versus the "working dad" and "ideal employee."

METHOD

Participants

Participants included 176 undergraduate students from a small New England campus recruited from three psychology and two management classes. Eight students did not pass the manipulation check and their data were eliminated from analysis, leaving a total sample size of 168 (124 females, 44 males). The mean age of the participants was 20 years (SD = 1.7, range 18-33). Ninety percent of the participants indicated that they were working;

11% reported working on a full-time basis while the majority (79%) was employed on a part-time basis. Almost all were single (99%) and all were childless.[1]

Design

The design of this study was a 2 x 2 factorial with employee gender (male/female) and parental leave request (request/no request) as the independent variables. Participants were randomly assigned to each of the four-experimental conditions, resulting in 44 participants in the male employee/request and 42 in the female employee/request conditions, with 39 participants in the male/no request condition and 43 participants in female/no request condition.

Procedure

The researchers informed participants that the study was part of a research project to learn about the process of evaluating job performance with the goal of helping to improve the effectiveness of the procedures used in organizations. They were asked to assume the role of a manager and told that they would be examining and evaluating performance data about an employee. They then received a packet of materials, the first page of which contained a vignette describing a fictitious purchasing manager for a multinational footwear manufacturing company. This job was rated gender neutral in a pretest conducted with 36 psychology undergraduates. Using a nine-point bipolar scale, these participants rated the masculinity/femininity of a series of 20 jobs selected from the Occupational Information Network or O★Net (National Center for O★Net Development) that were relevant to our footwear company. The employee background information included a brief educational and employment history, tenure at the company, and personal information such as the employee's age (29), marital status (married in all four conditions), and the experimental manipulations.

The following page of the packet included a completed performance evaluation form indicating the results of the employee's most recent annual review, ostensibly completed by the employee's superior. The employee's name and a summary of the job tasks upon which the evaluation was based appeared at the top of the form. This form also included the completed evaluation of the employee's performance on each of eight criteria (planning/organizing, quantity and quality of work, job knowledge, efficiency, responsibility, cooperation and enthusiasm). The five-point scale system used for the evaluation (1=poor,

---

[1] Although undergraduate students have relatively limited work experiences, a full 90% of our participants were employed. Previous research in this field suggests that students' views are not unlike those found in studies that utilize more professional samples (See Gungor and Biernat, 2009). We therefore expect the findings of the present study to reasonably approximate those in the general work population.

5=excellent) also appeared on the form. We controlled for the performance level by giving all employees, regardless of the gender or request manipulation, a rating of "good" on half of the scales and "very good" on the other half. After reviewing all the material, participants assessed the employee's competence on a seven-point bipolar scale and indicated the employee's likelihood of future job-related behaviors and success.

Experimental Manipulations

Employee gender. We varied the employee's name (Alison Caldwell, Andrew Caldwell) in the employee background information and on the annual evaluation form. In addition, we matched the appropriate gender pronoun to each target employee.

Parental leave request. As noted above, the parental leave request manipulation was intended to highlight the employee's impending status as a mother or father. We indicated the employee's request for parental leave twice; first, in the employee background information and, second, on the annual evaluation form. In the employee background information, we identified the employee as either "married with no children" or "married and expecting a child." (In the case of the male employee, his wife was noted as expecting the baby.) In the request condition we also mentioned that each employee "requested a 12-week parental leave to care for the infant and home."

Dependent Measures

Competence. We used a seven-point bipolar adjective scale (1=incompetent, 7= competent) to obtain participants' perceptions of the employee's competence.

Table 8.1 Dependent Measures: Correlations

	COMPETENT	PASSPROMO	JOBEXPECT	EXCEL	QUIT	SICK
Competent		.12	.26**	.21**	-.14	.03
PassPromo			.17*	-.31**	.22**	.62**
JobExpect				.48**	-.24**	-.01
Excel					-.21**	-.06
Quit						.12
Sick						

**Correlation is significant at the .01 level (two-tailed)
* Correlation is significant at the .05 level (two-tailed)

Future job behavior and success. Using seven-point scales in which 1=not likely and 7=very likely, participants rated the likelihood that the employee would "meet future job expectations," "quit the job," "pass on a promotion for family-related reasons," and "take time off to care for a sick child." Participants also rated the employee on the extent to which they "believe the employee has the potential to excel in his/her career" (1=not at all, 7=very much). Inter-correlations among these measures are presented in Table 8.1.

RESULTS

Manipulation Checks

The results of the manipulation check showed that 95% (168/176) of the participants correctly responded to questions about the gender of the employee and whether the employee requested a parental leave. We removed from further analysis the data of the eight subjects who did not provide the correct response to the two items.

Hypothesis Testing

A multivariate analysis of variance (MANOVA) was conducted on the competence and future job behavior and success measures. The multivariate F was significant for parental request, $F(6,152) = 42.14$, $p<.001$, and the employee gender x parental request interaction, $F(6, 152) = 3.99$, $p<.001$. Univariate analyses of variance (ANOVA) and inter-cell comparisons were conducted to examine our hypotheses.

Competence

Results of the ANOVA conducted to determine the effect of employee gender and parental leave request on perceptions of the employee's competence revealed a main effect for employee gender, $F(1,160) = 7.07$, $p<.01$, with the male targets (M=5.86, SD=.74) viewed as being more competent than the female targets (M=5.62, SD=.76). In other words, regardless of the employee's parental status, our participants viewed Andrew as more competent than Alison. Additionally, there was a significant gender x leave request interaction, $F(1, 160) = 12.49$, $p<.001$, that supports our first hypothesis. Comparisons of the cell means indicated that, as predicted, when leave is requested, Alison was perceived as significantly less competent (M=5.50, SD=.86) than Andrew (M=6.05, SD=.75), $F(1, 160) = 12.31$, $p<.001$, while there was no difference when leave was not requested $F(1, 160) = .42$, n.s. The difference in the perceived competence between Alison the parent (M=5.50, SD=.86) and Alison the nonparent (M=5.74, SD=.62) did not achieve significance, $F(1, 160) = 2.42$, n.s. Interestingly, as noted in Table 8.2, this difference was significant for

Table 8.2 Dependent Measures: Means and Standard Deviations

EXPERIMENTAL CONDITION & TARGET	COMPETENT		PASSPROMO		JOBEXPECT		EXCEL		QUIT		SICK	
	M	SD	M	SD	M	SD	M	SD	M	SD	M	SD
Employee Requesting												
Female	5.50	.86	4.76	1.34	5.43	.59	5.12	.80	3.32	1.47	6.19	.99
Male	6.05	.75	4.0	1.57	5.82	.84	5.57	1.11	2.57	1.30	5.73	1.25
Employee Not Requesting												
Female	5.74	.62	2.26	1.40	5.67	.52	5.47	1.08	2.79	1.87	1.88	1.37
Male	5.64	.67	2.77	1.23	5.62	.71	5.36	.90	2.82	1.16	2.18	1.67

Note: All ratings were done using 7-point scales. The higher the mean, the more likely the rating, that is, the more competent, likely to pass on a promotion, to meet job expectations, to quit the job, to excel at work, and to take time off to care for a sick child.

the male employees such that Andrew the parent (M=6.05, SD= .75) was perceived as more competent than Andrew the non parent (M=5.64, SD=.67) $F(1,160) = 6.54$, p<.05. Results of all analyses are presented in Table 8.2.

We added the participant's gender to the analysis to examine whether male and female participants viewed things differently. Indeed, the three-way interaction (target gender x leave request x participant gender) was significant, $F(1, 160) = 3.99$, p<.05. The employee gender x leave request interaction was significant for the males, $F(1, 40) = 8.99$, p<.01, but not for the females. Comparison of cell means revealed that, male participants viewed Andrew requesting leave (M=6.50, SD=.54) as significantly more competent compared to Alison who was also requesting leave (M=5.25, SD=1.06); $F(1, 40) = 12.50$, p<.01. However, the difference between employees in the non-request, non-parent condition continued to be insignificant $F(1, 40) = .30$, n.s. Results from male participants are presented in Table 8.3.

Future Job Behavior and Success

Pass on a promotion. A univariate ANOVA revealed a significant main effect for "request" such that parents requesting leave (M=4.37, SD=1.5) were seen as significantly more likely later to forego a promotion than employees who were not expecting a child (M=2.51, SD=1.33); $F(1,159) = 51.76$, p<.001. The employee gender x parental leave request interaction was also significant $F(1,159) = 8.17$, p<.01. Comparisons of cell means

Table 8.3 Dependent Measures: Male Participants

EXPERIMENTAL CONDITION & Target	COMPETENT		PASSPROMO		JOBEXPECT		EXCEL		QUIT		SICK	
	M	SD	M	SD	M	SD	M	SD	M	SD	M	SD
Employee Requesting												
Female	5.25	1.06	4.67	1.16	5.33	.49	4.83	.58	2.55	1.21	6.17	1.12
Male	6.50	.54	4.0	2.27	6.12	.99	6.00	1.41	2.25	1.28	5.75	1.39
Employee Not Requesting												
Female	5.64	.51	2.18	.75	5.82	.60	5.73	.91	2.82	1.40	2.27	1.79
Male	5.46	.78	3.38	1.56	5.31	.75	5.31	.63	3.46	1.20	2.77	1.83

Note: All ratings were done using 7-point scales. The higher the mean, the more likely the rating, that is, the more competent, likely to pass on a promotion, to meet job expectations, to quit the job, to excel at wofk, and to take time off to care for a sick child.

supported Hypothesis 2 and indicated that the Alison the parent (M= 4.76, SD= 1.34) was viewed as significantly more likely to pass on a promotion than Andrew the parent (M=4.0, SD=1.57; F(l,159) = 6.43 , p<.05). The difference between the non-parent targets was not significant, F(1,159) = 2.69, n.s. Consistent with our hypothesis, participants saw Alison the parent (M=4.76, SD=1.34) as significantly more likely to forego a promotion than Alison the nonparent, (M=2.26 SD=1.23; F(1,159) = 67.65, p<.01. The three-way interaction with participant gender was not significant F(l,159) =.82, indicating that both male and female participants had similar perceptions of the target employees.

Meet future job expectations. There was a significant employee gender x parental leave request interaction, F(l,160) = 9.07, p<.01. Consistent with Hypothesis 2, when leave was requested, the male target employee was viewed as significantly more likely to meet future job expectations (M=5.82, SD=.84) than was the female target (M=5.43, SD=.59; F(l,160) = 7.22, p<.01. There was no difference between Alison and Andrew who did not request a leave, F(l,160) = .16, n.s. The difference in ability to meet future job expectations between Alison the parent and Alison the nonparent was also not significant F(1,160) = 2.84, n.s.; however, the means were in the predicted direction. The three-way interaction was significant F(l,160) = 5.91 p<.05, and we examined the results for male and female participants separately. Male participants' results are presented in Table 8.3. Similar to the competence measure, only the male participants indicated a significant employee gender x leave request interaction, F(l,40) = 9.04, p<.01, such that the Andrew the parent was perceived as significantly more likely (M=6.12, SD=.99) than Alison the parent (M=5.33, SD=.49) to meet future job expectations, $F_{(1,40)} = 6.02$ p<.05, while the difference between the non-parents continued to be insignificant, $F_{(1, 40)} = 3.11$, n.s. Male participants perceived Andrew the parent to be more likely to meet future job expectations than Andrew the non-parent. An insignificant difference remained between Alison the parent and Alison the non-parent; however, the means were in the predicted direction.

Excel in career. Consistent with the other results presented thus far, the employee gender x parental status interaction was significant, $F_{(1,160)} = 6.73$, p<.01, with the mother seen as having the lower potential to excel in her career than the father, $F_{(1,160)} = 4.46$, p<.05. Neither the difference between Alison and Andrew the nonparents, $F_{(1,160)} = .24$, n.s., nor the difference between Alison the parent and Alison the nonparent, attained significance, $F_{(1,160)} = 2.63$, n.s. Means and standard deviations are presented in Table 8.2. The analysis of the three-way interaction with participant gender just missed significance at the .05 level, $F_{(1,160)} = 3.76$ p=.054, but was close enough to warrant further examination. Data from male and female participants were analyzed separately and, consistent with our other participant gender analyses, it is the male participants who view the differences among the target employees most extremely. The employee gender x leave request interaction was significant only for the male participants, $F_{(1,40)} = 8.74$ p<.01. As indicated in Table 8.3, male participants evaluated Andrew the parent as significantly more likely to excel in his career (M=6.0, SD=1.41) than Alison the parent (M=4.83, SD=.58; $(1,40) = 8.48$, p<.01. Their view of the potential for Alison the nonparent to excel was also significantly more positive (M=5.73, SD=.91) than that of Alison the parent, $F_{(1, 40)} = 5.95$, p<.05. We found no significant difference between male participants' perceptions of Andrew the parent compared to Andrew the non-parent.

Quit the job. The employee gender x parental leave interaction narrowly missed attaining significance, $F_{(1,158)} = 3.13$ p<.08; however, cell means are in the predicted direction and are presented in Table 8.2. Congruent with gender role prescriptions, participants viewed Alison the parent as more likely to quit the job than any of the other three other targets. Interestingly, the leave request x participant gender interaction was significant, $F_{(1, 158)} = 7.41$, p<.01, and further examination revealed that, compared with male participants, (M=2.42, SD=1.22) female participants perceived parents as significantly more likely to quit the job (M=3.08, SD=1.46); $F_{(1, 158)} = 4.01$, p<.05.

Time off to care for sick child. There was a main effect for parental status such that, unsurprisingly, employees expecting children were perceived as more likely to take time off to care for a sick child than child-free employees (M=5.95 vs. M=2.02 $F_{(1,159)} = 257.01$, p<.001.). Analyses of the employee gender x leave request interaction and the three-way interaction with participant gender were not significant.

DISCUSSION

As we have noted, several previous studies found support for the motherhood penalty. These studies utilize male-typed jobs that presume the male worker and, as a result, accentuate the lack of fit between mothers in those jobs and the traditional expectations and prescriptions for mothers in the larger culture. In contrast, our study sought evidence for the motherhood penalty in the context of a gender-neutral job. We chose the gender-neutral job in order to reduce the lack of fit perceptions and to explore a different condition in which the motherhood penalty operates. Due to the strength and ubiquity of gender ideology and its stereotypes, we predicted that the motherhood penalty would persist even in the context of occupational gender neutrality, and our results supported this prediction.

In support of Hypothesis 1, we found significant differences in perceptions of competence when comparing females and males in the parental leave condition and no differences between the non-parent employees who did not request leave. In other words, we found that our participants identified workers in the parental condition to be generally less competent than those in the non-parental condition. This finding is consistent with Heilman and Okimoto (2008) who found a motherhood penalty in a male gender-typed job when looking at competence ratings but no significant differences in perceptions of non-parents' expected competence. Our participants may have measured and judged our everyday working mother against a preconceived and well-entrenched notion of the ideal mother. The ideology of motherhood is deeply ingrained and includes a set of constructs that portray the ideal mother as a woman who has immeasurable empathy, engages in the total care of children and others in need, and subordinates her own needs and desires for those of others. The juxtaposition of the working mother to this ideal is sufficient enough to reveal a statistically significant difference when comparing female and male working parents. The male working parent remains closer perceptually to the prototypical ideal worker. We suspect that for the non-parents we have sufficiently reduced the lack-of-fit perceptions (by removing the parental status + leave request characteristics of the worker) so that no meaningful difference relative to our study remained between males and females.

We also found that participants assumed working parents would be less inclined to accept future promotions within the organization and, unsurprisingly, more inclined to take time off to care for a sick child than non-parents. In support of Hypothesis 2, our participants perceived women who ask for parental leave to be more likely to forego a promotion compared to men who make a similar request. This is similar to Gungor and Biernat's (2008) finding that married fathers were perceived to be more "available" for work than married mothers (p. 240). Also in support of Hypothesis 2, participants viewed males who ask for leave to be more likely to meet future job expectations and more likely to excel at work compared to females in a similar situation. Our participants may be tapping into a traditional societal expectation that fathers will take on the role of breadwinner and more likely be responsible for the financial well-being of the family compared to mothers. Women who ask for parental leave were also perceived as more likely to leave the job than men in the same condition. Although this difference did not attain significance, the results were in the predicted direction. Again, the ideology surrounding motherhood suggests that mothers are—and should be—the primary caregivers of children. Indeed, reality reflects, at least in part, this notion that women have the greater responsibility for childcare. Consequently, our participants may have made comparisons between the working mother in our study to what amounts to a reality for many mothers attempting to juggle work and family life. In so doing, they assume more family and childcare responsibilities for mothers in contrast to fathers, which would explain the above findings. Again, we suggest that the smaller differences we found between non-parents on these measures may be due to the weaker lack-of-fit perceptions for women who do not have children.

The reader will recall that the three-way interactions with the gender of our study participants revealed a motherhood penalty on some of our measures for the male participants only. More specifically, male participants viewed the mother as less competent, less likely to meet job expectations, and less likely to excel in her career than the father. That male participants appeared to hold less egalitarian views than our female participants may reflect males' greater tendency to endorse more traditional gender stereotypes (Spence & Hahn, 1997).

Hypotheses 3 and 4 predicted significant differences in perceptions of Alison in the parental leave condition compared to Alison in the non-parent condition. Significance was obtained for passing on a promotion; i.e., the mother was seen as more likely to forego a future promotion than was the female nonparent. On the other hand, and contrary to Cuddy et al. (2004) and Heilman and Okimoto (2008), we found no significant difference for competence or perceptions of future job expectations when making these comparisons, although both of these differences were in the predicted direction. Marginally significant measures that we examined also revealed differences in the predicted direction (i.e., quitting the job and excelling at work, which revealed a significant difference but only with male participants).

PRACTICAL IMPLICATIONS

The starting point for organizations is to ensure that performance criteria are job-related, developed from appropriate job analyses, and based on observable behavior (Malos, 1998). Stereotypes are over-generalizations based on group membership. We can diminish our reliance on stereotypes by individuating performance information about the employee (Landy, 2008), and managers and supervisors should promote conditions that enhance the use of such information.

Evaluators should also have sufficient time and opportunities to observe and document specific job behaviors organized by performance dimensions and to prepare final evaluations. This process can be facilitated by ensuring that evaluators have a clear understanding of behaviors that constitute effective and ineffective performance. Additional training to improve observational skills as well as the use of multiple evaluators may also be necessary (Hauenstein, 1998). Organizations can further improve the evaluation process by making it an ongoing process rather than merely an annual event. Frequent evaluations and feedback can improve communication, help to identify more clearly any weaknesses, and give the employee opportunities to improve before the final review. This increases the employee's perception of evaluation fairness which in turn enhances organizational commitment and reduces the likelihood of lawsuits. Managers can also improve the perception of fairness in their organizations by providing frequent, informal feedback throughout the review cycle, encouraging employee participation in the evaluation process, and incorporating opportunities for employees to respond to evaluations (Gilligand & Langdon, 1998).

LIMITATIONS AND SUGGESTIONS

First, due to the possible limitations inherent in our use of college undergraduates as participants, we suggest replicating the study with employees. Second, there was also a gender imbalance among our participant pool that may have influenced the results. Third, this study did not examine the extent to which negative perceptions would impact reward allocation decisions. Such information would provide further indication of the severity of discrimination against working parents and working mothers, in particular. Fourth, while other studies examine the motherhood penalty as it relates to initial hiring decisions, future research should do so in the context of a gender neutral job. Last, gender discrimination is a growing concern not only in the United States but around the world; future research should investigate the nature, extent, and effects of gender role expectations on performance evaluations cross-culturally.

CONCLUSION

The Family and Medical Leave Act (1993) requires that all public agencies and companies that employ over 50 employees provide up to 12 weeks of unpaid leave per year to qualified employees. One provision of this act is that leave may be requested for the birth or care of a newborn. For this legislation to be effective, no parent should fear that such requests will result in consequences that negatively impact their jobs or careers. We believe it is critical that organizations support family-friendly policies at all levels of management. When such policies are securely integrated into organizational practices, accepted, and used as a matter of course, they can reduce the stigma and negative stereotyping that currently affects workers taking them. In fact, as increasing numbers of workers use such policies, the traditional conception of the "ideal worker" may be reconfigured into something that more accurately reflects the contemporary realities of people's lives.

REFERENCES

Cook, E. P. (1994). Role salience and multiple roles: A gender perspective. *Career Development Quarterly*, 43, 85-95.

Correll, S.J., Benard, S. & Paik, I. (2007). Getting a job: Is there a motherhood penalty? *American Journal of Sociology*, 112(5), 1297-1338.

Cuddy, A., Fiske, S. & Glick, P. (2004). When professionals become mothers, warmth doesn't cut the ice. *Journal of Social Issues*, 60, 701-718

den Dulk, L. & de Ruijter, J. (2008). Managing work-life policies: Disruption versus dependency arguments. Explaining managerial attitudes towards employee utilization of work-life policies. *The International Journal of Human Resource Management*, 19(7), 1222-1236.

Etaugh, C. & Folger, D. (1998). Perceptions of parents whose work and parenting behaviors deviate from role expectations. *Sex Roles*, 39(3/4), 215-222.

Fuegan, K., Biernat, M., Haines, E. & Deaux, K. (2004). Mothers and fathers in the workplace: How gender and parental status influence judgments of job-related competence. *Journal of Social Issues*, 60(4), 737-754.

Gilligand, S.W. & Langdon, J.C. (1998). Creating performance management systems that promote perceptions of fairness. In J.W. Smither (Ed.) *Performance appraisal*. San Francisco: Jossey-Bass

Gunclius, S. (2009). New U.S. women in business statistics released by Catalyst. Retrieved on August 17, 2009 from http://www.womenonbusiness.com/new-us-women-in-business-statistics-released-by-catalyst/.

Gungor, G. & Biernat, M. (2009). Gender bias or motherhood disadvantage? Judgments of blue collar mothers and fathers in the workplace. *Sex Roles*, 60, 232-246.

Hauenstein, N.M.A. (1998). Training raters to increase the accuracy of appraisals and the usefulness of feedback. *Performance appraisal.* San Francisco: Jossey-Bass.

Heilman, M.E. (2001). Description and prescription: How gender stereotypes prevent women's ascent up the organizational ladder. *Journal of Social Issues,* 57(4), 657-674.

Heilman, M. E. & Okimoto, T.G. (2008). Motherhood: A potential source of bias in employment decisions. *Journal of Applied Psychology,* 93(1), 189-198.

Landy, F. J. (2008). Stereotypes, bias, and personnel decisions: Strange and stranger. *Industrial and Organizational Psychology: Perspectives on Science and Practice,* 1, 379-392.

Malos, S.B. (1998). Current legal issues in performance appraisal. In J.W. Smither (Ed.) *Performance appraisal.* San Francisco: Jossey-Bass.

Pelton, J. (2004). Habits of the gendered heart: Drawing connections between individualism, conformism, and gender. Paper presented at the annual meeting of the American Sociological Association, San Francisco, CA. Retrieved September 6, 2009, from http://www.allacademic.com/meta/p108955_index.html.

Ridgeway, C.L. & Correll, S.J. (2004). Motherhood as a status characteristic. *Journal of Social Issues,* 60(4), 683-700.

Schneer, J. A. & Reitman, F. (1994). Effects of early and mid-career employment gaps on career outcomes: A longitudinal study of MBAs. *Journal of Organizational Behavior,* 15, 199-207.

Spence, J.T. & Hahn, E.D. (1997). The attitudes toward women scale and attitude change in college students. *Psychology of Women Quarterly,* 21, 17-34.

Swanberg, J. E. (2004). Illuminating gendered organization assumptions: An important step in creating a family-friendly organization: a case study. *Community, Work & Family,* 7(1), 3-28.

GIRLS AND BOYS, WORK AND PLAY: GENDERED MEANINGS AND PARTICIPATION IN EARLY CHILDHOOD EDUCATION

By Sue Nichols

I'll get your name and you have to write it down, not now. Come with me.
—*four-year-old girl playing teacher quoted in Miller & Smith, 2004, p. 130*

What the teacher tells you to do even if you're not interested.
—*child defining "work" in Briggs & Nichols, 2001, p. 20*

When young children enter their first school classroom, most quickly learn that one of the most important activities taking place there is work. This special kind of work is different from what mom and/or dad do when they say they are going to work. School work is undertaken in a new social grouping, the class, and the formation of this collective is made possible through the activities of this specialized work (Kamler, Maclean, Reid, & Simpson, 1992). At the same time, play, which in the preschool years tends to be interwoven with daily activities in a fluid manner, is separated out and given its own time and space. Divisions between work and play become more starkly outlined.

It has often been noted that girls and boys have different orientations to school (Huston & Carpenter, 1985; Myhill, 2002; Thorne, 1992). This conclusion has generally been based on teacher perceptions and researcher observations. Young children's views are less often

Nichols, S. (2011). Girls and boys, work and play: gendered meanings and participation in early childhood education. In B. J. Irby & G. H. Brown (Eds.), *Gender and Early Learning Environments* (pp. 29-46). Information Age Publishing.

sought, but when they are, this impression is strengthened. An Australian study added weight to the view that experiences of school as a workplace are strongly associated with gender differences in children's orientations to school right from the start (Briggs & Nichols, 2001). In a structured interview study that sought to understand children's perspectives on their lives at home and at school, 311 children aged between 5 and 9 were asked how much they liked and disliked, and the "best" and "worst" things about, various contexts and activities.

Girls, overall, were more positive about school than were boys. Differences were most striking at school entry (five years old) when all the girls surveyed stated they liked school "all the time" compared to less than half the boys. For children who disliked school, the experience of school as work was central to their criticisms. At age five, more than half the boys compared to less than a quarter of the girls volunteered that work was the "worst thing" about school. The interviewers probed children's meanings by asking them, "What is work?" Some answers to this question were:

"What the teacher tells you to do even if you're not interested";
"What you have to do when you'd rather be doing something else";
"When she stops you from doing something you like doing and
makes you do something you don't want to do." (Briggs & Nichols,
2001 p. 20)

Thus, adult–child power relations were integral to children's understanding of the distinction between work and other activities. Even before school, many children experience these power relations when adults (particularly mothers) introduce literacy-related or school-like activities (Solsken, 1992).

The school activity termed *work* has changed little over many decades. More than 20 years prior to my current study, King found that children defined school work in the following terms: "listening to the teacher give directions; … listening to or participation in large group academic lessons during which teacher makes a didactic presentation; and … doing required, individual academic tasks" (1983, p. 68, quoted in Kamler et al., 1992, p. xx). Such *work* activities are central to a formal literacy curriculum, which is outcomes-oriented and reliant on explicit teacher direction.

Children's play is generally considered to be spontaneous, imaginative, and child-initiated; in contrast, children's *work* is imposed, structured, and adult-directed. When a progressive philosophy is ascendant in early education policy and practice, play assumes a privileged position as the key means by which children are considered to develop cognitive, emotional, and social competencies (Walkerdine, 1988). Absent this progressive philosophy, work becomes an inappropriate adult imposition on children. It has been argued that progressive pedagogies favor boys precisely because adult women's power is backgrounded (Clark, 1990; Walkerdine, 1994).

Under current accountability regimes, adult-directed formal learning is being strongly advocated, particularly in early literacy (Jeffrey, 2002). Some would argue that this swing of the pendulum is creating conditions that favor girls' orientations to schooling. In reality, neither the progressive nor the conservative models have been able to gain complete hegemony. This is probably because the qualities of children that each promote (autonomous and self-regulating vs. compliant and well trained) are insufficient in themselves to provide a picture of the complete adult-to-be. As evidence of compromise, in the UK, Early Learning Goals—an outcomes-oriented policy document—was, as a response to pressure, supplemented in 2000 by a set of guidelines that reintroduced the idea of play-based learning (Miller & Smith, 2004).

In this complex and shifting context, there is a need to understand how these reciprocally related domains of practice—work and play—impact young children as they adapt to the school environment. In this chapter, my particular interest is in how children accomplish gender identity formation within a context where the work/play relation is both central and in tension. I will argue that it is important to recognize children's ability to bring work into play and play into work. Specifically, playing at school work is a key aspect of boys' and girls' differential preparation for, and participation in, the social relations of schooling.

MASTERY AS SUBMISSION: BECOMING A WORKER IN SCHOOL

The nexus of forces around adult and child agendas, pleasures, and forms of accountability is the terrain within which I herein will explore relationships between gender and early learning. My analysis draws upon Butler's concept of performativity (Butler, 1990, 2004; Olsen & Wolsham, 2004), particularly as it has been applied by educational researchers (Davies, 2006; Hey, 2006; Renold, 2006). Butler (2004) defined performativity as "improvisation within a scene of constraint" (p. 1). This describes the work all social subjects do to produce meaningful identities. For example, children are producing their identities to make sense within the social context of school, a context within which adult–child and child–peer relationships are equally crucial. This way of understanding identity applies equally well to those experiences understood as play and to those understood as work. Viewing improvisation and constraint as integrally related results in a shift from binary views of the work–play relation, enabling one to see the improvisation in work and the constraint in play. Such a perspective cuts across polarized debates about the merits of adult-directed (work-oriented) and child-centred (play-based) pedagogies that inevitably reduce to power conflicts between adult and child agency. Butler (1997) wrote: "[P]ower is not simply what we oppose but also, in a strong sense, what we depend on for our existence and what we harbor and preserve in the beings that we are" (p. 2). Thus, both adults and children rely on the operations of power to provide social structures within which identity formation is at all possible.

Butler (1995) wrote, "The more a practice is mastered, the more fully subjection is achieved. Submission and mastery take place simultaneously... and mastery as submission, is the condition of possibility for the subject itself" (pp. 45–46). The early years of school, perhaps more so than any other, are a time when behaviors are explicitly taught and practiced. The teacher's objective, through explicit modeling and affording children repetitive practice, is for all children to adopt schooled subjectivities. Kamler and colleagues (1992) provided a vivid example in their study of the first month of school. For the first time ever, children were being trained to begin their seat work. The teacher handed each one a piece of paper and asked each child to hold their paper up. She demonstrated the wrong and right way to stand behind a chair. She directed them to stand behind their chairs, put their piece of paper on the table in front of the chair, pull out the chair and, finally, sit on it. The authors comment that this drilling is intended to downplay gender as central to children's identities; they claimed that the ideal disciplined body for school is a gender-neutral body. However, children are practiced in many activities and already at school entry have mastered other skills. They bring the subjectivities they have achieved through mastery in these other arenas. Some of these subjectivities are closely related to children's developing gender identities. In class, children run their social agendas simultaneously with the teacher's educational agenda (Dyson, 1994; Nichols, 2004).

King investigated views on play in the school context. She found children defined play at school as either what happened at recess time or "surreptitious talking and whispering to other children and other illicit behavior such as clowning around and silly laughing" (1983, p. 67, quoted in Kamler et al., 1993, p. 69). This indicates that children's play goes on through and around teacher-directed work, both providing in different ways spaces for performing gendered identities.

My discussion from this point will progress through a consideration of three themes arising from my analyses of children's activities in preschool and school settings. First, the notion of playing at school work is used to examine girls' and boys' differential preparation for the power relations of the classroom. Secondly, teacher surveillance of boy's work will be discussed as integral to the operation of performativity in the early years classroom.

Thirdly, the notion of giftedness is considered in terms of its impact on the framing of work and play with differential impacts on girls and boys.

"I'LL BE THE TEACHER":
GIRLS' PLAYFUL PREPARATION FOR SCHOOL WORK

While play and work may be constructed as opposites in order to reinforce divisions between children and adults, when children play, they often play at work. One of the functions of children's play is to enact imaginative identification with adult roles. Indeed, it is in this domain of children's lives that gendered behavior has frequently been observed. Girls' monopolization of the *home corner* is a familiar theme; playing the powerful and preferred role of *mom* entails the dramatic performance of work practices such as cooking, infant care, and event management (MacNaughton, 1995).

Boys' enactment of heroic identities in role play is often seen as the gendered opposite of these domestic scenarios. Some children's attempts to cross gender boundaries and take up roles within the *other* storyline have also been observed (Jones & Brown, 2001). Being able to enact acceptable performances of work activities (whether domestic, vocational, or heroic) is a part of a child's social competence as a play partner.

One of the scenarios available for children to appropriate in their play is that of the school classroom. This is particularly salient for preschool children who are aware of their immanent entry into this important domain (Skattebol, 2006). From reviewing the literature on children's play and from my own observations in preschool settings, I found a strong pattern of girls taking up the role of teacher in school-based play scenarios. For example, Dury (in Parke, Drury, Kenner, & Robertson, 2002) observed four-year-old Samia in both nursery school and home and was able to affirm that her play scenarios at home had a close affinity to the pedagogical practices she experienced in her preschool setting. At home, Samia had her younger brother play the student role while she took on the teacher role.

In a fascinating account of conflict in the kindergarten home corner, Jones and Brown (2001) described the attempts of two boys to enact a domestic scenario where one played the role of dad and the other of baby. Their play was soon entered by Shelby, who put in a bid to be the mom. When the boys resisted this move, she improvised the maternal strategy of bribing *baby* with a movie trip. Eventually this is successful in enticing the boys out of the home corner, but to prevent their return, Shelby then "gently pushes both boys onto the easy chairs [in the reading area of the kindergarten] and gives them each a book to read" (p. 718). The authors commented, "Shelby ensures complete obedience by taking on a 'teacher' role and thereby positioning boys within the discourse of schooling … where children are perceived as being powerless" (Jones & Brown, 2001, p. 720).

Here we see how the roles of mom and teacher readily transmute from one to another. Within both the domestic and the classroom play scenarios, adult forms of power are enacted by girls; boys need considerable peer support and imaginative dexterity to sustain these roles just as girls face real challenges in sustaining heroic play roles.

The following two examples provided by Miller and Smith (2004) are significant, not only just for their vividly described observations of children's school-like play, but also for their commentary, which makes an argument against formal learning in the early years. Essential to this argument is seeing the children's activities as free play and not as adult-imposed work. The first case involves two girls in a role- play situation in an area of the nursery school set up as an office. "Sabrina" approaches "Yohannah" and initiates an interaction as follows:

> **Sabrina:** I'm going to do some writing today—not reading. I'll get your name and you have to write it down, not now. Come with me. (She led the child to a table with magnetic names and a magnetic board.) Here are the letters, can you find your name—can you find Yohannah?

After Yohanna complies, Sabrina continues to give instruction:

> **Sabrina:** Don't use my book, I need to do my counting today. [. . .] OK what do you want to write then? (Miller & Smith, 2004, p. 130)

Miller and Smith commented that "Sabrina's independent play was supported by literacy resources and she could practice her emerging writing skills without pressure to achieve an outcome" (p. 130). Regarding this episode as a play scenario emphasizes the child's autonomy, consistent with a binary view of adult-imposed work and child-centered play. While they acknowledged that Sabrina was acting out the adult support model, they implied that adult power is absent from this interaction. This was made explicit when they then compared the episode with one in which an actual adult took the directive role and met with trenchant resistance from the (male) child. However, their view of a free unpressured child in a free play context only holds if one ignores the experience of the unremarked girl, Yohanna. While Sabrina took a directive role, using language and mannerisms highly reminiscent of those used by teachers, Yohannah followed her direction, saying little. From Yohanna's perspective, her role is the same regardless of whether a *real* or *pretend* adult is issuing directions.

Both girls were achieving mastery as submission through the power relations inherent in the practice of school work. Their positions within subject relations, however, were different. Sabrina practiced moving between the directive adult ("Come with me") and the autonomous child worker ("I need to do my counting today") and, thus, could be seen as developing the kind of dual subjectivity that will serve her well in negotiating the shifting terrain of the classroom. Yohanna, on the other hand, took up neither the directive adult nor the independent child subject position; rather, she was the directed child necessary for Sabrina's performance. On another occasion, perhaps their roles were reversed; no other examples were offered, so it is not possible to say. Even practicing the directed child offered a kind of mastery, however, and this becomes even clearer when authors' contrastive example is considered.

In the second case, a playgroup leader was observed working with a group of preschool children on a writing activity that was understood by her to prepare them for formal learning in school. Field notes described the interaction between Josh and the adult:

> Worksheets involving drawing along dotted lines are introduced and Josh says "I can't do it." He flicks his pencil away saying "Go away." The adult helps him to trace the line. She talks to him about writing his name, "Yes, a huge J." The children are then given shapes worksheets and Josh says "Go away, I don't want a pencil"—he pushes away the pencil and paper. (Miller & Smith, 2004, p. 131)

Josh employed various strategies to resist the adult-directed literacy work. He asserted his incompetence, attempted to get rid of his pencil, and a little later complained of tiredness. All of these responses could be understood as refusals to gain mastery of writing. All his references to himself were in the negative: "I can't, I don't want," and this negation operated to maintain a disjuncture between himself and the subject desired by his teacher (from her account)—the school-ready child. However, at the same time, Josh evidently complied with the directive to sit at the table and, rather than confront the adult directly, he vented at a safer target, his pencil. In this way, he also avoided stepping into the position of defiant, naughty boy.

In commenting on the case of Josh, the authors stressed the imposition of adult power, which they saw as the crucial distinction between the social relations of work and those of play. They saw work, in the sense of adult-imposed formal learning, as inappropriate to the preschool context. However, they seemed to assume and accept that formal learning is characteristic of the school context, indeed as what creates the essential difference between preschool and school. No comment was made on the gender dimension of the children's activities; the girls' appropriation of the teacher–student roles on the one hand, and the boy's resistance to school-like work on the other. Yet both examples are typical of gendered patterns that continue in the school entry classroom, an aspect of continuity that is rarely mentioned in the literature.

Josh, Sabrina, and Yohanna are doubtless aware that they will soon be stepping into a school classroom for real. Talk about school, imagining what school is like, is an integral part of children's lives in their preschool year. As Butler (2004) stated, "The act that one does, the act that one performs, is … an act that has been going on before one arrived on the scene" (xx). These children may not have arrived on the scene but they know it exists and some of them use this knowledge to performatively enact the social relations of schooling before their first day of school. Those children who play school, and particularly those who take powerful roles within these play scenarios, are working on identities which will enable their mastery (and submission) to be demonstrated when school life starts for real. There is plenty of evidence that girls, more than boys, experience this kind of playful work preparation.

WORKSHEETS, TABLE WORK, AND THE GENDERING OF PRODUCTIVITY

Earlier, I introduced some definitions of school work offered by children (Briggs & Nichols, 2001; King, 1983, cited in Kamler et al., 1993). These definitions stress two elements, the adult role in initiating and monitoring the activity and the individualized task focus. While it has been argued that a much more diverse range of activities should be considered work, including participating in sharing time, listening to stories, and manipulation of physical objects (Kamler et al., 1993), children clearly associate the term *work* with a more specific set of tasks.

School children experience strong cueing when a transition to work is about to occur. Examining some instances of this cueing can assist in further understanding the meaning of work in the early years classroom. The following examples are taken from a multiple case study project concerning children's transition from home to preschool to school, *Questioning Development in Literacy* (QD; Comber & Nichols, 2002; Hill, 2004; Nichols, 2003, 2004, 2008).

On one occasion in a Year 1 class, the author had been requested to assist the teacher by measuring some children, and Sally had been assigned as a helper. As soon as the teacher began to hand out worksheets, Sally said politely, "I think I'll stop helping now and go and do my work, OK? I'll come back later." Sally's statement shows she understood precisely when a transition to a work activity was taking place; it was signaled by the worksheet distribution.

Mrs. C, a reception teacher in the project, started each day with a structured routine, incorporating drawing, roll call, story reading, and guided discussion of concepts from the story text. However, she did not use the term "work" until it was time to send the children to their tables. The teacher stated, "Now we're getting to the serious side of things: our work for today." She then explained that children should first find the right page of their workbooks, the very next blank page following the previous working session. She held up the first of the day's worksheets which, on this occasion, featured drawings of several objects. Pointing to the graphic of an elephant, Mrs. C read its caption aloud, "I am an … " and described the task, "You've got to think of an 'e' word." Before sending them to their seats, Mrs. C reminded children to put finger spaces between words and to put the date on the sheet.

Mrs. C's instructions assist us in understanding what might be meant by the term "serious" in her characterization of work as an activity. Work is textual; it involves transformation of the incomplete text (the page with blanks spaces) to the complete text (the page with all blanks filled in by the child's textual traces). Work is specified down to the micro level; anything other than absolute compliance with all directions cannot be considered completion. Work is physically disciplined; the page holds the child's gaze and body. Work produces individual accountability; each child must complete his/her own sheet.

This definition of work produces definitions of the ideal worker and the problematic worker. The choice of non-worker is unavailable, despite some children's attempts to occupy this position. It is the problematic worker who becomes highly visible in a context in which every child is doing the same task over the same time-frame, sitting down while an adult circulates around the room.

Analysis of observations over the QD project reveals that teachers monitored boys' performance of table work more closely than girls and, correspondingly, that boys' strategies to escape this work or transform it into play were more visible than girls' avoidance strategies. This is consistent with research conducted mainly with older student populations which reports that teachers' concerns about boys' perceived underachievement are strongly associated with the issue of productivity, and, specifically, with the completion of text-based tasks. In the early years classrooms observed, teachers' explicit surveillance of boys during table work included such strategies as naming, standing alongside, overlooking, reminding, increasing the frequency of reminders, giving praise for each task element completed, and specifying times for task elements.

As an illustration of this monitoring, all teacher utterances made to a particular Year 1 boy over the duration of a writing task have been listed below. The task took the form of a worksheet which required responses to a story the teacher had previously read. The child, Toby, was a talkative boy considered to be easily distracted. Over the half hour allocated to the task, the teacher made the following comments to Toby:

1. Toby, your writing has just come along beautifully.
2. You started so beautifully Toby.

3. Would you find those animals in the city? They're more likely to be in the bush.
4. Toby, you have to finish your writing. So do you [names another child].
5. What I'd like to see now is you finishing your writing. Right now, quick! I'm going to sit here [squats beside Toby's chair]. What was the story about? Can you remember?
6. OK, finished Toby? I'm just about there to see that sentence done.
7. Toby, what have you been asked to do? [Toby replies "Finish the sentence"] Well do it. Now.
8. That's two minutes to finish this.

In the first four interactions, the teacher began with positive feedback, encouragement, and questioning. She used the child's name, perhaps with the intention of reinforcing his agency, and refrained from any first person invocations of her own agenda. In the fifth interaction, these strategies were discarded and the teacher's agency was invoked: "What *I'd* like to see now is you finishing your writing. Right now, quick! *I'm* going to sit here." She employed her body in an attempt to compel action through close proximity.

From the fourth exchange, every teacher utterance included the word "finish." Toby was not able to escape being made aware of the teacher's view of the problem of his low productivity. This exchange was typical of interactions between teachers and those boys considered unproductive during seat work.

Toby's View

The case of Toby offers a rare opportunity to hear a child articulate a view of his positioning within the classroom as a workplace (Nichols, 2004).

His views, expressed regularly in informal conversations with the researcher over two years, are consistent with the view of work expressed in the child survey (Briggs & Nichols, 2001). Toby's views, however, add an element of complexity since Toby does not take a stance of simple or direct resistance. Rather, there is a sense in which he attempts to maintain both a playful and a productive orientation to school, even though this never seems to translate into the product desired by his teachers—the written task completed independently within the time allocated.

During a worksheet activity in his Reception class, Toby addressed the researcher, who was busy writing field notes, as follows:

> **Toby:** Are you *still* here?
> **Researcher:** Yes. I'll be hanging around a bit longer too.
> **Toby:** You must be having fun, *not*.

In the conversation that followed, Toby and his friends compared the *here* of the Reception classroom to the *there* of the ELC (Early Learning Center), a flexible play-oriented preschool:

> **Toby:** We want to go back to the ELC; don't we Connor?
> **Connor:** Yes!
> **Researcher:** Why's that?
> **Toby:** It's bigger. It's *much* bigger. Isn't it Connor?
> **Connor:** Yes.
> **Toby:** And you don't have to do work there. Only play.
> **Martin:** More toys.
> **Toby:** We have to work *all the time* here.

Toby's Reception teacher, while she was aware of the restricted space in the classroom and its impact on the children's movement, could have disputed the notion that she made the children work *all the time*. Many of the learning activities were framed as fun and playful, and there were numerous play objects in the room and its adjoining outdoor space, such as construction sets, blocks, painting gear, and so on. However, for Toby and the other boys at his table, play, as they had previously understood it, was associated with freedom of movement, ample provision of toys, and the absence of demands for productivity. In this sense, it was unlike the school-oriented role play carried out by girls such as cases of Susannah and Yoshana. This is not to suggest that girls did not also appreciate the scope for movement and spontaneity offered by the ELC, but rather that many girls, unlike most boys, also experienced the kinds of peer play that recreated school-like work practices and social relations.

In the Reception classroom, Toby and his peers were learning that the meaning of play had to be understood in relation to work:

> **Researcher:** Don't you get to play?
> **Toby:** Yes. We do get to play after we've done our work. … In fact (*raises eyebrows*) I'm starting to think this work might be a bit fun. I think I'm getting onto this. Because I think, "Get your work done, then you can play." (*Shrugs like it's no hassle.*)

Toby had clearly come to understand the message that play was not the primary activity in this new space. Work was the focal activity, and play was the reward for work. This also entailed understanding that activities were sequenced in time; some came first (work) and others afterwards (play).

Toby's words represent him during his Reception year as a transitional subject—someone who is starting to think in a new way and getting into a new role. The self-consciousness with which he enacted this process was striking. Toby created a self-regulatory voice that took the teacher's position—get your work done, then you can play. The eyebrow raising, voicing, and shrugging all show him performing the part of one who is able to puzzle out a situation and handle a new challenge. Toby was observed enacting work preparation without actually completing much of the task. He spent time getting work tools (pencils), maintaining the tools (sharpening the pencils) and adjusting the furniture (shaking his plastic chair to make it more comfortable).

Toby drew on his ability to play, to perform a role, as a resource in what was evidently the difficult task of becoming a successful school subject. At home he spent much of his time in solo play and was reported by his parents to act a whole case of characters in extended imaginary scenarios. At preschool, he exerted energy enlisting other children into, and maintaining the flow of, similar scenarios. However, it seemed that Toby had no experience prior to school of playing the teacher in relation to a child subject and of switching roles between the director and the directed in a school-like play context. Thus, his ability to play did not parlay effectively into the social relations of school work.

However, there are other contexts in early years schooling in which the social relations of work and play shift, creating the possibility of differently gendered positions. One of these is the specialist gifted class. Here, it seems that pedagogic practices and task structures may enable many boys to draw on their play subjectivities and, correspondingly, position girls versed in teacher-play as less successful.

GOOD IDEAS OR FAIR EFFORT? BOYS AND GIRLS IN THE GIFTED CLASS

The notion of giftedness has introduced another discourse into early childhood education, one which interacts in interesting ways with ideas of schoolwork, play and gender. The concept of intellectual potential is central to the attribution of giftedness. As Walkerdine's (1988, 1994) analysis has shown, the notion of potential has an antithetical relationship to the notion of effort. Potential is understood by teachers, and middle-class parents, as an untapped resource of natural intelligence that is inside children, particularly gifted children. Effort, on the other hand, is the work a child does to perform a task. This work enables achievement to be better than it would have been if the child did not make an effort but, for those with potential, not as good as it could be if that untapped intelligence had simply flowed out. Teachers in Walkerdine's (1994) study explained bright girls' performance as "based on hard work and rule-following rather than brains or brilliance" (p. 58).

When asked how they could recognize a gifted student, early years teachers cited a list of classroom behaviors, including:

- adapting quickly and effectively to change in the environment
- shaping the environment to suit them better in ways that were successful
- selecting alternative environments by isolating themselves and withdrawing from peers and the teacher
- rebelling in class by verbal and/or physical means (Lee, 2002).

For all but the first descriptor, it was overwhelmingly boys who became noticeable for these behaviors. In terms of orientations to school work, it was precisely boys' lack of compliance with classroom work norms (quietness, remaining seated) and their questioning of set tasks that made them more visible to teachers. Indeed, Lee's study was prompted by the fact that five times as many boys as girls had been nominated by their early years teachers for a specialist gifted program.

One of the schools in the QD Project ran a twice-weekly program for Reception children identified by their teachers as having high intellectual potential. Observing in these sessions enabled me to understand how the pedagogic relations of gifted methodology produced gendered relations to work and play different to, and in a sense a reversal of, those in the regular class. In the example below, I focus mainly on one girl.

Prudence had not initially been selected by her regular teacher for inclusion in the gifted program; she entered via a psychological assessment organized by her parents. Thus, I could assume that in the classroom she did not fit the image of a gifted child. Observations indicated she did all her work exactly as instructed and, indeed, was particularly concerned about completing it correctly. At the same time, she kept a playful social orientation with her peers, particularly through the popular scenario of imaginary romances. Work on task was often accompanied by talk about boyfriends and domestic futures of marriage and children. Owing to her productivity, Prudence was not the subject of the kind of surveillance and regulation experienced by boys like her peer, Toby.

One particular day, the gifted session began with a story concerned with the attempts of a little old lady and a little old man to transport their worldly possessions across a stony desert by reluctant camels. The children were given the task of inventing a vehicle capable of carrying the old couple and all their belongings across what the teacher described as rough country with no roads. Mrs M, the teacher, encouraged each child to design and draw something that had not been invented yet.

For many of the boys, this task put them in familiar territory. They were used to constructing and playing with vehicles, often in competitive ways, and their talk during the task had a similar flavor to their play interactions. They threw out challenges to each other, giving their vehicles impressive sounding names and claiming the superior advantages of the qualities with which they would be endowed. On one occasion, a girl was heard attempting to participate in this kind of challenge:

Boy 1: I know what! A flying motorbike.
Girl 1: Mine can fly up as well.
Boy 1: Oh, that's just a normal one. That's a normal one.

Prudence seemed particularly concerned about her ability to complete this task. At the start of the invention activity, she twice called out to the teacher, "I don't know how to draw a car." Mrs. M did nor respond directly to Prudence's appeal for help but circulated around the room, emphasizing the importance of originality by asking children to add something new and make it different. Prudence said little and drew a conventional looking sedan car. Underneath the car, she drew a road which stretched from one side of the page to the other and had a dotted line dividing its two lanes. She seemed satisfied with this and spent the next ten minutes coloring the car before looking up and seeming to register what the teacher was saying about the necessity for new and different creations. She then added what looked like a long streamer and quietly announced to her table mate, "It's a wedding car."

When it was sharing time, two girls refused to participate. Gabi said, "I'm not showing mine." Her table mate, Ashleigh, added, "Mine isn't finished." Like Prudence, these girls were normally successful task completers in their regular classroom. All the boys seemed eager to talk about their invented vehicles. The different reactions of girls and boys to the task, and the invitation to share, indicate that pedagogic relations may be differently gendered in the gifted compared to the regular class. Examining teacher responses to the children's outcomes adds weight to this view.

Table 2.1 contains the teacher's verbal responses to each child's display and descriptions of their creations. All the girls were given responses that either suggested or explicitly stated that their inventions required more work. In contrast, only two out of the five boys received suggestions, and in only one case was this directive. Two of the girls received no positive feedback from the teacher, but only directions to do more work. None of the boys received this kind of response—when suggestions were given, so was praise. So, not only were girls' productions seen as less satisfactory, but the deficiencies were to be remedied by work; girls were positioned as workers rather than as successful inventors.

Table 9.1 Teacher's Verbal Response in the Gifted Classroom

	RESPONSE TO GIRLS	RESPONSES TO BOYS
1.	1) You're going to be well and truly protected. 2) You'll have to work on that. But I think it will be very good if you want to go through enemy territory.	
2.	So that's what you need to work on next	1) Good idea 2) You'll need to put that in.
3.	1) What a good idea. 2) You forgot it was in the country. Perhaps you could turn it into a paddock.	[Not noted owing to noise from girls sitting out and from Ollie]
4.	So that's what you have to work on next.	1) You might like to write a little label. 2) I don't think there are any questions. Everyone has understood your explanation and is happy with it.
5.	Thank you, Ollie.	1) Wonderful! 2) That would look very pretty wouldn't it? Then people could see it coming.

While the boys' habits of play held them in good stead in this activity, such was not the case for Prudence. This is not because she only did the work, but because the play scenarios familiar to her (i.e., playing at weddings) did not translate into the kind of mechanical inventiveness emphasized by the teacher. The task of designing an all-terrain vehicle clashed with Prudence's fantasy of the ideal wedding trip, which presumably involved a smooth ride for the bride, a problem she solved by adding a paved road. Mrs. M's response, however, did not reward this initiative, but rather positioned Prudence as having failed to understand the task: "You forgot it was in the country." After this exchange, Prudence returned to her seat, put her head down on the table and did not move for some minutes. After a while, she rubbed out the road and drew rocks around her wedding car. Submission was only belatedly achieved; the pleasure afforded by being recognized as having mastered the role was not to be hers.

CONCLUSION

The relationship between work and play in early childhood is complex and contested, involving both adult and child agendas connected to broader social forces related to gender and productivity. A view of play as a zone of freedom oppositional to the zone of adult-imposed work can prevent early childhood researchers and practitioners from seeing these complexities. Simple comparisons are not adequate to describe girls' and boys' different orientations to, and participation in, early schooling. Describing girls as compliant and boys as resistant, or boys as playful and girls as good workers, does not do justice to all children's efforts to succeed within the social relations of schooling. Success is a difficult negotiation, as it involves being accountable both to the teacher and to peers.

It is clear, though, that girls and boys enter school for the first time with different experiences of play and that this impacts significantly on their positioning in the classroom as a workplace. Girls are more likely to have played at school work and, thus, to have imaginatively entered into the social relations of school either as teacher, student, or both. Boys also draw on their play repertoires, not only to entertain themselves in the classroom, but also, in the transition to an unfamiliar zone, to act out possible personas. Toby optimistically attempted to perform work-like postures as if that, and not actual productivity, might suffice. After all, if at home he acted the part of a scientist, no one expected him to *actually* do experiments. Trying to teach boys like Toby the meaning of productivity exercises their teachers in continual surveillance and regulation during those activities designated as work.

The introduction of a discourse of giftedness and its associated pedagogic practices into the early years classroom changes gendered relations to work and play. Young girls who are positioned as good workers in the regular class may experience themselves as unsuccessful in the gifted class. When regular classroom teachers describe the young gifted child, they emphasize behaviors that are at odds with the subject of the good worker and, consequently, are much more likely to identify boys as gifted (Lee, 2002). Ironically, in the gifted class when girls exhibit such behaviors as refusal, withdrawal, or reshaping the task to suit their own agendas, they are unable to benefit from being seen as possessing potential. Boys' playful modes of participation, which may put them at odds with the teacher's agenda in the regular class, enable their smooth positioning into the pedagogic relations of the gifted classroom.

Debates about the relative merits of teacher-centered and child-centered curricula, and their (dis)advantages for girls and boys will not go far towards addressing issues of early childhood gendered work and play. Rethinking the nature of work and play, and their relation, in the light of what is known about gendered patterns of participation may offer possibilities. Such rethinking should involve disrupting the work–play binary in order to open up new ways of relating to education and social participation. Becoming a successful social actor in early childhood education involves strategy, effort, imagination, compliance, persistence and daring— qualities children and adults can bring to both work and play.

ACKNOWLEDGEMENTS

The Questioning Development Project was funded by the Australian Research Council. Chief investigators: Barbara Comber, Susan Hill, William Louden, JoAnn Reid, Judith Rivalland.

REFERENCES

Briggs, F. & Nichols, S. (2001). Pleasing yourself and working for the teacher: Children's perceptions of school. *Early Childhood Development and Care, 170*, 13–30.

Butler, J. (1990) Gender trouble, feminist theory, and psychoanalytic discourse. In L. Nicholson (Ed.), *Feminist/Postmodernism* (pp. 201–211). London: Routledge.

Butler, J. (1995). Contingent foundations: Feminism and the question of postmodernism. In S. Benhabib, J. Butler, D. Cornell, & N. Fraser (Eds.), *Feminist contentions: A philosophical exchange* (pp. 35–57). New York: Routledge.

Butler, J. (1997). *The psychic life of power.* Stanford: Stanford University Press.

Butler, J. (2004). *Undoing gender.* New York: Taylor & Francis Routledge.

Clark, M. (1990). *The great divide: The construction of gender in the primary school.* Carl-ton, Victoria: Curriculum Corporation.

Comber, B. & Nichols, S. (2003). Getting the big picture: Regulating knowledge in the early childhood literacy curriculum. *Journal of Early Childhood Literacy, 4*(1), 43–63.

Davies, B. (2006). Subjectification: the relevance of Butler's analysis for education. *British Journal of Sociology of Education, 27*(4), 425–438.

Dyson, A. H. (1994). The ninjas, the x-men, and the ladies: Playing with power and identity in an urban primary school. *Teachers College Record, 96*(2), 219–239.

Hey, V. (2006). The politics of resignification: Translating Judith Butler's theoretical discourse and its potential for a sociology of education. *British Journal of Sociology of Education, 27*(4), 439–457.

Hill, S. (2004). Privileged literacy in preschool. *Australian Journal of Literacy and Language, 27*(2), 159–171.

Huston, A., & Carpenter, C. (1985). Gender differences in preschool classrooms: The effects of sex-typed activity choices. In L. Wilkinson & C. Marret (Eds.), *Gender influences in classroom interaction* (pp. 143–165). London: Academic Press.

Jeffrey, B. (2002). Performativity and primary teacher relations. *Journal of Education Policy, 17*(5), 531–546.

Jones, L. & Brown, T. (2001). Reading' the nursery classroom: A Foucauldian perspective. *Qualitative Studies in Education, 14*(6), 713–725.

King, N. (1988) Play in the workplace. In M. Apple & L. Weis (Eds.), *Ideology and practice in schooling* (pp. 262–280). Philadelphia: Temple University Press.

Kamler, B., Maclean, R., Reid, J., & Simpson, A. (1992). *Shaping up nicely: The formation of schoolgirls and schoolboys in the first month of school*. Canberra: Department of Employment Education and Training.

Lee, L. (2002). Young gifted girls and boys: perspectives through the lens of gender. *Contemporary Issues in Early Childhood, 3*(3), 383–399.

MacNaughton, G. (1995). *The power of mum! Gender and power at play*. Watson: Australian Early Childhood Association.

Miller, L., & Smith, A. P. (2004). Practitioners' beliefs and children's experiences of literacy in four early years settings. *Early Years, 24*(2), 122–133.

Myhill, D. (2002). Bad boys and good girls? Patterns of interaction and response in whole class teaching. *British Educational Research Journal, 28*(3), 339–352.

Nichols, S. (2003). Reading the social world. In J. Barnett & B. Comber (Eds.) *Look Again: Longitudinal case studies of children learning literacy* (pp. 85–98). Rozelle: PETA.

Nichols, S. (2004). Literacy learning and children's social agendas in the school entry classroom. *Australian Journal of Literacy and Language, 27*(2), 101–113.

Nichols, S. (2008). Ghosts, houses and the psycho brother: A young girl working on gendered and schooled identities through text production. *Redress*

Parke, T., Drury, R., Kenner, C., & Robertson, L. H. (2002). Revealing invisible worlds: Connecting the mainstream with bilingual children's home and community learning. *Journal of Early Childhood Literacy, 2*(2), 195–220.

Olsen, G. & Worsham, L. (2004). Changing the subject: Judith Butler's politics of radical resignification. In S. Salih (Ed.), *The Judith Butler reader*. London: Blackwell.

Renold, E. (2006). They won't let us play … unless you're going out with one of them': Girls, boys and Butler's 'heterosexual matrix' in the primary years. *British Journal of Sociology of Education, 27*(4), 489–509.

Skattebol, J. (2006). Playing boys: The body, identity and belonging in the early years. *Gender and Education, 18*(3), 507–522.

Solsken, J. (1992). *Literacy, gender, and work in families and in schools*. Norwood, NJ: Ablex.

Thorne, B. (1992). Girls and boys together … but mostly apart. In J. Wrigley (Ed.), *Education and gender equality* (pp. 115–130). London: The Falmer Press.

Walkerdine, V. (1988). *The mastery of reason*. London: Routledge.

Walkerdine, V. (1994). Developmental psychology and the child-centered pedagogy: The insertion of Piaget into early education. In J. Henriques, W. Hollway, C. Urwin, C. Venn, & V. Walkerdine (Eds.), *Changing the subject* (pp. 153–202). London: Methuen.

❧ ten ❧

THE HETEROSEXUAL QUESTIONNAIRE

By Martin Rochlin

Purpose: The purpose of this exercise is to examine the manner in which the use of heterosexual norms may bias the study of gay men's and lesbians' lives.

Instructions: Heterosexism is a form of bias in which heterosexual norms are used in studies of homosexual relationships. Gay men and lesbians are seen as deviating from a heterosexual norm, and this often leads to marginalization and pathologizing of their behavior. Read the questionnaire below with this definition in mind. Then respond to the questions.

1. What do you think caused your heterosexuality?
2. When and how did you first decide you were a heterosexual?
3. Is it possible that your heterosexuality is just a phase you may grow out of?
4. Is it possible that your heterosexuality stems from a neurotic fear of others of the same sex?
5. If you have never slept with a person of the same sex, is it possible that all you need is a good gay lover?
6. Do your parents know that you are straight? Do your friends and/or roommate(s) know? How did they react?
7. Why do you insist on flaunting your heterosexuality? Can't you just be who you are and keep it quiet?
8. Why do heterosexuals place so much emphasis on sex?
9. Why do heterosexuals feel compelled to seduce others into their lifestyle?

Rochlin, M. (1972). *The heterosexual questionnaire.*

10. A disproportionate majority of child molesters are heterosexual. Do you consider it safe to expose children to heterosexual teachers?

11. Just what do men and women *do* in bed together? How can they truly know how to please each other, being so an atomically different?

12. With all the societal support marriage receives, the divorce rate is spiraling. Why are there so few stable relationships among heterosexuals?

13. Statistics show that lesbians have the lowest incidence of sexually transmitted diseases. Is it really safe for a woman to maintain a heterosexual life style and run the risk of disease and pregnancy?

14. How can you become a whole person if you limit yourself to compulsive, exclusive heterosexuality?

15. Considering the menace of over population, how could the human race survive if everyone were heterosexual?

16. Could you trust a heterosexual therapist to be objective? Don't you feel s/he might be inclined to influence you in the direction of her/his own leanings?

17. There seem to be very few happy heterosexuals. Techniques have been developed that might enable you to change if you really want to. Have you considered trying aversion therapy?

18. Would you want your child to be heterosexual, knowing the problems that s/he would face?

19. What were your first reactions upon reading this questionnaire?

Education

Equalizer or Replicator

These three articles were selected for their diverse approaches to a shared theme of inequality in our educational system. The first two articles focus on various aspects of K–12 public education in the United States. We encourage the reader to identify the key concepts (see Chapter 2) relevant in each article. To what degree are they clearly defined and does this aid the points made in the article?

Haimson and Ravitch (2013) discuss Mayor Bloomberg's controversial policies in New York City in the article "Unequal Schools" and whether these policies were effective. We think the points made and criticisms provided could give impetus for closer examination of other school systems in the United States. In what ways do you think the educational achievement gap in the United States could be remedied? Can you apply the routine of identify, apply, evaluate, and integrate recommended in Chapter 3? For instance, can you identify what you believe is the problem? What needs to be done (applied) to impact that problem? How would you evaluate effectiveness? What other skills can you integrate into your plan for solving this issue?

For several decades, educators and researchers alike have pointed to parental involvement as being an important factor in academic success. In the article "Defining Parental Involvement," what is meant by "parental involvement" and how it relates to student success is explored. Is this an answer to inequality in our schools? Do you agree with Young, Austin, and Rowe (2013) regarding who the stakeholders are in schools today?

Finally, "10 Myths About Legacy Preferences in College Admissions" considers inequality in higher education, specifically myths associated with college admissions legacy preferences, and, indirectly, gender, racial, and economic inequalities relative to higher education admissions. Regardless of which area of education we reflect upon, considering and understanding that inequalities exist as well as how they continue to impact education success and subsequent achievements in society is important as we apply critical and creative thinking to the institution of education.

Questions for Consideration:

1. Earlier in this book, we addressed the use of language and how this impacts our understanding of the world around us. How is this demonstrated in Young, Austin, and Growe's (2013) discussion of defining parental involvement?
2. How should our schools be addressing inequality, according to Haimson and Ravitch? Do you think this is attainable?
3. What do you think is important relative to parental involvement and the educational success of students?
4. How well do you think the authors of these articles present their position? How would you assess the *clarity* of the reasoning and evidence provided?
5. What are your thoughts about the statement "legacy preferences introduce an aristocratic snake into the democratic Garden of Eden" found in the article "10 Myths About Legacy Preferences in College Admissions"?

☙ eleven ❧

UNEQUAL SCHOOLS

By Leonie Haimson and Diane Ravitch

I n 2008, Mayor Michael Bloomberg and his schools chancellor at the time, Joel Klein, testified before Congress that their policies had led to a substantial narrowing of the racial achievement gap, meaning the gap in test scores between white students and those of color: "Over the past six years, we've done everything possible to narrow the achievement gap—and we have. In some cases, we've reduced it by half," said Bloomberg. He repeated that claim in 2012, saying, "We have closed the gap between black and Latino kids and white and Asian kids," he said. "We have cut it in half."

The notion that there had been a great improvement in the public schools, leading to sharp increases in achievement among minority children—the majority of the city's public school students—was echoed in the mainstream media. It helped Bloomberg retain mayoral control of the public schools, which the state legislature had granted him shortly after his election in 2002, and to win a third term in 2009 (a campaign in which he spent a record $108 million).

Unfortunately, his claims of closing the achievement gap proved misleading. On the reliable national assessment known as the NAEP, there had been no significant increase in scores or narrowing of the gap since 2003, when the mayor's policies were first imposed. In 2010, the state Education Department finally admitted what observers had long suspected: that the state exams had become overly predictable and that scoring well had grown easier over time.

After New York State acknowledged that test score inflation had occurred, scores across the state were recalibrated and declined dramatically. The achievement gap was revealed to

Haimson, L., & Ravitch, D. (2013). Unequal schools. *The Nation*, 41–43.

be as wide as it had been before Bloomberg implemented his policies. The black–white test proficiency gap in eighth-grade reading actually increased. By last year, 29 percent of black students were proficient in reading, compared with 62 percent of white students. If one compares the gains on the NAEP since 2003 of all economic, racial and ethnic student subgroups, New York comes out second to last of the large cities—only Cleveland, one of the nation's lowest-scoring cities, has seen less progress.

DATA AND DIVERSITY

The mayor has sought to manage the city's 1,500 or so schools and 1.1 million students as if he were running a business. Data, derived mainly from standardized tests, are his primary management tools. While focused on test scores, Bloomberg has allowed class sizes to increase, despite the fact that class-size reduction is one of only a handful of reforms proven to narrow the achievement gap (and is the top priority of parents, according to the Education Department's own surveys).

In a December 2011 speech, Bloomberg said that he would double class size if he could by firing half of the teachers, and that it would be "a good deal for the students." On his weekly radio show in March, he claimed that even if classes were so overcrowded that students were forced to stand, the result would be fine as long as they had quality teachers: "that human being that looks the student in the eye" and "adjusts the curriculum" based on an "instinct" for "what's in the child's interest."

Numerous studies show that black and Hispanic children receive twice the academic gains from smaller classes as white children. Though the state's highest court concluded in 2003 that the city's children were denied their constitutional right to an adequate education based in large part on excessive class size, the size of classes in the early grades are now the largest in fourteen years, and about half of middle and high school students are in classes of thirty or more. Many teachers have 150 students, making it all but impossible for them to look students "in the eye" and give them the individual attention they need—especially students who are disadvantaged.

Meanwhile, the mayor has put relentless pressure on schools to raise their test scores. As a result, while allegations of cheating have spiked, many schools have seen a narrowing of the curriculum and have dropped their project-based learning and field trips. According to a 2011 audit by the city comptroller, not one of the schools in his sample complied with the state-required minimum amount of physical education.

In 2007, the mayor eliminated funding for the program known as "Project Arts." Since that time, spending on art supplies, equipment and partnerships with cultural institutions has declined. Between 2006 and 2010, the amount spent on art and music equipment and supplies was cut by 79 percent. The number of arts teachers has also fallen as a result of repeated budget cuts. In New York City, the arts capital of the nation, nearly one-fourth of all public schools have not a single art, music, theater or dance teacher on staff.

New York is the only city in the country where admissions to elite high schools are based on the results of a single exam. Bloomberg has not only aggressively defended this policy, but has also expanded the number of selective schools that make decisions based upon a single score. During his administration, the number of minority students admitted to selective high schools has dropped precipitously. At Brooklyn Tech, 24 percent of the students were black in 1999–2000, compared with 10 percent during the 2011–2012 school year. At Bronx Science, the share of black students dropped from 9 to 3.5 percent over the same period. At Stuyvesant, the city's most selective high school, the number of black students fell from 109 in 2000 to forty in 2012, out of more than 3,000 students. Only nine have been accepted into the school for next year.

Though black and Hispanic students make up about 71 percent of public and charter school students citywide, they received just 12 percent of specialized high school offers this year. The NAACP Legal Defense Fund has filed a civil rights complaint with the federal Office of Civil Rights on the grounds that the city's admissions policy is racially discriminatory.

For the first time, Bloomberg also imposed a test-based policy for admissions into gifted and talented programs, which caused the percentage of minority children in these programs to plummet. Before 2006, community school districts devised their own policies and relied on more holistic measures. In 2006, 53 percent of students in these programs were black or Hispanic; now less than one-third are. Last year, in some large areas of the Bronx, too few children tested "gifted" for a single gifted class to be offered, while in wealthier parts of the city—where parents send their 4-year-olds to expensive test-prep programs—more than half of the children are deemed gifted.

The expansion of charter schools has been another source of widening inequity. Bloomberg has been an aggressive proponent of charter schools, which receive public funds but are run by private corporate boards. The mayor, together with a set of wealthy philanthropists, successfully lobbied to have the cap raised on charter schools in 2007 and again in 2010. Recently, it was revealed that he plans to start his own chain of such schools when he leaves office, and has assigned city employees to the task of designing them.

Charter schools enroll fewer special-needs students, English-language learners and children in extreme poverty than do public schools in the same communities. In the Bronx, they enroll half as many ELLs and children with disabilities as the neighborhood public schools. As the number of charter schools has proliferated, the concentration of the most at-risk students in nearby public schools has risen, with less space and fewer resources to serve them.

The siting of charter schools in public school buildings has led in many cases to such overcrowding that the pre-existing schools have lost pre-K programs, classrooms, art rooms and libraries, forcing students with disabilities to receive their services in hallways and closets. Many parents and students perceive separate but unequal conditions, as the charter schools often have refurbished classrooms and bathrooms and more computers and white-boards, as well as smaller classes and more staff. In addition, many of the higher-performing charters have a "no excuses" philosophy, with rigid disciplinary policies and long school days, which in turn contributes to a high rate of suspensions and children who are "pushed out"—especially those with special needs. Teacher and principal attrition rates also tend to be very high, signaling dissatisfaction with the harsh working conditions and classroom environment.

WINNERS AND LOSERS

Another signature Bloomberg policy with disparate effects is school closures. During his administration, he has closed more than 150 schools, most of which have had dis-proportionate numbers of at-risk students, with higher percentages of students who are over age for their grade because they have been previously held back, are poor or need special education services. The high schools slated for closure have been shown to have larger rates of homeless students as well. Schools with large proportions of students receiv-ing free lunches are eleven times more likely to receive failing grades on the city's "progress reports" and become eligible for closure, as are schools with more over-age ninth graders. Few parents with means want to send their children to such schools. Thus, the competition model creates winners and losers, and the most disadvantaged and at-risk students are the ones who lose the most.

As schools are phased out, the majority of students who remain are prevented from transferring elsewhere and thus lose access to many programs and courses they need to graduate or to be prepared for college. Dropout and discharge rates surge. Struggling students who would have attended these schools are sent to other nearby schools, overcrowding them and causing them to spiral downward in a domino effect. Some commentators have likened the current practice of closing large numbers of schools to the now-discredited policy of "urban renewal," when whole neighborhoods in the 1950s and early '60s were flattened and the displaced residents sent to live in worse conditions elsewhere. Bloomberg has scoffed at parents who have criticized these policies. In 2011, on his weekly radio program, he said: "Unfortunately, there are some parents who just come from—they never had a formal education, and they don't understand the value of education."

REINFORCING INEQUITIES

Overall, the city's graduation rate has increased—a fact touted by the mayor in his recent State of the City address. However, this is partly the result of lowered standards—including "credit recovery" programs that allow students to gain the credits they need to graduate via software programs where they can look up the answers to multiple-choice questions with little or no oversight. Moreover, according to the administration's own statistics, in 2010, when the city claimed a 61 percent four-year graduation rate, only 21 percent of all students who had entered high school four years earlier were college-ready. In 2011, only 13 to 15 percent of black and Latino students were. As a result of poor preparation, nearly 80 percent of the city's public high school graduates who enroll in community colleges require remediation. The number of high school graduates needing triple remediation (in reading, writing and math) has doubled in recent years.

Under Bloomberg's direction, and now the state's as well, the bureaucracy operates with a slavish devotion to "data," but an indifference to the actual human beings the data represent. The public is weary of this approach. The Quinnipiac public opinion poll in January found that only 18 percent of the city's voters want the next mayor to have the unilateral control over schools that Bloomberg has wielded. No economic, ethnic or racial group supports continuing mayoral control.

Only by rescinding mayoral control and instituting progressive reforms can we make our schools what they should be: centers of learning, collaboration, and humane interaction among children and adults—and a force for diminishing, rather than reinforcing, the dramatic inequality that has come to define our city.

❧ twelve ❧

DEFINING PARENTAL INVOLVEMENT: PERCEPTION OF SCHOOL ADMINISTRATION

By Clara Young, Sheila Austin, and Roslin Growe

INTRODUCTION

Researchers and writers have noted that parental involvement is associated with academic achievement (Mandara, 2006; Toldson, 2008); is a primary contributor to a student's success (Rumberger, 1995); and is widely accepted as important to a students' academic performance (Reutzal, Fawson & Smith, 2006; Senechal, 2006; St. Clair & Jackson, 2006). Randall, Shin & Spoth (2008) revealed in their research that less risky behavior in adolescents was manifested through declining drug usage when parents displayed active involvement.

Parental involvement boosts a child's perceived level of competence and autonomy, offers a sense of security and connectedness, and helps to internalize the value of an education and performance. Parental influences can have considerable impact from Kindergarten up to the high school levels. According to Gonzales-DeHass, Willems, & Doan Holbein, 2005, parents who are involved with their child's education directly support learning while indirectly encouraging achievement. Since the results of parental involvement are positive, why is parental involvement low for ethnic-minority, language-minority, and lower resource families? In fact, encouraging these parents is a challenge noting that race, ethnicity, and linguistically characteristics of these parents often fail to participate in parenting activities (Shin, 2004). The same argument applies to the lower resource families. There is a tendency

Young, C., Austin, S., & Growe, R. (2013). Defining parental involvement: Perception of school administrators. *Education, 133*(3), 291-297.

for the lower resource family to react differently when it comes to parental involvement than families that have greater resources (Anderson, Minke, 2007).

A significant aspect to closing the achievement gap for ethnic-minority students and to address one of the goals of No Child Left Behind (2002) is that parents become involved. Issues related to the lack of parental involvement include lack of a clear definition of parental involvement; parents not knowing how to help a child academically; lack of encouragement from the teachers; parents are only contacted when something is wrong; and teacher treatment of parents. Teachers want parents involved based on what was experienced as a child when his or her parent was involved or is defined by what the teacher wants. However, since what is desired, based on parental involvement varies from teacher to teacher and even the school's administrator, can be confusing to parents of multiple children.

If this issue is ever going to be resolved, then the school, which includes the school's administrator, teachers, parents and stakeholders, need to define parental involvement so that a consistent message can be conveyed to parents regarding the expectation of involvement. In addition, teachers and school leaders will have to devise nontraditional ways to motivate parents to become involved so these parents can become advocates for their child's learning. When parents come to the school and get involved, then a system of reward should be implemented to encourage more involvement.

PARENTAL INVOLVEMENT

A concept that seems to garner universal agreement is that parents should be involved in his or her child's education (Nichol-Solomon, 2001); however, what defines parents being involved? What is parental involvement as defined by the school's administrator, teachers and parents vary. Some theorist and practitioners define parental involvement as home-school partnerships; parental participation; and parents as partners (Lloyd-Smith & Baron, 2010). Based on a study conducted by Deslandes, Royer, Turcotte and Berttrand (1997—as listed in Lloyd-Smith & Baron) parental involvement is defined as presence at school, communicating with the teachers, or helping at home with homework. Abdul-Adil and Fanner (2006) defined parental involvement as any parental attitudes, behaviors, style, or activities that occur within or outside the school setting to support children's academic and/or behavioral success in their currently enrolled school. Based on the literature reviewed, definitions have been devised by researchers due to the lack of a consensus definition of parental involvement, especially addressing African-American parents of inner city students.

Even though researchers have defined parental involvement, motivations by which parents are involved have been assessed as a related factor. Based on a qualitative study conducted by Huang and Mason (2008), parents of preschool age students are motivated to become involved based on the affiliations in the school, the power to influence their child's learning and their belief of education as being the key to achieve success. If parents can experience affiliations with teachers, other parents and educational administrators, then actual involvement happens. Green, Walker, Hoover-Dempsey and Sandler (2007) developed constructs to examine motivations of parental involvement The three major psychological constructs identified were parents' motivational beliefs, perceptions of invitations for involvement from others, and perceived life context. The results of the study suggested that the three major constructs prompted parents home-based and school- based involvement. More specifically, parents became involved in home-based activities by specific child invitations, self-efficacy and self-perceived time and energy for involvement.

Defining parental involvement is not enough to get parents involved because there are challenges in involving parents. Based on information obtained from a newsletter published by the Center for Comprehensive School Reform and Improvement, there are challenges to getting parents involved. The barriers include parents not knowing how to be involved and parents not feeling welcomed in the school based on past experiences. Personalizing parental involvement programs based on the needs of the community and the school is another means of encouraging involvement. However, successful parent-school partnerships are well integrated with the school's overall mission and are not stand-alone or add-on programs. In addition, getting parents involved may not only require a specific definition but parent's input is instrumental in devising a definition of parental involvement and what motivates parents to become involved.

School Administrators and Parental Involvement

Parental involvement seems to primarily be implemented by teachers, but the school's administrator is an integral part of effective parental involvement programs. Efforts must be made by administrators, teachers and parents to realize the positive effects of parental involvement. Studies conducted by SEDL (2000) and Wynn, Meyer, & Richards-Schuster (2000) results supported the idea that collaborative teams and collaborative processes were a key to the success of increased family involvement in the education of children. According to Ferguson (2005) the school's administrator plays a key role in creating a school culture where parents involved is not only accepted but valued. Strong leaders can create a cohesive partnership among the school's stakeholders which includes schools, families and communities. The administrator should have a desire to involve parents in the partnership of school. In order to realize this desire, then it is important that a communication process is implemented that reaches out to family and community through multiple pathways, both informal and formal. Zarate (2007) conducted interviews with teachers, principals and counselors related to parental involvement of Latina parents resulted in identifying that there was a lack of organized focus on creating long-term, sustainable, or innovative parental involvement programs for parents. The interview also revealed that parents of high achieving students were more involved as a result of parents having more opportunities to be involved.

Even though the school's administrator value parental involvement primarily for its power in increasing student achievement (Auerbach, 2007), the empirical literature examining the intersection of parental involvement and leadership is underdeveloped (Auerbach, 2010). In a historical case study conducted by Horvat, Curci and Partlow (2010) of three different school administrators in one school, over three decades, related to the administrator managing parental involvement. The results reported three different styles of leadership each garnered parental involvement. The parental involvement garnered in Era 1 (1974–1989) continued under two additional leadership principles in Era 2 (1989–1993) and Era 3 (1993–2006). The parent's perception of the school's administrator supported parents being involved. As such, administrators may be able to foster parental involvement based on how parents perceive the school's administrator and the administrator must become acquainted with parents to obtain information needed to encourage parental involvement.

The purpose of this study was to assess how school administrators, teachers and parents define parental involvement using a qualitative research approach. Thus, the design used in this study was a grounded theory, which was developed by Glaser and Strauss in 1967 (Creswell, 2007). The grounded theory design was chosen because a key idea in this design is that theory-development is generated or "grounded" in data from participants who have experienced the process and is shaped by views of a large number of participants (Strauss and Corbin, 1998 as cited in Creswell, 2007). The data that will be reported in this aspect of the study is based on information obtained from school administrators. The primary objectives were to assess how administrators define parental involvement and to assess if how parental involvement is defined impacts the lack of involvement. The premise of the researchers is if each group primarily defines parental involvement differently, then parents may be confused in terms of what is expected and thereby causing the school to have ineffective parental involvement programs.

METHODOLOGY

Sample

The population of this study consisted of participants attending three different presentations by the researchers: one major conference with over 3000 attendees, one professional development program in a local school district and a state association conference. The sample size consisted of participants who submitted a definition of parental involvement. The number of attendees for the total venues was 400 and 100 attendees submitted a written response to the question. Half or 50% of the submitted responses were generated from school administrators. The School Administrators is defined as the principal of the school. Data Collection.

Attendees in the three venues were asked to write a definition to the following question, "How do you define parental involvement?" In addition, the attendees also listed the state presently residing in and job title. The written responses were collected by the researchers and organized into categories based on the job title of the attendees. The categories included school administrator, parent, parent liaison, parent as a teacher, teachers and parents as administrator. Attendees were from various states, north, south, east and west in the United States. The data collected from school administrators are reported in these results.

Analysis

The qualitative data were collected and analyzed by reducing the data into themes through a process of coding, condensing the codes and then finally presenting the analysis in figures, tables or discussion (Creswell, 2007). The process was used to analyze the data from each of the categories. However, of particular concern was from school administrators defining parental involvement.

Results

Several categories emerged based on the definition submitted by school administrators. These categories included parents actively engaged, parents supporting, parents as advocates, parents being knowledgeable, and parents communication (see Appendix). The two categories that generated the most responses were parents actively engaged and parents supporting. Active engagement is defined as parents participating in school-based activities. In other words, active engagement is when parents are participating in activities at school. Activities for active engagement included attending conferences, in-school activities, volunteering in the school, knowing what takes place during the school day, seeking information regarding the school, participating in school decisions, understanding the curriculum, and parents working with parents.

The second category was parental support which includes home-based activities. Parental support includes helping the child with homework, making sure homework is completed, creating an environment at home to complete homework, promoting the importance of an education, making an investment in the child's education, understanding how to best provide support to the child, developing a partnership with the school/

teacher, parents having hands-on in the child's education, helping to guide and motivate the child to reach academic goals, parents taking an active role in the education of their child by providing resources, parents showing an interest in their child's education, and working collaboratively to increase student achievement. Two definitions were given by parents who also served as administrators. The definition given was:

> "Parental involvement is when the parent starts at home by instilling the value of an education. Then the parent introduces reading and social behavior at birth to school age and beyond. The parent attends school functions that relate to the child's academic career, communicates with the child's teacher and administrator. In addition, the parent is also aware that policies and procedures are to be adhered. The parent supports and respects the school's policies and procedures" (parent/ school administrator—North Dakota). A second definition written by a parent/ school administrator was; concerned about your child's education and future by helping the child to reach his or her goals.

A third category was communication. Many of those surveyed indicated that communication should be two-way on the part of the school and the parents. That is the school needs to communicate more effectively with the parents and parents should learn how to communicate with educators and their child. One administrator wrote that "Parents should communicate actively about needs and desires of their child and listen to needs and desires of both their child's teacher and the child."

The last category developed was parents being advocates. School administrators believed that parents should also become advocates for their child's social, emotional, spiritual and psychological development. Advocacy should encompass not only academics but social and emotional well-being. The final category that emerged is that parents should have knowledge or information. Parents should know about the curriculum, know about the decision making process in the school, and what takes place during the school day. Whether having the above listed information will enlist parental involvement, school administrators believe parents should have the information. Analysis of the data collected identified a myriad of activities that include parental engagement and involvement. As such, the list can go on and on; however, if parents are going to become involved based on the expectations of school administrators more specific explanations in terms of how parents can actually fulfill supportive criteria listed above will be required.

CONCLUSION

It appears as if what school administrators desire for parental involvement are concepts that relate to effective parenting. So, is the lack of involvement related to parents not parenting children effectively, parents parenting the way he or she was parented, or parents lacking knowledge in terms of how to parent children. If school administrators desire parental engagement and support in his or her respective school, then the administrator will have to utilize one definition to be employed by school and not individual perspectives. The school administrator should then devise the definition, with the assistance of stakeholders a (i.e. teachers, parents, community leaders), convey the definition for the school and share the leadership of parental involvement with parents. This strategy may be the first step to establishing and improving communications between parents and the school personnel and parents becoming more engaged and supportive.

REFERENCES

Abdul-Adil, J. K. & Farmer, A. D. (2006). Inner-City African American Parental Involvement in Elementary Schools: Getting beyond Urban legends of Apathy. *School Psychology Quarterly, 21 (1)*, 1–12.

Anderson, K. J. & Minke, K. M. (2007). Parent involvement in education: toward an understanding of parents' decision making. *Journal of Educational Research. 100(5)*, 311–323.

Auerbach, S. (2007). From moral supporters to struggling advocates: Reconceptualizing parent roles in education through the experience of working-class families of color. *Urban Education, 42 (3)*, 250–283

Auerbach, S. (2010). Beyond coffee with the principal: Toward leadership for authentic school-family partnerships. *Journal of School Leadership, 20(6)*, 728–759.

Creswell, J. W. (2007). *Qualitative inquiry and research design.* Sage Publications: Thousand Oaks, CA

Ferguson, C. (2005). National Center for Family & Community connections with schools. *Southwest Educational Development Laboratory*, 1–7. http://www.sedl.org/connections/

Gonzales-DeHass, A. R, Willems, P. P. & Doan, M. F. (2005). Examining the relationship between parental involvement and student motivation. *Educational Psychology Review, 17(2)*, 99–123.

Green, C. L, Walker, J. T., Hoover-Dempsey, K. V. & Sandier, H. M. (2007). Parents' Motivation for Involvement in Children's Education: An Empirical Test of a Theoretical Model of Parental Involvement. *Journal of Educational Psychology, 99 (3)*, 532–544.

Horvat, E. M, Curci, J. D & Partlow, M . C. (2010). Parents, Principals and Power: A Historical Case Study of "Managing" Parental Involvement. *The Journal of School Leadership, 20(6)*, 707–727.

Huang, G. & Mason, K. (2008). Motivations of Parental Involvement in Children's Learning: Voices from Urban African American Families of Preschoolers. *Multicultural Education, 15*, 20–27.

Lloyd-Smith, L & Baron, M. (2010). Beyond Conferences: Attitudes of High School Administrators toward Parental Involvement in One Small Midwestern State. *The School Community Journal, 20 (2),* 23–44.

Mandaro, J. (2006). The impact of family functioning on African American males' academic achievement: A review and clarification of the empirical literature. *Teachers College Record, 108,* 206–223.

Nichol-Solomon, R. (2001). Barriers to serious parent involvement. *The Education Digest. 66(5)* 33–37.

No Child Left Behind (2001) PL-107-110, Sec. 1118 U.S. Department of Education, 2001

Randall, G., Shin, C., & Spoth, R. (2008). Increasing school success through partnership-based family competency training: experimental study of long-term outcomes. *School Psychology Quarterly. 23 (1),* 70–89.

Rumberger, R. W. (1995). Dropping out of middle school: A multilevel analysis of students and schools. *American Educational Research Journal, 32,* 583–625.

Reutzal, D. R., Fawson, P. C. & Smith, J. A. (2006). Words to go!: Evaluating a first- grade parent involvement program for "making" words at home. *Reading Research and Instruction, 45(2),* 119–159.

Senechal, M. (2006). Testing the home literacy model: Parent involvement in kindergarten is differentially related to grade 4 reading comprehension, fluency, spelling, and reading for pleasure. *Scientific Studies of Reading, 10(1),* 59–87.

St. Clair, L. & Jackson, B. (2006). Effect of family involvement training on the language skills of young elementary children from migrant families. *School Community Journal, 6(1),* 31–41.

Shin, H. J. (2004). *"Parent Involvement and its influence on children's School Performance: A Comparative study between Asian (Chinese & Korean) American and Mexican Americans."* Ph.D Dissertation. Columbia University

Tolston, I.A. (2008). Breaking barriers: Plotting the path to academic success for school-age African American males. Washington, DC: Congressional Black Caucus Foundation, Inc.

Zarate, M. E. (2007). Understanding Latino Parental Involvement in Education. Tomas Rivera Policy Institute: Columbia University, New York

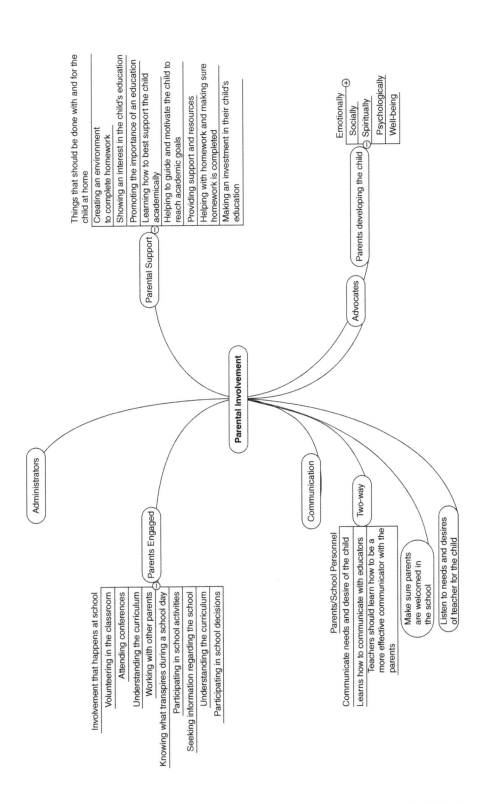

10 MYTHS ABOUT LEGACY PREFERENCES IN COLLEGE ADMISSIONS

By Richard D. Kahlenberg

Legacy preferences, which provide a leg up in college admissions to applicants who are the offspring of alumni, are employed at almost three-quarters of selective research universities and virtually all elite liberal-arts colleges. Yet legacy preferences have received relatively little public attention, especially when compared with race-based affirmative-action programs, which have given rise to hundreds of books and law-review articles, numerous court decisions, and several state initiatives to ban the practice.

The secrecy surrounding legacy preferences has perpetuated a number of myths, including the following:

1. Legacy preferences are just a "tie breaker" in close calls.

While some colleges and universities try to play down the impact of legacy preferences, calling them "tie breakers." research from Princeton's Thomas Espenshade suggests that their weight is significant, on the order of adding 160 SAT points to a candidate's record (on a scale of 400–1600). Likewise, William Bowen, of the Andrew W. Mellon Foundation, and colleagues found that, within a given SAT-score range, being a legacy increased one's chances of admission to a selective institution by 19.7 percentage points. That is to say, a given student whose academic record gave her a 40 percent chance of admission would have nearly a 60 percent chance if she were a legacy.

Kahlenberg, R. D. (2010). 10 myths about legacy preferences in college admissions. *Chronicle of Higher Education*.

The children of alumni generally make up 10 to 25 percent of the student body at selective institutions. The proportion varies little from year to year, suggesting "an informal quota system," says the former *Wall Street Journal* reporter Daniel Golden. By contrast, at the California Institute of Technology, which does not use legacy preferences, only 1.5 percent of students are children of alumni.

2. **Legacy preferences have an honorable history of fostering loyalty at America's great institutions of higher learning.**

In fact, as Peter Schmidt, of *The Chronicle,* notes, legacies originated following World War I as a reaction to an influx of immigrant students, particularly Jews, into America's selective colleges. As Jews often outcompeted traditional constituencies on standard meritocratic criteria, universities adopted Jewish quotas. When explicit quotas became hard to defend, the universities began to use more indirect means to limit Jewish enrollment, including considerations of "character," geographic diversity, and legacy status.

3. **Legacy preferences are a necessary evil to support the financial vitality of colleges and universities—including the ability to provide scholarships for low-income and working-class students.**

While universities claim that legacy preferences are necessary to improve fund raising, there is little empirical evidence to support the contention. In fact, several colleges and universities that do not employ legacy preferences nevertheless do well financially. As Golden notes, Caltech raised $71 million in alumni donations in 2008, almost as much as the Massachusetts Institute of Technology ($77 million), even though MIT, which does provide legacy preferences, is five times the size and has many more alumni to tap. Berea College, in Kentucky, favors low-income students, not alumni, yet has a larger endowment than Middlebury, Oberlin, Vassar, and Bowdoin. And Cooper Union, in New York City, does not provide legacy preference but has an endowment larger than that of Bucknell, Haverford, and Davidson.

Moreover, a study included in our book, *Affirmative Action for the Rich,* finds no evidence that alumni preferences increase giving. Chad Coffman, of Winnemac Consulting, and his co-authors examined alumni giving from 1998 to 2007 at the top 100 national universities (as ranked by *U.S. News & World Report*) to test the relationship between giving and the existence of alumni preferences in admissions. They found that institutions with preferences for children of alumni did have higher annual giving per alumnus ($317 versus $201), but that the advantage resulted because the alumni in colleges with alumni preferences tended to be wealthier. Controlling for the wealth of alumni, they found "no evidence that legacy-preference policies themselves exert an influence on giving behavior." After controls, alumni of legacy-granting institutions gave only $15.39 more per year, on average, but even that slight advantage was uncertain from a statistical perspective. Coffman and his colleagues conclude: "After inclusion of appropriate controls, including wealth, there is no statistically significant evidence of a causal relationship between legacy-preference policies and total alumni giving at top universities."

The researchers also examined giving at seven institutions that dropped legacy preferences during the period of the study. They found "no short-term measurable reduction in alumni giving as a result of abolishing legacy preferences." For example, after Texas A&M eliminated the use of legacy preferences, in 2004, donations took a small hit, but then they increased substantially from 2005 to 2007.

Nor can legacy preferences be said to be necessary for colleges to maintain high standards of excellence. It is intriguing to note that, among the top 10 universities in the world in 2008, according to the widely cited Shanghai Jiao Tong University rankings, are four (Caltech, the University of California at Berkeley, the University of Oxford, and the University of Cambridge) that do not employ legacy preferences.

4. **After a generation of affirmative action, legacy preferences are finally beginning to help families of color. Pulling the rug out now would hurt minority students.**

In fact, legacy preferences continue to disproportionately hurt students of color. John Brittain, a former chief counsel at the Lawyers Committee for Civil Rights, and the attorney Eric Bloom note that underrepresented minorities make up 12.5 percent of the applicant pool at selective colleges and universities but only 6.7 percent of the legacy-applicant pool. At Texas A&M, 321 of the legacy admits in 2002 were white, while only three were black and 25 Hispanic. At Harvard, only 7.6 percent of legacy admits in 2002 were underrepresented minorities, compared with 17.8 percent of all students. At the University of Virginia, 91 percent of early-decision legacy admits in 2002 were white, 1.6 percent black, and 0.5 percent Hispanic.

Moreover, this disparate impact is likely to extend far into the future. In 2008, African-Americans and Latinos made up more than 30 percent of the traditional college-aged population but little more than 10 percent of the enrollees at the *U.S. News's* top 50 national universities.

5. **An attack on legacy preferences could indirectly hurt affirmative-action policies by suggesting that "merit" is the only permissible basis for admissions.**

The elimination of legacy preferences would not threaten the future of affirmative action, because the justifications are entirely different. Affirmative-action policies to date have survived strict scrutiny because they enhance educational diversity. (For some members of the Supreme Court, though not a majority, affirmative action also has been justified as a remedy for centuries of brutal discrimination.) Legacy preferences, by contrast, have no such justification.

Because they disproportionately benefit whites, legacy preferences reduce, rather than enhance, racial and ethnic diversity in higher education. And rather than being a remedy for discrimination, they were born of discrimination. Affirmative action engenders enormous controversy because it pits two great principles against each other—the antidiscrimination principle, which says we should not classify people by ancestry, and the antisubordination principle, which says we must make efforts to stamp out illegitimate hierarchies. Legacy preferences, by contrast, advance neither principle: They explicitly classify individuals by bloodline and do so in a way that compounds existing hierarchy.

6. **Legacy preferences may be unfair, but they are not illegal. Unlike discrimination based on race, which is forbidden under the 14th Amendment, it is perfectly legal to discriminate based on legacy status, as the courts have held.**

Remarkably, legacy preferences have been litigated only once in federal court, by an applicant to the University of North Carolina at Chapel Hill named Jane Cheryl Rosenstock, in the 1970s. A New York resident whose application was rejected, she claimed that her constitutional rights were violated by a variety of preferences, including those for in-state applicants, minorities, low-income students, athletes, and legacies. Rosenstock was not a particularly compelling candidate—her combined SAT score was about 850 on a 1600-point scale, substantially lower than most out-of-state applicants—and she was also a weak litigant. She never argued that, because legacy preferences are hereditary, they presented a "suspect" classification that should be judged by the "strict scrutiny" standard under the amendment's equal-protection clause.

The district court judge in the case, *Rosenstock v. Board of Governors of the University of North Carolina,* held that it was rational to believe that alumni preferences translate into additional revenue to universities, although absolutely no evidence was provided for that contention. The decision was never appealed. As Judge Boyce F. Martin Jr. of the US Court of Appeals for the Sixth Circuit notes, the 1976 opinion upholding legacy preferences in *Rosenstock* addressed the issue "in a scant five sentences" and is "neither binding nor persuasive to future courts."

A generation later, two new legal theories are available to challenge legacy preferences. First, Carlton Larson, a law professor at the University of California at Davis, lays out the case that legacy preferences at public universities violate a little-litigated constitutional provision that "no state shall ... grant any Title of Nobility." Examining the early history of the country, Larson makes a compelling case that this prohibition should not be interpreted narrowly as simply prohibiting the naming of individuals as dukes or earls, but more broadly, to prohibit "government-sponsored hereditary privileges"—including legacy preferences at public universities. Reviewing debates in the Revolutionary era, he concludes: "Legacy preferences at exclusive public universities were precisely the type of hereditary privilege that the Revolutionary generation sought to destroy forever." The founders, Larson writes, would have resisted "with every fiber of their being" the idea of state-supported-university admissions based even in part on ancestry.

Second, the attorneys Steve Shadowen and Sozi Tulante argue that legacy preferences are a violation of the 14th Amendment's equal-protection clause. While the amendment was aimed primarily at stamping out discrimination against black Americans, it also extends more broadly to what Justice Potter Stewart called "preference based on lineage." Individuals are to be judged on their own merits, not by what their parents do, which is why the courts have applied heightened scrutiny to laws that punish children born out of wedlock, or whose parents came to this country illegally.

Shadowen and Tulante argue that legacy preferences at private universities, too, are illegal, under the Civil Rights Act of 1866. Unlike Title VI of the 1964 Civil Rights Act, which outlaws discrimination only on the basis of "race, color, or national origin," the 1866 law prohibits discrimination on the basis of both "race" and "ancestry."

7. **Legacy preferences—like affirmative action, geographic preferences, and athletics preferences—are protected by academic freedom, especially at private universities and colleges.**

It is true that the courts have recognized that colleges and universities should be given leeway in admissions in order to promote academic freedom. But that freedom is not unlimited, even at private institutions. As Peter Schmidt notes, the Supreme Court held, in *Runyon v. McCrary* (1976), that private schools could not engage in racial discrimination in admissions. In *Regents of the University of California v. Bakke* (1978), it struck down the use of racial quotas. And in the 2003 *Gratz v. Bollinger* decision, the court invalidated a policy that awarded bonus points to minority students. Ancestry discrimination—providing a leg up in admissions based not on merit but on whether a student's parents or grandparents attended a particular university or college—likewise falls outside the protected zone of academic freedom.

8. **Legacy preferences have been around a long time and are unlikely to ever go away, because powerful political forces support them.**

In fact, legacy preferences are not only legally vulnerable; they are politically vulnerable as well. Polls find that Americans oppose legacy preferences by 75 percent to 23 percent, and in the past decade or so, 16 leading institutions have abandoned them. As affirmative-action programs come under increasing attack, legacy preferences become even harder to justify politically.

Moreover, as a matter of tax law, legacy preferences are fundamentally unstable. Assuming it is true that they entice alumni to provide larger donations than they otherwise would—a claim that has not been empirically proven—then IRS regulations raise questions about whether those donations should be tax deductible. If universities and colleges are conferring a monetary benefit in exchange for donations, then the arrangement, writes the journalist Peter Sacks, "shatters the first principle underlying the charitable deduction, that donations to nonprofit organizations not 'enrich the giver.'" The IRS regulations place universities in a legal Catch-22: Either donations are not linked to legacy preferences, in which case the fundamental rationale for ancestry discrimination is flawed; or giving is linked to legacy preferences, in which case donations should not be tax deductible.

9. **Legacy preferences don't keep nonlegacy applicants out of college entirely. They just reduce the chances of going to a particular selective college, so the stakes are low.**

True, legacy preferences don't bar students from attending college at all. But the benefits of attending a selective institution are substantial. For one thing, wealthy selective colleges tend to spend a great deal more on students' education. Research finds that the least-selective colleges spend about $12,000 per student annually, compared with $92,000 per student at the most-selective ones. In addition, wealthy selective institutions provide much greater subsidies for families. At the wealthiest 10 percent of institutions, students pay, on average, just 20 cents in fees for every dollar the college spends on them, while at the poorest 10 percent of institutions, students pay 78 cents for every dollar spent on them. Furthermore, selective colleges are better than less-selective institutions at graduating equally qualified students. And future earnings are, on average, 45 percent higher for students who graduated from more-selective institutions than for those from less-selective ones, and the difference in earnings ends up being widest among low-income students. Finally, according to research by the political scientist Thomas Dye, 54 percent of America's corporate leaders and 42 percent of governmental leaders are graduates of just 12 institutions. For all those reasons, legacy preferences matter.

10. **Everyone does it. Legacies are just an inherent reality in higher education throughout the world.**

In fact, as Daniel Golden writes, legacy preferences are "virtually unknown in the rest of the world"; they are "an almost exclusively American custom." The irony, of course, is that while legacies are uniquely American, they are also deeply un-American, as Michael Lind, of the New America Foundation, has argued.

Thomas Jefferson famously sought to promote in America a "natural aristocracy" based on "virtue and talent," rather than an "artificial aristocracy" based on wealth. "By reserving places on campus for members of the pseudo-aristocracy of 'wealth and birth,'" Lind writes, "legacy preferences introduce an aristocratic snake into the democratic republican Garden of Eden."

For the most part, American higher education has sought to democratize, opening its doors to women, to people of color, and to the financially needy. Legacy preferences are an outlier in that trend, a relic that has no place in American society. In a fundamental sense, this nation's first two great wars—the Revolution and the Civil War—were fought to defeat different forms of aristocracy. That this remnant of ancestry-based discrimination still survives—in American higher education, of all places—is truly breathtaking.

Race and Immigration

Confusion and Illusion

In this selection of readings, we once again explore the importance of the use and meaning of various concepts (i.e., race, racism). After the election of President Barack Hussein Obama in 2008, many news journalists, and others, stated that we are now in a "post-racial" America. What do you think they mean by this? Hartigan (2010) wrote in the Chronicle of Higher Education that 2010 was a "busy year for news stories about race" (para. 1). How does our culture shape how we talk and understand race? Based on *What's Race Got to Do with It?* (http://www.newsweek.com/what-role-race-health-care-78335) consider what some would argue is the biological basis of race or how race is socially constructed. [Newsweek has changed the title of the article to *What Role for Race in Health Care?* since its original publication in 2009.] Hopefully, this challenges you to think not only about how the author constructs the argument presented but also about the issue of race and discrimination in modern society.

Finding an effective answer to how to prepare students to "work effectively with diverse populations" is an important issue for many disciplines. Social work is one field that has done research and offers many different strategies for achieving this. The case-study and role-play approach is one that could be incorporated across many disciplines to develop culturally sensitive college graduates regardless of the field they are pursuing. Understanding how the concept of race intersects with other concepts, such as class and gender inequality, maximizes our potential to eradicate racism nationally and globally. Therefore, "Can You Call It Racism? An Educational Case Study and Role-Play Approach" is included to provide an example of something we (educators and students alike) can do to impact intergroup relations and confront stereotypes while promoting social justice in our learning environments.

We have included two essays that relate to immigration in different ways. Moylan (2014) considers the connection and disconnection created when one changes their geographical location away from their family, whether that is across national or state lines, or from one community to another. A common thread between her essay and Bowie's (2014) is the experience of leaving one's home. His narrative as an immigrant to the United States sheds light on an experience that many may relate to and yet is uniquely his. When reading these narratives, what new understandings are created for you relative to current issues of immigration? We encourage the reader to once again attempt to apply elements and standards of critical and creative thinking (see Chapter 3) while reflecting on the micro, meso, and macro levels of the immigrant experience.

Our understanding of language and its use is important. If the soldiers fighting are on the side of what "we" believe, they are referred to as **Freedom Fighters**. Not surprisingly, if soldiers are acting in the interest of a people "we" are at odds with, they are called **Insurgents**. So too, a "patriot" belongs to "us," while "our" enemies are called "terrorists." The article "Top Ten Differences Between White Terrorists and Others" can be used to raise awareness of stereotypes we have of terrorists and our attitudes, assumptions, and behaviors toward people of Middle Eastern or Muslim descent. When considering critical and creative thinking relative to these issues, one might consider where our construction of race and "whiteness" and how we relate to each other due to these constructs intersect. We hope these articles will launch inquiry upon their reading, and dialogue during in-class discussions.

Questions for Consideration:

1. In what ways do you think political, social, cultural, and economic factors contributed to the construction of our modern conception of race? What impact do you think our current conceptualization of race is having on our society?
2. How has the understanding of the immigrant experience influenced US policy(ies) on immigration?
3. Using this subset of articles as a starting point, what do you think the dialogue regarding race, ethnicity, immigration and culture will be like in a hundred years from now?

CAN YOU CALL IT RACISM? AN EDUCATIONAL CASE STUDY AND ROLE-PLAY APPROACH

By Eun-Kyoung Othelia Lee, Betty Blythe, and Kassie Goforth

Social work education has long struggled to acknowledge cultural diversity and identify teaching methods to prepare students to work effectively with diverse populations (Council on Social Work Education, 2001). Garcia and Van Soest (2006) provide a conceptual framework that unites cultural competency and social justice in social work education. According to their model, the first steps are recognizing the centrality of the social construction of race and the practice of racism at personal, institutional, and cultural levels. This leads, in turn, to acknowledging racism as a mode of everyday human interaction, involving domination and exploitation, which reinforces an unequal socioeconomic system. During this process social workers must be willing to confront and work through unresolved conflicts in relation to their own role, status, and participation in an oppressive system (Van Soest & Garcia, 2003).

In this Teaching Note, we present an innovative case study and role-play approach to promoting student learning on diversity issues; to teaching diversity content; and to facilitating intelligent dialogue on such sensitive issues as race, ethnicity, and gender. One class session of a multicultural social work course was devoted to a case study and role-play based on a real incident that took place in a nongovernmental organization (NGO) in the state of Chiapas, Mexico. One of the authors lived in Chiapas and was affiliated with the NGO. The report of the case study and role-play are based on direct observation and participation.

Lee, E. K. O., Blythe, B., & Goforth, K. (2009). Teaching note: Can you call it racism? An educational case study and role-play approach. *Journal of Social Work Education, 45*(1), 123-129.

Here, we report on the ways in which MSW students experienced the educational case study and role-play approach and how they assessed the value of the intervention for understanding diversity and social justice. Student feedback and our observations address the merit of this multicultural educational intervention.

AN EDUCATIONAL CASE STUDY

The case study was set in Chiapas, the southernmost state in Mexico, home to many indigenous Mayan peoples. More than 90% of the population in the highlands of Chiapas is Mayan, and most inhabitants maintain their traditional language, clothing, and customs. Despite a wealth of natural resources, the Mayan population barely ekes out a living (Weller, 2000). Typically, they are subsistence farmers, but they must compete for land with highland cattle ranchers and often must grow their crops on steep terrain and in poor soil. Since the early 16th century, the Mayan people of Chiapas have experienced oppression because of their race and ethnicity (Stephen, 2003).

The setting for this case study is the Human Rights Center (HRC), which is located in a small town in Chiapas and is run by Jesuit priests. The HRC serves more than 200,000 people in the 500 Mayan communities within the Jesuit parish. The HRC has 25 fulltime employees, and many more people from other community groups work closely with the HRC. These faith-based groups include Jesuit priests and deacons and a community of Catholic nuns, many of whom are indigenous. When the deacons, tribal judges, and health and human rights promoters who work in the different communities that the center serves are included, hundreds of people collaborate with the HRC. Mayan religious life is inseparable from public and political life, so the HRC uses existing church structures to carry out its work, and staff members collaborate closely with the deacons and health and human right promoters to reach the communities.

The central issue in the role play is a wage dispute, first acknowledged by the Mayan members of the HRC. The paid workers at the HRC are about one-fourth indigenous and three-fourths Mestizo. Most of the Mestizo workers come from other states in Mexico and are professionally trained; they come to the HRC because they are committed to working for justice for the indigenous people of Chiapas. The other Mestizo workers tend to be technical staff or secretaries. With a few exceptions, these staff members are less motivated by the ideal of working for justice than by having full-time, paid employment, which is rare in the small towns of Chiapas. Because of the HRC's youth and rapid growth, formal personnel policies and a salary structure have not been established. Each employee was hired by the HRC director, Father Juan, and negotiated his or her salary with him.

In the Mayan tradition, leaders who serve the community are chosen by consensus and work for free.

Indigenous people who work for the HRC want to help their communities; they are also essential to the organization for their knowledge of the communities as well as their ability to speak the local dialect, Tseltal.

THE ROLE PLAY

Students were provided with educational case study materials that included background information on Chiapas, the HRC, and the personnel issue a week before the in-class role play (set up as a staff meeting) took place. The personnel issue, based on a real incident, was the fact that the Mayan employees learned that they were paid at a rate that was about one-half the rate of the Mestizo employees. Each student was assigned a role along with a detailed description of his or her character; they were not given such information about other characters. There were 23 to 26 characters in the role play, including both Mestizo and Mayan roles.

EXAMPLES OF CHARACTER DESCRIPTIONS

A full list of characters is available from the first author, along with notes on information each character should not share, on each character's goal in the meeting, and on points each character should make during the meeting. Following are some examples of the descriptions of characters that were provided to students.

Father Juan: A Mestizo Character

- Your role: You have a bachelor-level university education. Many of the workers at the HRC are young people whom you met in your travels around Mexico. As a priest, you try to be a spiritual father to your employees as well as their boss. You are extremely overworked, persuasive, and charismatic.
- Do not share with the group: You believe that most of the employees are there because you personally invited them. You feel that lay peoples' commitment to indigenous people is not as valuable as that of the priests, who gave up secular life entirely, whereas lay people tend to stay only for a few years. You privately feel that you would never be able to work for a female supervisor. People tend to follow your advice and you believe that you know what is best for others. Your goals in this meeting: To

retain control of the decision-making process and the salaries of HRC employees; to defuse the argument without making more work for yourself; and to make sure that the issue of racism is not raised or ascribed to your leadership or to the HRC.

- Points you must make in the meeting:
  - The staff can make recommendations to the coordinating council, but they cannot vote on decisions as a staff. You do not explicitly state this last point.
  - There are no funds to increase salaries. People with higher salaries are free to donate a portion of their salaries to people with lower salaries.
  - The salary policy is not racist. People must be very careful to avoid deciding that a situation that appears to be defined by race is, in fact, racist.
  - It is necessary to offer professional staff (such as lawyers) a salary that competes with the salary they might receive in the city.

Miguel: A Mayan Character

- Your role: You have been working for the HRC for 8 years as a community organizer. You know the Mayan communities intimately, and are well-known and trusted by the people. You also are a practitioner of traditional herbal medicine, which you learned from a "wise man" in your village. You play the guitar and write your own songs. At community events, you are sought after to sing, because there are not many popular songs available in Mayan languages.
- Your oldest son, Geronimo, is extremely ill with leukemia, and you and your wife frequently have to take him to the capital of Chiapas, 5 hours away, for treatment at a public hospital. Father Juan has been very supportive of you in this, giving you as much time off as you need, and sometimes lending you a car or visiting your son himself.
- Do not share with others in the group: You secretly dislike another HRC employer, Esequiel, who is from your village, whom you suspect of flirting with your wife when you are not around. However, in this group you and Esequiel are united as Mayan people in a Mestizo organization, and you would never openly disagree with his points or discredit him, because the stakes for the community are too high.
- Your goal in this meeting: To achieve a fair standard of payment that reduces the difference between the amounts that Mayans and Mestizos are paid, and to do it in a way that promotes a deeper understanding of indigenous culture.
- Points you must make in the meeting:
  - At the beginning of the meeting, you mention that you'd like to discuss the issue of salaries, because it seems to you that the Mayan employees are making less than the Mestizos. You also indicate that you would like to open up a discussion about the values suggested by the salary differential.

- Because the Mayan employees of HRC work full time and do not have time to farm their land, they need the salary to feed their families.
- You want to continue to respect the Mayan tradition in which people serve the communities without being compensated, but you also need to provide for your family.

Josue: A Mestizo Character

- Your role: You have a PhD in biology. The current leader of the Agriculture Department wants to hand over the leadership to you, but you have only worked at the HRC for a year. You are beginning to learn the Tseltal language. You hope to devote the rest of your working life to this organization. You believe strongly in consensus decision-making and in building community among coworkers.
- Your goal in this meeting: To support the Mayans' request for more equitable salaries, and to call on the agency to be fair and transparent in its dealings.
- Point you must make during the meeting: At an appropriate point, suggest that everyone reveal their salaries, as an exercise in "transparency."

Prior to the role play, the instructor explained the source of conflict. During a staff meeting, a Mayan employee, Miguel, had raised the issue of the salary inequity. Father Juan's main reaction was to clarify that everyone in the organization had had a chance to negotiate his or her salary, and had chosen to take the offered salary rather than reject the job. Father Juan had stressed that although the discrepancy appeared to be divided along racial lines, this did not mean that the situation was racist, because that would imply intention to discriminate against a certain group based on race. Given that Father Juan was solely responsible for the salary scale in the agency, it is no wonder that he wanted to squelch any discussion of racism.

In Mayan culture, it is difficult to challenge the authority of a member of the dominant Mestizo culture, and a priest, aggressively. Outside their community, Mayans often are punished for speaking their minds. On the other hand, Mestizo staff are secretly ashamed of how they treat their Mayan coworkers, perhaps because they themselves feel out of touch with their own indigenous heritage. Father Juan had clarified that members of one ethnicity being routinely paid less than members of the other was not racism. So the question remained: What was the problem, and how could it be solved?

The entire class was engaged in the role play, an exercise that lasted about 45 minutes. Afterward, the following questions were discussed in class.

1. What was your experience of the meeting?
2. What was most helpful about participating in the role play? What was least helpful?

3. Do you think this is a racist situation? Why or why not? If you think it is, what is the source of the racism? How could the racism be changed?
4. Do you find it easy or difficult to talk about a race issue that occurred in a foreign country?
5. What other factors besides race and culture are at play here, and how do they affect the overall picture?
6. What should the Center do to solve its problem? Would you like to propose a solution?

DISCUSSION

Student feedback was collected through in-class responses to discussion questions and voluntarily written postings on the Blackboard course management system. Overall, students' perceptions of the role-play exercise were favorable. They described it as "a fun, interactive activity" and "a great teaching asset." They found it helpful to review background information on the region and the organization before class, as this allowed them to represent their characters in a more realistic manner. Students appeared to benefit from the experiential component of the learning process, as indicated in the following comment: "I learn better through hands-on activities such as this and it was nice to see everyone in the class take a role and then later learn why they acted the way that they did."

Students expressed discomfort about "not knowing enough about the cultural and political context" in a relatively remote region such as Chiapas. One student commented, "It was hard for me to grasp the reality of the situation but even if it was hypothetical I still think the activity was successful in educating the class about a topic I know I was previously unaware of." Some students reported their difficulties in relating to incidents in a foreign country and in reacting without knowing the specific cultural contexts. In spite of students' concerns about their lack of knowledge of the indigenous culture of Mexico, students took the risk of thinking out loud and putting themselves in the shoes of dominant or oppressed groups.

We observed that MSW students in courses on racism often struggle with emotional baggage regarding historical events in the United States, such as racial segregation and slavery, for which they are not personally responsible. Hence, in multicultural education, it is critical to help students to move beyond their guilt and self-censorship; this can be done by reducing the cognitive and emotional barriers students perceive when confronted with the oppression embodied in the dominant culture and their privileged social status in it (Abrams & Gibson, 2007; Mildred & Zúñiga, 2004). Consequently, students especially appreciated the fact that the role play was based on a real and contemporary situation. A student commented "[instructors'] insight into the situation, because [author] was there, made it more powerful than just an exercise that was in a book for diversity classes."

Apparently, the role-play approach helped students extend empathy not only to the characters they played but also to the group dynamics and the power structure of the HRC. Characters in the dominant group were sanctioned to speak their unconscious, prejudiced remarks, which students would be extremely hesitant to do in a class setting. For those who played members of the oppressed group, it was a valuable experience to extend their empathy and try to understand the struggle of a vulnerable population. Hence, this teaching method has parallel emphases on the history and effect of oppression and the strengths and joys of diversity (Van Soest & Garcia, 2003).

This role play addressed a social problem in Mexico, but there are certainly parallels of the case study in the U.S. context. As a young White woman with a privileged background, the following student was able to identify with the character of Josue, who is an upper-middle-class Mestizo, while still feeling empathy for the indigenous characters. Her character plays a critical role by suggesting that everyone tell everyone else what salary they make, as an exercise in "transparency."

> I feel as if I could relate to [Josue's] perspective. I wonder what it might have felt like for some people to play the role of a Mayan, who in their own lives, have experienced little oppression and more privilege. I think it is critical to have the discussions about racism, oppression, and privilege in class, but we also need to make it more practical and think about what we will do when we are in situations outside the classroom.

The educational value of this role play is to help students strengthen their commitment to the promotion of social justice, which it may do more successfully than a more traditional approach to learning about historical oppression. As Van Soest and Garcia (2003) argued, exposure to content about social injustice and inequality forces students to reexamine many of the values and beliefs they have held about themselves and the dominant paradigm. It also evokes deepened awareness of social justice among students, providing a perfect moment for teaching.

After the role play, students identified unfair organizational structure as a root cause that influenced the distribution of money and power; weakened the traditional culture, which had no decision-making power; and perpetuated unequal gender roles. This identification of problems motivated them to come up with suggested solutions, including decentralizing the Center's leadership, establishing clear guidelines for a salary scale, creating a merit-based reward system, and establishing an antidiscrimination policy at the HRC.

It is important to note that this report of this case study and role play are based on the authors' understanding of the situation and do not represent the multiple realities experienced by many HRC members. Yet, the value of the educational case study and role-play approach lies in its use as a pedagogical technique rather than in its application to the particular circumstances in Chiapas.

Developing a case study requires an educator to think through the key issues involved in terms of conceptual frameworks, people, and the social environment, and to construct proactive rationales and strategies for the best resolution (Haulotte & Kretzschmar, 2001; Rivas & Hull, 2000). Toward this end, an educator should state the major problem, define the objective of the case study, describe key players within the organization, and identify the process of service delivery and decision-making. More creative educational interventions such as this should be designed with a goal of strengthening social workers' cultural competence and their capacity to work across multiple paradigms, and to find new ways to engage with clients.

REFERENCES

Abrams, L. S., & Gibson, P. (2007). Reframing multicultural education: Teaching White privilege in social work curriculum. *Journal of Social Work Education, 43*, 147–160.

Council on Social Work Education. (2001). *Educational policy and accreditation standards.* Alexandria, VA: Author.

Garcia, B., & Van Soest, D. (2006). *Social work practice for social justice: Cultural competence in action.* Alexandria, VA: Council on Social Work Education.

Haulotte, S. M. & Kretzschmar, J. A. (2001). *Case studies for teaching and learning social work practice.* Alexandria, VA: Council on Social Work Education.

Mildred, J., & Zúñiga, X. (2004). Working with resistance to diversity issues in the classroom: Lessons from teacher training and multicultural education. *Smith College Studies in Social Work. Special Issue: Pedagogy and Diversity, 74*, 359–375.

Rivas, R. F, & Hull, G. H. (2000). *Case studies in generalist practice.* Belmont, Ca: Wadsworth/Thomson Learning.

Stephen, L. (2003). *Zapata lives! History and cultural politics in southern Mexico.* Berkeley, CA: University of California Press.

Van Soest, D., & Garcia, B. (2003). *Diversity education for social justice: Mastering teaching skills* (lst ed.). Alexandria, VA: Council on Social Work Education.

Weller, W. H. (2000). *Conflict in Chiapas: Understanding the modern Mayan world.* North Manchester, IN: DeWitt Books.

THE ONE WHO LEFT

By Ann Moylan

I had been thinking about what it means to be "the one who left" as I sat down with a friend for lunch in a campus eatery. Sitting across from her, our Panda Express bowls between us, it dawned on me that she might have a story to contribute to the essay I was writing. I knew that she had moved from her home country to the United States many years ago in order to attend graduate school; and that upon completion of her graduate studies, she had remained in the U.S. I believed that she was the only person in her immediate family to be living in the U.S., so I asked her this question: "Do you think of yourself, and does your family think of you, as 'the one who left'?" Here is her story.

THE TREE

"Yes, I think of myself as the one who left, and my family also thinks of me in those terms. When I was leaving my home in South Korea to attend graduate school in the United States, we all believed I would be away for seven years—two years for the Masters degree and an additional five years for the PhD.

"I am the only daughter in a family with three sons. When I was preparing to leave South Korea, my father especially was very sad. So he planted a little tree. 'This', he told me 'will help me mark the years until you return home.' And so for seven years my father would visit the tree. As it grew in size, he had a concrete reminder that he could see and

Moylan, A. (2014). The one who left. In S. Torres, Jr. (Ed.), *Palabra: The Book of Living Essays* (pp. 88-109). Sacramento, CA: Petraglyph Publishing.

touch, of how long I had been away; and the larger the tree, the closer we were to the time of my return.

"But during those seven years, I met the man I would marry. My husband, who is also from Korea, wanted to stay in the U.S. and raise our family here. It was not an easy decision for me because I knew how desperately my parents missed me. This was such hard news to break to my family. My father cried each time we would speak on the phone and I knew that I was breaking his heart.

"Year after year he reminded me that he still goes to stand beside my tree. It was not until this past year, 19 years since I left Korea, that he finally made the trip to visit me in the U.S. It helped him so much to see how and where we live; the home we live in, the school our children attend. He now understands why we decided to stay in the U.S. and raise our children here. For the first time, now when I speak with him he does not cry.

"Fortunately, in the year since his visit, I have started to engage with my brothers and their wives via social media. We send text messages and photos frequently. If they take my parents out to lunch or dinner, they share a photo of the food and tell me what a nice time they all had. I am still the one who left, but I am beginning to feel more a part of the family. I believe my father's visit and my family's use of social media have begun to bring us closer again."

As she finished the story, tears rolled down her cheeks. I also was moved by the sweet, sad story and the image in my mind of her father, on his hands and knees, digging in the soil to plant this tiny tree that would remind him of his beloved daughter. I could see her father returning to that tree, so firmly planted on Korean soil while his daughter was not. I imagined that he was aware over the years of the roots that were becoming deeper and stronger, reaching out to secure this little tree to its home. And I felt in my heart what he must have felt watching the tree grow taller and wider like his longing for his daughter.

I share this friend's story because I believe it speaks to an experience many of us share. In some version or variation this experience of leaving home and longing for those from whom we are separated is at the heart of our lives. Those of us in California, in particular, live in a state with a large percentage of recent immigrants and what some refer to as "transplants," those who have relocated from another part of the country. Some of us moved here with family, but many of us moved here on our own. In either case we may share a sense of being the "one who left," which can play a large part in our identity, significantly impact our life experiences, and in some cases be a source of unresolved grief.

This defining characteristic that separates us from our families, that makes us the odd one out, the one far from home, the one others may believe turned our backs on our family, is the same characteristic that helps many of us to understand each other. It helps me to better understand the challenges faced by those who have immigrated to the U. S.

It helps me to better understand students who are the first generation to attend college, and those who are the first to move away from their home communities. And importantly, acknowledging this aspect of my own history has helped me to understand myself better. It has helped me to find a framework for some of the loss and longing that I harbor within me. I carry a sweet, incessant nostalgia for the smells of the salt marshes, the family gatherings, my brother and my sister. Not a day goes by that I don't think of my family on the East Coast. And I wonder, how often do they think of me?

A few years ago, I was in a professional training on the topic of children and trauma. The leader of the training was particularly interested in exploring how children can be impacted, and sometimes traumatized, by circumstances surrounding their immigration, or even, in some cases, the immigration of their parents. As a group we explored case studies of mothers who were struggling with attachment issues related to trauma experienced during their immigration and how the mother's trauma was playing out in her relationship with the infant. Participants were then asked to consider our selves as immigrants, even if our own relocation had not involved crossing U. S. borders, or even state borders. We were asked to reflect upon what it was like to leave the old place; our journey to the new place; arriving in the new place; which customs and practices were the same in the old place and the new place; which customs and practices were new to us; what it had felt like to be in the "foreign" land; how we had established new support systems, and so on.

This was the first time I had considered my experience in terms of immigration. Up until then, immigrants were other people. I had ancestors who were immigrants, but I did not use that term to describe my self or my experience. Even now it is easy to dismiss the significance of my "immigration" or more accurately, migration. Particularly when I hold it up in comparison to the immigration stories of those who have risked life and limb to cross borders, who have entered a land where they do not speak the language, where they have been driven due to persecution or lack of opportunity in their homeland, where they may live in fear of deportation. None of those circumstances apply to me yet there is some aspect of the immigration stories that resonates with me, that seems to reflect my experience.

INDIVIDUALISM AND FAMILISM

Many families, communities, societies or cultural groups expect that one should stay geographically close to one's roots. This is an aspect of *familism*, in which the good of the family as a unit is to be placed above that of the individual or it is believed that it is in the best interest of the individual to remain geographically close to the family. This concept of familism is often discussed in relation to or in opposition to *individualism,* in which the individual's needs trump those of the family or it is believed that it is in the best interest of the individual to strike out on their own. There are variations in the degree to which familism and individualism are embraced and how they are applied to norms regarding moving away from family, leaving home. In some families the expectation is that you don't move away at all. Those who move away will be shunned—family connections will be cut off. In other families, you may move away for school or other time-limited opportunities, but you are expected to come back home. Or, as was the case for me, I felt no pressure to stay close to home and learned only after leaving that I had unrealistic expectations regarding how that move would play out across time.

Twenty-seven years ago, when I made the decision to move 3000 miles across the country, from South Carolina to California, I was not aware of how this decision would play out in my life or the lives of the children I would later have. I was not aware of the many ways in which this one decision would impact so many experiences and relationships and eventually come to define, in large part, the person I am today. I was neither aware nor concerned that the trip away from home might be one way.

ORIGINS OF LEAVING

Early Signs I'd Be The One

I am eight years old, holding in my hands a glossy publication from Camp Illahee—page after page of beautiful, inviting photographs—the cabins with bunk beds, the dining hall with tables stretching across the entire room, archery, canoeing, the swimming lake, and horses; oh, the horses. There are pictures of campers of all ages, starting with little ones not more than five or six years old, and going through the high-school-aged kids, college-aged counselors, and the adult directors. Everyone is in their Sunday Whites camp uniform: white shorts, a white collared shirt with a little tie at the neck; standing or sitting shoulder to shoulder, arranged by age group. I don't know how many times I studied that publication, envisioning myself there. I had to get to that magical place.

For people outside the Carolinas, North and South Carolina may seem to be pretty much one and the same. But that is not true to Carolinians. Even at age eight I knew that going to summer camp in the North Carolina mountains would take me a long, long way from home. The land of evergreen firs and waterfalls was a different world than the sandy-soiled "low-country" of South Carolina where I was from.

My father was a local merchant and my mother was a schoolteacher. Dad sold and repaired household appliances and had a gift shop; Mom taught English at the Junior High.

My older sister, my younger brother and I had everything we needed, but when it came to things like summer camp, that was extra. And Illahee was expensive. I started saving my money so that I could attend camp. My grandparents would send me a crisp five-dollar bill inside a greeting card for most holidays, and I would save these and other cash gifts and small allowances. Maybe it's true and maybe it isn't, but I believe I saved up about half of the money needed to spend two weeks at Camp Illahee's "Pre-Camp." Most girls would go for a month or even two months. That was out of the question for me. But "Pre-Camp" seemed an obtainable goal. I didn't know anyone who had ever been there. I didn't know anyone who was planning to go there. That didn't matter, and may have even added to the intrigue. I wanted to experience camp at Illahee. By the time I finished 5th grade in 1966, having just turned 11, I was on my way.

Later Signs I'd Be The One

Years later I was still living in that small town in South Carolina, now a senior in high school. The pressing question for my friends and me was where to go to college. I was not drawn to the likely state schools where most of my friends would be attending—Clemson, Carolina (University of South Carolina), and the College of Charleston; nor was I drawn to the schools where my parents or older sister had attended.

I remember one day sitting under the white canopy of my bed, surrounded by Pepto-Bismol® pink walls and peppermint shag carpet and reading through descriptions of colleges in the back of the dictionary. I had only a vague idea of what I wanted in a college: small, but not too small; co-ed; and good school spirit. With those parameters, I selected Wake Forest.

It was my dad who took me up to visit Wake Forest, a five-hour drive from our home. He remarked that he had taken both my brother and my sister on trips by themselves, but that he and I had missed out until now. I could tell that this was an important trip for him, but I was not sharing the same significance he felt. The importance of the trip to me had to do with me, not with us. I was excited about having found this school and worried about whether or not I could get in. Looking back, I imagine now that he recognized on a greater scale the meaning of this move for me, and for him, and what it would mean in terms of my future, my connection to him and to all of my family. I imagine he was thinking about what it would be like to have me leave home. We shared a special bond, which I will discuss later. I appreciate now how bitter sweet it must have been for him.

Mine had not been a trouble-free adolescence and I saw leaving for college as an opportunity to repair myself, perhaps to reinvent myself. Fortunately, I was admitted and when it came time to go, both my parents drove me to North Carolina. I can still see my mother sitting on my bed in the dorm that day. She was teary, sitting on the bed beside my teddy bear, Charmin. But I didn't share her feelings. Her tears puzzled me then. Wasn't this the happiest moment ever? Now, as a mother myself, I understand those complicated tears. I wish I could reach out and give her the comfort and the thanks that she so deserved on that day.

The Final Move, So Far

I believe those two departures set the stage for my move years later to California. If my parents were saddened by my departure for California, they did not let on to me. They showed excitement that I had been offered a position that I was excited about. I had been teaching in at a small college in Georgia for the seven years prior, three hours and fifteen minutes from home. Getting home was easy and I made the trip regularly. You may think I had a similar motivation to get to California as I did to get to Illahee and Wake Forest. That was not the case. During the time that I was teaching in Georgia, the college decided to phase out the program I had been teaching in. I would no longer have a job. Fortunately, I had been working on my PhD, which turned out to be my ticket to ride. So while there was nothing calling me to California, there was a boot to my backside to find another job. I realize now that all it takes to get far away from home is allowing that to be a possibility.

When it came time for me to pack up the house I had been living in, my mother drove the three hours to help. In fact, she did most of the packing, as I was very distracted, preoccupied with the many goodbyes and loose ends. I packed my microwave oven, television, and clothes into my 1983 Honda Accord; and little else except for my miniature schnauzer, Dietrich, who rode in a laundry basket wedged between a full front seat and the dashboard. During my five days on the road I grew sick and tired of the same songs on the radio playing over and over again, but I was comforted by the repeating ad for Motel 6—"we'll leave the light on for you." Exactly what my parents would have said had they been awaiting my arrival.

My Father's Daughter

While I have thought before about the early signs that I would be the one who left, I had always thought about my early decisions and my inclinations. It was in writing this essay that I traced the story back another step—to my father's influence.

In his family, my father was the one who stayed. The second of four children, he left home to attend college, join the Navy, and then return to college on the GI Bill. But he is the one, and the only one in his family, who returned home to work in his father's business in South Carolina. His siblings moved away to North Carolina, Virginia, New York; but my father returned home. He returned after college graduation and stayed there until he died at age 78.

Dad told lots of "could have been" stories: he could have been a doctor—loved and excelled in biology; could have been a teacher—actually was a teacher in many ways. I remember riding with Dad in the cab of his pickup truck, windows down, no air conditioner, no seat belts. And he'd explain things to me. Like why we have daylight savings time—so the workers could enjoy some daylight with their families at the end of the day; and why he ran a business—not just to make money and provide for his family, he said, but to provide a needed service to his community.

Dad wasn't a doctor or a teacher. He was a dedicated merchant who also serviced all the appliances he sold. I loved how he could fix anything. Washing machines. Radios. Stoves. Refrigerators. How many times did I take him a plastic horse, a tangled necklace, a finger with a splinter, and he would fix those too?

Significant to this story is that like my dad, I am also the second born. And my father and I share the same birthday. My sister had been born on my mother's birthday, and, as my dad would tell it, he wanted a birthday present too. There was clearly a strong connection and identification between the two of us on these and other grounds. We both had older sisters. We both had younger brothers. We were middle kids! He understood me, he would say.

It comes to me now that my being the one who left had origins with my dad. He raised me to not only see the windows of opportunity, but also to pry them open and go through them. He encouraged me to reach, to pursue my dreams, to live my life wherever it took me. I was working in my father's store by the time I was in junior high school. This provided even more opportunity to be taught by him. For example, he allowed my sister and me to have a teen corner in his store and sell things we thought our friends would like. We sold big soft pom-pom key chains alongside the 45rpm records, and learned about pricing and selling and understanding your target customer. I learned other lessons too. One day the store was too cold, so I put on my raincoat. He came in and really let me have it. "What are you doing with your raincoat on?" "I was cold." "But you can't wait on people in your raincoat, it looks like you are leaving." Hmmm. I never thought of that.

Dad worked hard to impart the knowledge and skills I would need to succeed. I don't know if he had regrets about his own choice to stay in that little town, I didn't sense that he did. But I believe he consciously positioned himself to extend the horizon I would see before me. I remember being little, not even up to his waist yet. He scooped me up and placed me on his shoulders in our house on Honeysuckle Lane. He walked around the house, going from room to room, and pointing out the difference in our perspectives. He walked into the little galley kitchen—did I realize, he asked, that when he walked into the kitchen he could see what was on top of the refrigerator? Really? No, actually, I had never thought of that. And when I was in high school and I said I wanted to be a kindergarten teacher, he replied, "why not be a teacher of teachers?" The message I received was, shoot a little higher. Go a little farther. And I guess I did just that.

Back Another Step

I think now of the generations before my father. While I am the one who left in my family, I am the descendent of many ones who left. Whether they left Ireland, or New York, or Baltimore, or Wilmington; I have only followed a pattern so clearly established before me. In my "western exile," as one of my friends calls our state of being and living so far from our East Coast families, I feel the connection to all these ancestors. How similar were their experiences to my own, I wonder. Did they leave with family in tow? Or did they leave all family behind? Did they leave and then return? Or did they leave never to return? Did their families expect them to come back home? Were they able to maintain relationships from afar?

THREE STAGES OF DENIAL

When I Have Children

When I first moved to California I was single. My sister made a trip out with her two children, ages 7 and 11 at the time. My brother made a trip out with his wife before they had children. I was traveling across country two to three times a year, and I wished they would come out my way more than they did. I wished that, as I imagined adult friends would do, they'd share the financial burden, the physical stress, and the emotional cost of traveling, closing the gap of miles that separated our family. But, I told myself, it makes sense for me to be the one who travels. After all, I am single. It is easier and less expensive for me to be the one who covers the miles. I bet they will travel out this way more when I have kids.

My parents and my brother and sister and their spouses and children all came out to California to attend my wedding six years after I arrived in California. One year later I had my first child and the year after that I had my second child. I had expected that having kids would change how my family dealt with getting together. But, I was wrong. Twice a year I would fly to the East Coast with my two children in tow. When they were one and an infant. When they were two and one. When they were three and two. Often I would be traveling without my husband. It was hard. Really hard. Hard on my parents, hard on my kids, hard on me. But, I reasoned, even though I had little kids, there were still more family members on the East Coast. It made more sense for me to fly there than for them to come see me. And anyway, I wanted my children to know the sights and smells of my homeland.

We would rent a cottage at the beach near my South Carolina home and coordinate our trip to coincide with when my siblings would be there with their kids, each of us in a different beach house. I loved those times and I cherish the photos of the cousins together on the beach, and memories of boat rides, Bingo, fried shrimp and hush puppies, collecting shells, building sand castles, soothing sun burns.

They will come out when they have the time, when they have the money, when … When?

When Their Schedules Allow

I longed for my siblings to help me cover the miles. Maybe, I thought, things will be different once they don't have kids at home. Maybe they don't come because it is so hard to work out everyone's schedules. This will sound crazy, but I never entertained the possibility that they didn't come because they chose not to, because they didn't want to. I always thought there must be some other good reason. And I was able to continue this line of reasoning, this denial, when I realized that as long as our parents were alive I would make the effort to fly back. My siblings could just wait for me to come home. They knew I would not be gone too long. Our parents were aging. It was difficult for them to travel. My siblings did not need to travel out here to see me; they could just see me when I traveled back home. Things would be different, I thought, once our parents were no longer alive. Then we would be three grown children, three adults with no one having more or less reason to cross the miles than the other.

Once Mom and Dad Passed Away

My father passed away in 2005 and my mother in 2010. But my parents' deaths didn't change much of anything with regard to my siblings traveling out here more. Finally, after 27 years, I have had to face the fact that there is nothing I can say or do to make them want to come out here, make them want to put forth the effort to close the gap, make them invested in knowing my children better. Both my siblings have always made me feel welcome when I visit them, but as my sister has pointedly told me on occasion, "You are the one who left." And I am just now starting to understand the significance of that remark, to see the reality as she sees it. It was my decision to move away. My choice should not create any obligation for her or her family to spend their time and money getting to me. It actually makes sense to me now. But will where I lived forty years ago define our relationship as adults? Have I committed a moving violation for which I will never be able to pay the fine?

AT WHAT GAIN, AT WHAT COST

I have, on many occasions, asked myself these two questions: At what gain? At what cost? The clearest gain for me has been in the personal and professional growth I have enjoyed. It is in California that I have learned more about the richness that diversity offers a community. My classes look to me like the United Nations. I have learned so much from the life experiences of my students, their perspectives. My children have enjoyed a state that, for all its flaws, is much more accepting of "otherness" in its many forms. In California, no matter what you are like, you will find people like yourself. This was so freeing, so affirming. I wanted this for my children.

The greatest loss for me has been in not having the day-to-day extended family interactions. Growing up as children of the one who stayed, my siblings and I were the only grandchildren who lived in the same town with our paternal grandparents. We had grandparents to sit with in church, to visit after school, and who would attend our birthday parties. When I worked in my father's store, after school or on weekends, my grandfather was there, too. I would spend the night with my grandmother when my grandfather was away on a trip or in the hospital. I think of my grandmother when I eat cream cheese on ginger snaps, when I hold in my hands one of her colorful silk scarves that I have squirreled away all these years, when I smell her perfume bottle I saved. I remember her braiding my hair and telling me that I reminded her of her daughter. This is something that my children have missed. They did not know their grandparents well. They may or may not get to know their aunts, uncles and cousins well. I wish they could have this. I wish I could have given them this and I will continue to try. This is the source of greatest sadness. But maybe just for me.

A COMMON STORY

I have been listening to others tell their stories of being the one who left. I am surprised by how often I hear the story even when I did not ask for it. Just this past week, I posed the following question to my class in Family Studies: "How has race or ethnicity impacted your life experience and/or the experience of your family?" One student shared that the biggest impact of her ethnicity was her family's belief that she would not move away from home. She explained that her move from Fresno to Sacramento, (a move of less than 200 miles), was outside the norm for members of her family. She saw herself as having broken a family rule, made a transgression; the moving violation.

I was surprised that this was the story she shared based on the question I had posed. I had not mentioned the essay I was writing or my own family experience. This experience of being the one who left was most salient in her mind, the experience she saw as being most closely related to family ethnicity – this expectation that she would not leave; but then she did.

Just last night I was at a party and I mentioned this essay to a friend. As I gave a brief overview of what I was writing about, I felt she was listening more intently than I would have expected in a causal conversation over a glass of wine. Then she said, "I am the daughter of the one who left. My father moved away from New Orleans and came to the West Coast. Growing up here, we didn't know our family in Louisiana very well. Now I make the trek back to try to have a relationship with our family there. I don't expect that they will ever visit us out here in California. I feel they still hold it against him that he left, and he has been dead for several years now."

I have also read many migration and immigration stories: *The Death of Josseline: Immigration Stories from the Arizona-Mexico Borderlands* by Margaret Regan; *The Warmth of Other Suns: The Epic Story of America's Great Migration* by Isabel Wilkerson; *Enrique's Journey* by Sonia Nazario; *Common Boundary: Stories of Immigration* by Gregory F. Tague. Each of these has added to my understanding of how immigration and migration have impacted the lives of others, some positively, some negatively; for most, a mixed bag. One perspective that has been helpful to me is in Sara Lawrence-Lightfoot's *Exit: The Endings That Set Us Free,* in which she contemplates a lack of rituals for our exits.

> Our societal neglect of the rituals and purposes of exits is not only a puzzling contemporary phenomenon; it is also strange when we consider the history of our country—a history that has been primarily defined by leave-takings, departures, and journeys away from home. (Lawrence-Lightfoot, 2012, p. 7.)

In reflecting on her own exits, some more emotional than physical, Lawrence-Lightfoot notes, "I remember, in each case, searching for cultural rituals and social scripts, a set of protocols, ceremonies, or practices that might offer me support and guidance or bring me into community with others who were charting similar exits" (p. 6).

But do these endings necessarily set us free, as she suggests in the title of her book? Not always. I find myself surrounded by friends who are also the ones who left. They left New Jersey, Florida, Texas. We don't all harbor the same sadness and longing. In some of their cases, others in the family also headed out to California. But for many of us who are out here, living both at home and away from home at the same time, we may entertain, as one friend does, that "there is another view to why families shouldn't disperse: Not because the good of the individual is subservient to the family's needs, but because, perhaps, the good of the individual in the long run is enhanced by the close proximity of family."

I have thought of establishing a club for those of us a long way from home. I have played around with what I'd call this club. Far From Home (FFH)? The Ones Who Left (TOWL)? Siblings at a Distance (SAAD)?

CONCLUSION?

I have just reached the stage in my life in which I am pondering all of these questions from a different perspective. This time I am the mother whose children are leaving home. I have a daughter in college and a son who leaves for college in a few months. I can't imagine what it will be like if they move far away from me. Will I once again be separated from family, but this time I stay and they leave? Will I plant a tree to count the years until they return? Or will I, at some point, move back to South Carolina; closer to one family, but leaving the place my children know as home, and perhaps my children?

I want my children to feel the freedom to make their own choices and not be overly influenced by my experiences—my years of longing for my siblings, or perhaps in years to come, longing for my children. And yet I know that they will be impacted by the life they have seen me live. In what ways may I already have helped to lay the groundwork for their journey? Set an example they will follow. They are native-born Californians, and they are children of two parents who left families back on the East Coast. I am from South Carolina and their father is from New York. Who will be their family? Can the chasm be undone? When should I have asked these questions? Is it too late to ask them now?

REFERENCES

Lawrence-Lightfoot, S. (2012). Exit: The endings that set us free. New York: Sarah Crichton Books.

Nazario, S. (2006). Enrique's journey: The story of a boy's dangerous odyssey to reunite with his mother. New York: Random House.

Regan, M. (2010). The death of Josseline: Immigration stories from the Arizona-Mexico borderlands. Boston: Beacon Press.

Tague, G. F. (2011). Common boundary: Stories of immigration. New York: Editions Bibliotekos, Inc.

Wilkerson, I. (2010). The warmth of other suns: The epic story of America's great migration. New York: Random House.

Inspiration for the Essay

I chose to address the topic of being "the one who left" because this issue has weighed heaviest on my heart for the past twenty-seven years, the years that I have lived across the country from my family of origin. Addressing the topic in this essay forced me to confront my own perceptions and misperceptions, my stubborn as well as changing expectations, and the perceptions and expectations of others. Sharing my thoughts and feelings about this topic in discussion with others has drawn me closer to many of my students, friends, and colleagues and others who are living out their lives far from home, with "far" and "home" being relative and subjective terms. The question of what it is to be a migrant or an immigrant confounds the issue for me, yet it aligns my experiences with those whose lives have brought them to a new world. I am intrigued by the similarities in our seemingly disparate experiences.

About the Author

Ann Moylan, PhD, CCLS, CFLE, has been a professor at Sacramento State since January 1987. She has focused her professional projects on infant mental health, early intervention, adoption, hospitalized children, parent education and sexuality education, in line with her certifications in Child Life and in Family Life Education. She was previously on the faculty at Georgia College and later served as the Education Director of Planned Parenthood, San Francisco/Alameda. Ann lives in Davis, CA with her partner of twenty-one years, two children, two dogs and three cats.

❧ sixteen ❧

IN SEARCH OF COUNTRY: HOW CHASING THE AMERICAN DREAM CAN BECOME A NIGHTMARE

By Sylvester Bowie

Ellis Island is maybe the most famous of immigrant entry point is the United States and possibly the world. According to the website Scholastic Inc. the record shows that over 12 million people made their first stop as immigrants to the United States at Ellis Island (http://teacher.scholastic.com/activities/immigration/tour/). As an immigrant, I did not enter the United States through Ellis Island. I suspect that my own journey could not be compared to those pioneering immigrants who did, but nonetheless I believe that there are many shared feelings about the new and old home and the sense of "homelessness" or not belonging that must visit many immigrants as efforts are made to deconstruct the experiences of the migrants coming to America ("Coming to America" is also the name of a popular comedic film).

It was Emma Lazarus, the poet writing in 1883 about the joys and wonders that the Land of Liberty has to offer, when she uttered the most famous words that might be associated with immigration when she wrote:

> Give me your tired, your poor
> Your huddled masses yearning to breathe free,
> The wretched refuse of your teeming shore.
> Send these, the homeless, tempest-tossed to me
> I lift my lamp besides the golden door

Bowie, S. (2014). In search of country: how chasing the american dream can become a nightmare. In S. Torres, Jr. (Ed.), *Palabra: The Book of Living Essays* (pp. 250–263). Sacramento, CA: Petraglyph Publishing.

The portion about the huddled masses and the wretched refuse is quoted frequently to highlight and promote the idea that the United States of America is the land of opportunity and it is the country that will take the "huddled masses and wretched refuse" (you could be excused for not thinking that it is true in light of the current ongoing debates about what to do with 12 million undocumented people currently living in the US). Even such awe-inspiring words will not capture the range and extent of the experience of the immigrant should more accurately say, well it does not capture mine. This missive is about my thoughts, experiences and feelings as an immigrant and my inability to edit the stories as a way of changing narratives. I will explore certain questions and make attempts to illustrate the points based on personal experiences accrued over more than twenty-five years of living in the place I call "the in-between". I was listening to one of my favorite National Public Radio Programs (NPR), when I heard about the concept of "story editing". That is when the idea hit me, maybe I should be examining and telling this narrative about my immigrant experience with the question: Could I have edited my story and would it have changed the narrative and thus the experiences I have had since emigrating from Jamaica to the United States? The question is to self because I have spent almost half of my life thinking, experiencing and wondering where do, I belong and how could I make a better fit. I have been thinking about being an immigrant and what it has meant to me for a very long time. After all, I moved to the United States more than 26 years ago on June 21, 1988.

It all started while I was in San Diego on vacation listening to NPR when I heard a piece being told about editing the story to create a new narrative. The NPR piece went on to discuss Psychologist and researcher James Pennebaker and the pioneering work he has done encouraging others to edit their stories and in the process create new or different narratives. The NPR story mentioned the research of Pennebaker & Seagal (1999) in which they concluded that: "Once an experience has structure and meaning, it would follow that the emotional effects of that experience are more manageable" (p. 1243). This NPR piece had me wondering if I too needed to edit the story of my immigrant experience to create a different or new narrative for meaningfulness and I said to myself what a wonderful world. Yes, is it wonderfully confusing or do I mean perplexing? Whatever the appropriate synonym for this idea, the reality is that being an immigrant has been baffling to and for me. I know why I came to the United States of America and I did come on my own volition. I was never forced to be an immigrant and I was not an economic refugee. I left Jamaica to live in the USA with my wife and my plans were to travel, study and have a better life with more opportunities and I have. I am still married to the same person, I have traveled all over Europe and made it to Africa (Ghana and Nigeria), studied and earned a doctorate and I have lived the kind of life that many can only dream about, but I am still living in that space in between and not fully belonging.

Since the early days of my immigrant experiences I was aware that I had entered the twilight zone of my personhood. After all I was thirty-two years old, graduated from college, worked as a classroom teacher and salesman before moving from my country of birth to the land of the free and the home of the brave. If the truth is to be told, I felt neither free nor brave; it was more trapped and timid when I first arrived in the US. What would I do and how could I do it, were some of the more prominent thoughts occupying my head over these years.

I had arrived in Vacaville, California on June 21, 1988 and a drought was still in effect, it was hot and there was no rain in sight. Did I say it was hot? That is an understatement, it was very hot and I was experiencing my first bout of doubt. Would I be able to survive this heat much less live in this place? Maybe if I knew about the story editing approach, I could have adjusted my outlook by changing my narrative. In response to the unbearable heat, I traveled to Toronto, to attend the "Caribana Festivals". These festivals are enjoyed not just by people of Caribbean decent, but also by nationals from all parts of the globe. This is an event I discovered and I have been attending for all but one year (2012 the year Jamaica celebrated 50 years of independence from Britain) since then. I returned from Canada and it was even hotter than before I left and did I mention that it had not rained in my newly adopted hometown since my arrival. I wonder now if story editing would have been utilitarian under the circumstances. Would I be able to edit away the reality that where I came from it would rain even for a few minutes in the heights of summer for no explainable reason? Not to worry, I had not yet encountered the idea, nor was I even exposed to NPR, so it does not even matter. What mattered was my adjustment to my new place of abode and that was not going well.

In August of the same year, I went back to the place I had called home for my entire thirty-two years of existence and I realized that after less than 90 days living abroad, things had changed dramatically. I did not own a car, nor did I have furniture, or even a "home". I had sold all the items that could/should not be given away and I was renting the house I lived in, so it was given up when I packed my bag for the land of opportunity. Yes, it was real I was in the place of "in between". Unfortunately, that is the feeling and experience I have felt and had for the last 25 years. When the question is asked where do I belong and where and how do I fit in with my new home environment I have never been sure. The answer might come out one way or the other, but the feeling is the same, I might be a man without a country because I am caught up in the "in between". Could I have edited the story, can the story be edited or is the in between my reality and destiny? I am sure I used the feeling as an escape also. I could avoid getting involved with my civic duty because I was not at "home".

My stay away from Vacaville, California while I visited Jamaica, the place where I did not own furniture, car, or even have a place to call my own was brief because of the cost of being away from home. After less than 90 days abroad everything seems to cost much more than I could remember and I doubt that my memory was already failing me after such a short time away. To the contrary, this experience was the beginning of many to come where you learn that one of the downsides of living abroad is that you could and will pay more for basic goods and services than do the locals. This might have been my baptism of fire when I was forced to face the reality that I have not been able to edit the story to make the experience other than it is. Part of the challenge is the attitude of some of the people you encounter who are willing to treat you as if you are so out of touch with the current reality that there is no way you can know or fully understand what is going on. Because you are from abroad or you live in the "other place" (the subtle message is/was you do not belong). Even though I had only left the country for less than 90 days the tales about needing money were as long as they were tall and the expectation is that you would be giving people money to ameliorate their circumstances. Since you were now living in America you must have the "strong green back dollars" and you should or must want to give some away. Upon returning to the US from my brief trip to Jamaica, I now had to face the reality that I was living in a foreign land and was destined to be a foreigner as my otherness increased, improved or just became more obvious.

Even though I arrived in the US on June 21, 1988 it was November that same year before I first experienced rainfall in Vacaville and the questions lingered. What kind of place is this? There are so many days when it was more than 100 degrees for days in a row and then more than ninety days had passed and still no rain was in sight. What would have happened if I could edit the story and change the narrative? Maybe not much as being an immigrant is a journey into the in between. A destination where being conflicted, not be-longing and "not knowing" or understanding nuances is par for the course. After 25 years of thinking, feeling, experiencing and always wondering I am told that editing the story is a way to create a new narrative and in the process an understanding. I was going to talk with a few of my fellow sojourners to hear from them what they felt and are feeling about this phenomenon of being an immigrant. I wanted to understand how they approached the in between status and its accompanying challenges. Did they edit their stories to change the narratives or, did they like me, face the chasm of being caught in a maelstrom in-between spaces and places?

While I did not ask my fellow sojourners if they have had to encounter questions about the old country that are bewildering. Questions such as, "why did you leave such a beautiful country to live in the United States? Or "you speak such good English, what language do they speak in Jamaica?" One question I did ask goes to the core of my deepest emotions, fears, confusion, experience and challenge. It is a question that I am unlikely to want to discuss with some casual contact. Yet in the innocence of "small talk" and sometimes with a genuine desire to know, an innocent encounter could expose the fragility of the immigrant experience. It is the question about citizenship. The issue of citizenship might be the most confusing narrative that cannot be edited. Merriam Webster online dictionary (Merriam-Webster, n.d.) describes citizenship as: the fact or status of being a citizen of a particular place the qualities that a person is expected to have as a responsible member of a community (http://www.merriam-webster.com/). I, like my fellow sojourners are responsible members of our communities. I have advanced degrees and work as a Professor of Social Work. I volunteer as a Court Appointed Special Advocate (CASA) and have been an active and productive member of the National Association of Social Work (NASW) California Chapter, where I was elected as a 1st Vice President in 2012. Yet, for me citizenship means much less than is explained by Merriam-Webster. I, and many of the people I have asked, find no comfort in thinking or saying that I/we are (in my case) Americans. After more than 20 years traveling on an American Passport, I have no idea what it feels like to be "a proud American" yet, I have no reservation nor do I hesitate to defend and discuss the belief that the United States is the greatest country in the history of the world. If I believe that the USA is the greatest country in the history of mankind to be true, and I do, then why not embrace the citizenship that I have legally qualified for more than 20 years ago? Maybe I do need to explore and edit the narrative of belonging and citizenship for my own mental health. One person who has lived in the United States for more than 30 years and has been a citizen for more than 25 of those years echoed my sentiments when she said that she has no intention of going back to Jamaica to live on a permanent basis, but she neither feels 100 percent Jamaican nor 100 percent American. Rather she feels like a woman without a country. She concluded that whenever she thinks of home she thinks Jamaica, the very place she has no intention of living in. It is uncertain if the person in question was positing that she wanted to be 100 percent Jamaican as well as 100 percent American. Maybe she wanted to straddle the fence and be fully Jamaican and fully American at the same time. That sounds like the recipe for a split personality. I do get the point she was making, she was saying in essence that in trying to belong she feels neither fully Jamaican, nor American. Her words were; "I feel like a woman without a country." She was voicing my feelings, belief and experience that as an immigrant, I have been caught in the in between spaces belonging neither fully here in the US nor there in Jamaica. I wish story editing was the fix that we and especially me deserve, but I am not able to see and identify how the editing would have made the desired difference. On the other hand, I do think that there might need to be an editing of the narrative to ensure that we do have healthy perceptions of the story because the current view of our/my status as a citizen is still too murky to be sustainable.

I wonder if I/we feel the way we do because many of the people we encounter in our adopted home react differentially to accents, foreigners, people of color, do not listen well (constantly asking you to repeat what you have just said), question your ability to appreciate the nuances of the American ethos, want to send you home at the first sign of disagreement/provocation even when you travel on an American Passport, blame you (mostly indirectly) for all that ails the country but want your cheap labor, song and dance and your addition of diversity to the American experimentation?

I want some sanity; I must stop living in no man's land (the in-between), but is editing the story and narrative the answer? As I listened to that NPR story on that December Morning in 2013, I got hopeful that there was some answer in the field of Psychology to treat what ails me and it is called story editing. Unfortunately, as I contemplated, listened and talked with other travelers on the same immigrant road I am not feeling more hopeful because I realize like Sisyphus that the experience of being an immigrant will always take you back down to earth. You will climb the steep terrain and then almost at the top someone will innocently ask: So, when are you going back home? That question will be asked of you with the same earnestness in Jamaica as it will be in the US and that is when you realize that your story cannot be edited to change the narrative. Once you have taken the faithful plunge to become an immigrant you can never go back. I will continue to look forward to going "home" knowing that it will only be an illusion, the figment of a fertile imagination and not an actual place. When I sold my possessions and gave up my dwelling place more than twenty-six years ago, I entered in an abyss and I am destined to be stuck in that place until there is a new invention maybe even an app, but currently I know assuredly the way out is not through story editing.

Inspiration for the Essay

The theme for the essay was selected because of what I live everyday as an immigrant, dealing with what I would call the place that most natives have never been. Having the feeling or sense of not belonging and uncertain how one fits in the schema or should be seen, accepted or just be, did influence me as I settled on a theme for the essay. The theme speaks to the constant reminder that enough ground is not being covered to ensure one authentically belongs. So, exploration of the change of narrative as discussed in the work of Pennebaker & Seagal (1999) is not only appealing, but raises the important question can one be authentic if the narrative has to be deliberately changed? What is wrong with keeping the hand that one has been dealt? The theme might be the result of the author's search for meaning, place and identity.

About the Author

The author is an optimistic social work professor with positive views of the world who is mostly looking to extract a laugh in any situation he is faced with (there is no situation too serious that should not first be explored for its laughter content). The author has travelled to Ghana and Nigeria in Africa and many countries in the Caribbean to share his love for and belief in the idea of using mediation for peace and conflict resolution. He has visited England to watch cricket at Lords (regarded as the headquarters of the game) famous grounds; participated in the famous football wave in stadiums in France while watching World Cup soccer, and he continues to enjoy teaching social work policy and practice while challenging students to become comfortable not just identifying the pathologies in their clients, but being mindful of the systemic and social conditions that cause or significantly incapacitate these clients and must be change to the benefit of the clients. The author has also travelled back to Jamaica with frequency and has the habit of truthfully boasting that he has never been absent from either country for six (6) months. It might be a reassuring way to claim to be in touch with the goings on in both places.

TOP TEN DIFFERENCES BETWEEN WHITE TERRORISTS AND OTHERS

By Juan Cole

1. White terrorists are called "gunmen."[1] What does that even mean? A person with a gun? Wouldn't that be, like, everyone in the US? Other terrorists are called, like, "terrorists."
2. White terrorists are "troubled loners." Other terrorists are always suspected of being part of a global plot, even when they are obviously troubled loners.
3. Doing a study on the danger of white terrorists at the Department of Homeland Security will get you sidelined by angry white congressmen.[2] Doing studies on other kinds of terrorists is a guaranteed promotion.
4. The family of a white terrorist is interviewed, weeping as they wonder where he went wrong. The families of other terrorists are almost never interviewed.
5. White terrorists are part of a "fringe." Other terrorists are apparently mainstream.
6. White terrorists are random events, like tornadoes. Other terrorists are long-running conspiracies.
7. White terrorists are never called "white." But other terrorists are given ethnic affiliations.
8. Nobody thinks white terrorists are typical of white people. But other terrorists are considered paragons of their societies.
9. White terrorists are alcoholics, addicts, or mentally ill. Other terrorists are apparently clean-living and perfectly sane.
10. There is nothing you can do about white terrorists. Gun control won't stop them. No policy you could make, no government program, could possibly have an impact on them. But hundreds of billions of dollars must be spent on police and on the

Cole, J. (2012, August 9). Top ten differences between white terrorists and others. Retrieved from http://www.juancole.com/2012/08/top-ten-differences-between-white-terrorists-and-others.html.

Department of Defense, and on TSA, which must virtually strip-search 60 million people a year, to deal with other terrorists.

NOTES

1. www.latimes.com/news/nation/nationnow/la-na-nn-sikh-temple-gunman-20120808,0,6572009.story.
2. www.wired.com/dangerroom/2012/08/dhs/all.

Inequality

A Burden Shared by All

Circumstances of birth can create privilege or the lack thereof. Privilege is a concept that cuts across gender, race, and class. These articles address "social capital" and how it helps in the examination of the social structure in society as well as how it maintains and legitimizes placing those with less social capital in less influential positions to negotiate relationships in society (e.g., education, work, housing). A broad understanding of power, oppression, and privilege is important to move to a position of advocacy that enhances people's lives. How can we use this information to empower those with less social capital to better navigate systems in their lives and empower them as they activate resources that are available to them? A game-changer perspective when considering oppression and discrimination and other corollary terms is that it is all about the narrowing of opportunity for some and the expanding of opportunity for others.

The article "The American Dream: Slipping Away?" discusses family income disparities from 1977 to 2007 and unemployment among those with a high school diploma or less as well as residential segregation. While the discussion in many ways focuses on educational inequality, Neuman (2013) seems to propose that educational equity is what will open up the American Dream for all Americans. Yet, "to recapture the American dream" implies that it once existed. What do you think? What specific critical and creative thinking skills (see Chapters 1–3) can you identify as you consider this question?

Garcia and McDowell (2010) examine how families are affected by limited social capital as well as interventions that could be incorporated when working with families to increase their well-being and maximize or increase their social capital in the article "Mapping Social Conflict: A Critical Contextual Approach for Working with Low Status Families."

The authors suggest that interventions to assist those who work with disadvantaged families "limit constraints and optimize opportunities" versus strategies that may contribute to the maintenance of the status quo of inequity. In what ways might applying the *Nine Approaches to Creative Problem Solving* (see Chapter 3) be useful when considering strategies for helping disadvantaged families?

One might think the article "Should the Government Promote Marriage?" is about marriage, but it focuses on social inequality as well. In 2002 there was an initiative supported by the Bush Administration for states to develop programs that, by offering a monetary incentive, encouraged TANF welfare recipients to marry. The focus of this initiative is that single mothers who are in need of government assistance need to be married, and that marriage will contribute positively in resolving other social issues such as academic success of children, behavioral problems demonstrated by children, and juvenile delinquency and crime, as well as finding and keeping employment. What may be ignored is that many of the "problems" cited have more to do with the low-income and socioeconomic status of the families and are not caused by there being only one parent in the home (or "single" as a marital status).

We recommend to once again identify the structure of argument for each of these articles, if you are not already in the habit of doing so. Can you also identify the components of the author(s) research approach (see Chapter 2)? How does information from Chapter 2 about research design help you evaluate the quality of the argument and reasoning?

Questions for Consideration:

1. Are there settings other than therapy or helping relationships in which the use of the *critical contextual perspective* might prove useful?
2. What does your *social map*, as described by Garcia and McDowell, look like? How would you assess your level of social capital?
3. What questions arise for you as you consider the different aspects of inequality raised in these articles?

⊗ eighteen ⊗

THE AMERICAN DREAM: SLIPPING AWAY?

By Susan Neuman

Economic inequality is real and growing. It can place low-income and high-income children on separate trajectories throughout school.

There is a national ethos among Americans that captures our faith in progress, opportunity, and striving. It's the belief that if you work hard and play by the rules, you can succeed and prosper regardless of your original social status or the circumstances of your birth. This American dream has given hope to people born without privilege, and it's one of the main reasons people have often struggled to come to the United States from around the world.

But many people are now beginning to fear that the American dream is slipping away. Economic inequality is real and growing. Between 1977 and 2007, the income of families at the 99th percentile increased by 90 percent; the income of those at the bottom 20th percentile, by just 7 percent (Duncan & Murnane, 2011). Further, the unemployment rate remains dispiritingly high. Especially among those with a high school education or less, the Great Recession wreaked havoc among working-class families' employment (Carnevale & Rose, 2011).

Astonishing increases in the degree of residential segregation are exacerbating these circumstances, according to demographer Douglas Massey (2007). Those with money are more likely to live in homogeneously privileged neighborhoods and interact almost exclusively with other affluent people. Those without money are increasingly confined

Neuman, S. B. (2013). The American dream: slipping away?. *Educational Leadership, 70*(8), 18–22.

to homogeneously poor neighborhoods, yielding a density of material deprivation that is unprecedented in U.S. history.

These stark inequalities have become fodder for increasingly intractable debates among politicians and pundits. More important, however, is what these statistics mean for educating our children and keeping the hope of upward mobility through hard work alive. Are there still real opportunities for all children? Or is the American dream now an empty promise?

EARLY EXPERIENCES AND INEQUALITY

On the basis a 10-year study that my colleagues and I conducted of two neighborhoods within the confines of Philadelphia, one of poverty and the other of privilege (Neuman & Celano, 2012), one could argue that our fears are real. Although the dream of upward mobility still exists, it has become far more difficult for many to accomplish.

Our work in these two neighborhoods was guided by the theory that the amount of early access to print and the quality of adult support young children receive set in motion a process that either accelerates or delays literacy development and knowledge acquisition (Stanovich, 1986). Children learn about literacy through experiences and observations of the written language they encounter in their everyday lives. They construct an understanding of how print works through independent explorations of print and signs, interactions around books and other print resources, and participation with others engaged in both enjoyable and purposeful literacy activities. These early experiences provide opportunities to learn about the spelling-to-sound code, building preparatory skills that are essential for learning to read.

Those who are not initiated early on through such environmental print exposure are likely to experience greater difficulty in breaking the spelling-to-sound code. They come to school needing specialized help, and the remediation exercises they receive expose them to less text than the reading exercises that are given to their more skilled peers. They often find themselves working with materials that are too difficult for them to read—or too easy for them to learn from. This combination of difficulties in decoding, lack of practice, and inappropriate materials results in unrewarding early reading experiences. Children struggle to develop fluency in reading, further draining their capacity for comprehending text.

But it doesn't end there. The vicious cycle accelerates. As the Common Core State Standards emphasize, children gain knowledge through text. Knowledge disparities, therefore, grow as a result of these differences in reading experiences. Those who read more are creating and using greater pools of knowledge. Greater knowledge use enhances students' speed of information acquisition, which over time is likely to accelerate a knowledge gap between those who have access and those who do not (Neuman & Celano, 2006). Although the have-nots gain knowledge, the haves gain it faster. By gaining faster, they gain more. The result, we hypothesized, leads to the social stratification of information capital that occurs among those who live in affluent and poor communities.

Unfortunately, this is what we found.

TWO NEIGHBORHOODS

Like many cities throughout the United States, Philadelphia is a city of contrasts. It has become home to many immigrants (Polish, Italian, Irish, Russian, Hispanic, Chinese, and Southeast Asian) and African Americans as a result of industrialization in the late 19th and early 20th centuries. Philadelphia is known as a city of neighborhoods: Its residents live in neat brick row homes as well as back alleys and decaying buildings. Some children in this city will grow up in abject poverty; others, in highly privileged circumstances.

We chose to study two neighborhoods that were representative of these contrasts. Kensington, also known as the Badlands, is a dense, multiethnic community consisting of Puerto Rican, black, Vietnamese, Eastern European, and Caucasian residents with a poverty rate of 90 percent, almost 29 percent unemployment, and approximately 5,000 children under age 17. In contrast, Chestnut Hill is a highly gentrified neighborhood, 80 percent Caucasian and 20 percent black, with a child population of about 1,200. Families there tend to be educated professionals, with the average home costing in the $400,000s. The neighborhood borders several large parks and is somewhat geographically isolated from the rest of the city.

For more than 10 years, we examined how these contrasting ecologies of affluence and poverty might contribute to disparities in reading and the develop ment of information capital (see details in Neuman & Celano, 2012). We engaged in observations, interviews, and activities, using many different analytic tools to understand how these environments might influence children's opportunities for education.

STARK DIFFERENCES

Differences in Print Resources

Right from the beginning, there are differences in the amount and quality of print children in these two neighborhoods are exposed to in their worlds. For example, a 3-year-old in Chestnut Hill would likely see signs with iconic symbols in good readable condition, professionally designed with clear colors and strong graphics. In contrast, many of the signs in the Badlands neighbor hood are covered with graffiti with taggers' distinctive signatures, rendering them impossible for a young child to decipher. We found that 74 percent of signs in the Badlands were in poor condition, compared with 1 percent in Chestnut Hill.

The disparities continue when it comes to the availability of print resources appropriate for young children. In Chestnut Hill, we found 11 stores that sold print materials for children, 7 of which even had special sections just for children. In contrast, the Badlands, with a far greater density of children, had only 4 places that carried children's print materials.

Even more troubling were the differences in choices available to a parent selecting a book for a child. Children in Chestnut Hill had access to thousands of book, magazine, and comic book titles, whereas children in the Badlands could access only a small fraction of materials. Our calculations indicated about 13 titles for every child in the community of privilege, and about 1 title for about every 20 children in the community of poverty.

Schools and outside institutions, like the library—often considered safety nets for those who lack resources—did not alter this pattern. In Chestnut Hill preschools, average book condition was excellent, with a wide assortment to choose from; book condition for those in the Badlands was merely adequate, with a limited selection. Differences were even more stark in elementary school libraries. Schools in Chestnut Hill had more than two times the selection of books compared to those in the Badlands. Further, other resources to support children's reading, like computers and trained librarians, were missing in the Badlands.

In short, differences in the economic circumstances of children who live in these neighborhoods translated into extraordinary differences in the availability of print resources.

Differences in Adult Supports

Material resources represent only one kind of support in creating an environment for reading and the development of information capital. Even more important is the type of adult support and mentoring that children receive.

In a now-classic study, Annette Lareau (2003) identified parenting practices associated with social class. According to her research, parents from middle- and upper-middle-class families typically engage in a child-rearing strategy known as *concerted cultivation*, consciously developing children's use of language, reasoning skills, and negotiation abilities. In contrast, working-class and poor parents tend to practice—not necessarily by choice—a more hands-off type of child rearing known as *natural growth*. These parents generally have less education and time to impress on their children the values that will give them an advantage in school. Their children often spend less time in the company of adults and more time with other children in self-directed, open-ended play. The differing strategies reinforce class divisions.

Spending hundreds of hours in the public libraries in each neighborhood watching parent–child behaviors, we found a consistent pattern. In the spirit of concerted cultivation, toddlers and preschoolers in Chestnut Hill were carefully guided in selecting appropriate reading materials. Activities were highly focused, with the accompanying adult suggesting books, videos, or audiobooks to check out. The parent clearly appeared to be the arbiter for book selection, noting, "That book is too hard for you," "That is too easy," or "This one might be better."

In contrast, children in the Badlands largely entered the library alone or with a peer, sometimes with a sibling, but rarely with an adult. They would wander in, maybe flip through some pages of a book, and wander out. Without adult assistance, a child would pick up a book, look at the cover, pause for a moment to try to figure it out, and then put it down. Occasionally an older child might help locate a book or read to a younger child. But more often than not, preschooler activity would appear as short bursts, almost frenetic in nature.

To examine how these patterns may influence early reading development, we counted the age of the child, whether the child was accompanied by an adult, and the content and amount of text that might be read to children in each community. We found a disturbing pattern: For every hour we spent observing at the library in Chestnut Hill, more than three-quarters of the time—47 minutes—was spent with an adult reading to a child. During the same time period, not one adult entered the preschool area in the Badlands. By our estimate, children in Chestnut Hill heard nearly 14 times the number of words read in print per library visit as children in the Badlands.

Differences in Independent Reading

We suspected that the early years established a pattern of reading behavior that would affect later development. Consequently, we next focused on the tween years (ages 10–13), when students need to read challenging informational text independently and use self-teaching strategies to learn essential academic vocabulary and concepts.

To examine independent reading, we spent hours in the public library in each neighborhood, recording what students were reading, the average grade level of the text, and whether it was informational or entertainment reading activity. We then conducted a similar analysis of students' use of the computers.

We found an all-too-predictable pattern. Perhaps most alarming was the difference in the challenge level of the texts students selected to read. Students in the Badlands tended to select easy materials. Although 58 percent of the materials read were at grade level, 42 percent were designed for younger children. It was not uncommon to see a 13-year-old boy reading *Highlights* magazine or *Arthur's Eyes,* a book typically favored by the preschool crowd. Challenging words related to academic disciplines are rarely found in these kinds of books and magazines. In contrast, 93 percent of students from Chestnut Hill tended to read at their age level, with a small percentage (7 percent) reading more-challenging above-level materials.

Further, there were striking differences in the amount of time spent reading and the genre of text selected. Students from the Badlands spent considerably less time reading than students from Chestnut Hill, and the majority of reading time in the Badlands was spent with entertainment materials. A similar pattern occurred with computers and the Internet in the Badlands library: the majority of time was spent watching movies or game-like shows. For students in Chestnut Hill, these patterns were reversed. Most of the students' time was spent on informational texts. In fact, these students spent about 12 times the amount of time on informational reading materials in print and about 5 times more on informational websites than they spent on entertainment content in print and online.

Consequently, by the time students are in their tweens, we see a pattern of reading that leads to a knowledge gap. Reading challenging informational text enhances the speed of information gathering and knowledge acquisition. Reading low-level text of questionable value is likely to keep one at status quo, or worse, be a waste of time.

Continued unabated, this gap between the "information haves" and "information have-nots" could lead to even greater social and economic inequality in our society that will be difficult, if not impossible, to reverse.

CHANGING THE TRAJECTORY

I have painted a bleak picture of the gap between poverty and privilege not to suggest its inevitability but to galvanize people to action. So what can we do? Consider the following steps.

Un-level the Playing Field

Programs like Title I are based on a policy of "leveling the playing field," ensuring that education resources for poor communities are equal to those for the more affluent. But the notion of providing equal resources is only helpful when none of the competing partners has an advantage at the outset. As we have seen, that is certainly not the case for students who come from poor neighborhoods when compared with more affluent peers.

We need to tip the balance not by equalizing funding but by providing more resources and additional supports to students in poor neighborhoods. Not just extra funding, but additional human resources are needed. Training paraprofessionals for such simple activities as reading one-on-one with children in libraries like those in the Badlands could have enormous benefits later on.

Strengthen Parent Involvement

School programs often profess the importance of parent involvement, but schools rarely offer sustained, intensive parent involvement training programs. We need programs that help parents become the advocates they wish to be by teaching them about the skills and strategies children will need to be successful in school. Such programs will help them make judgments about what kinds of language and literacy experiences to look for in preschool and childcare settings, what to look for in initial reading instruction in kindergarten and the early grades, what to ask principals and other policymakers who make decisions regarding reading instruction, and how to determine whether their child is making adequate progress in reading or needs additional instruction.

Engage Students' Minds

Far too often, people underestimate the capabilities of students who live in poor neighborhoods, equating poverty with low ability. In reality, however, these students are eager to learn and develop greater expertise when given opportunities to do so.

In public policy, our targets for these students have been to help them graduate from high school and become college-ready. In fact, if students from poor families are to have a fighting chance, they will need far more. They will need a rich knowledge base. They will need to learn how to participate in a new kind of information fabric in which learning, playing, and creative thinking interact in ways that not only use existing knowledge, but also advance it in new directions. We deceive them and ourselves if we expect any less.

Economically Integrate Schools

Schools today reflect their neighborhoods. Throughout the United States, schools are economically segregated, exacerbating the problems of inequality.

Schools in poor areas struggle for many reasons, but among the most prominent are their rotating faculty of inexperienced teachers and administrators and their low-level curriculum. In contrast, schools in affluent areas are more stable, with more highly trained teachers, rigorous curriculum, fewer discipline problems, and more support from volunteers. Studies have shown that economic integration can begin to change this scenario (Kahlenberg, 2001).

RECLAIMING THE DREAM

Americans are a resilient people. We remain a formidable force in the knowledge economy. Nevertheless, the last decade's economic chaos and rising inequality has led some to question whether there is a future for the American dream. For those of us who believe that this concept is still what defines us and makes America great, it is time to renew our determination to recapture the American dream and make it a reality for all our children.

REFERENCES

Carnevale, A., & Rose, S. (2011). *The under-educated American.* Washington, DC: Georgetown Center on Education and the Workforce.

Duncan, G., & Murnane, R. (Eds.). (2011). *Whither opportunity?* New York: Russell Sage Foundation.

Kahlenberg, R. (2001). *All together now.* Washington, DC: Brookings.

Lareau, A. (2003). *Unequal childhoods.* Berkeley: University of California Press.

Massey, D. (2007). *Categorically unequal.* New York: Russell Sage Foundation.

Neuman, S. B., & Celano, D. (2006). The knowledge gap: Implications of leveling the playing field for low-income and middle-income children. *Reading Research Quarterly, 41,* 176–201.

Neuman, S. B., & Celano, D. (2012). *Giving our children a fighting chance: Affluence, literacy, and the development of information capital.* New York: Teachers College Press.

Stanovich, K. E. (1986). Matthew effects in reading: Some consequences of individual differences in the acquisition of literacy. *Reading Research Quarterly, 21,* 360–406.

MAPPING SOCIAL CAPITAL: A CRITICAL CONTEXTUAL APPROACH FOR WORKING WITH LOW STATUS FAMILIES

By Marisol Garcia and Teresa McDowell

Family therapists are often called upon to help solve social problems. Acting as agents of social control is part of our daily work when we report child abuse, testify on behalf of victims, and help prevent domestic violence. At times, however, we can become inadvertently complicit in maintaining unjust and inequitable social arrangements. Therapy can serve to maintain the status quo of inequity by effectively solving social conflicts while maintaining and reproducing existing social order (Martín-Baró, 1994). This is particularly true when we fail to interrogate how systems of class privilege shape our worldviews, our social role as therapists, and the life worlds of those with whom we work.

In this article, we describe our developing framework for using critical contextual perspectives to inform our work as family therapists. We explore our understanding of how social capital and therefore access to social and material resources are gained and/or lost through participating in and crossing multiple systems. In particular, we share a method for mapping social capital that can guide interventions aimed at helping clients secure necessary resources for solving problems. Finally, we offer a case example of therapeutic work with a low-status Puerto Rican family and retrospectively apply social capital mapping.

We restrict most of our discussion and the case example to low-status families out of concern for how lack of resources (adequate housing, employment, transportation, avail-

Garcia, M., & McDowell, T. (2010). Mapping social capital: A critical contextual approach for working with low-status families. *Journal of marital and family therapy, 36*(1), 96–107.

ability of parents, etc.) contributes to the reproduction of inequality. We use the term "low status" to refer to the intersection of class, race, ethnicity, sexual orientation, abilities, nation of origin, and language that places some at significant social and economic disadvantage.

A critical contextual perspective is not a model of therapy, but a lens that can inform therapeutic decisions in ways that raise social awareness and support social equity. This perspective builds on ecosystemic and multiple systems concepts (Aponte, 1976; Auerswald, 1968; Boyd-Franklin, 1989; Brofenbrenner, 1977) that emphasize power relative to intersecting identities and the exchange of social capital within and across structural contexts. Viewing multiple systems through a critical lens offers a framework for understanding not only the influence of our multiple intersecting identities (e.g., race, class, gender, sexual orientation, nation of origin) relative to power within specific local structural contexts (McDowell et al., 2006), but also how influence and access to resources are built, lost, and exchanged across contexts or systems.

Early in the development of family therapy, Auerswald (1968) argued for an ecosystemic approach as an effective way to work with poor families, challenging the assumption that individuals and families are the sole owners of problems. A number of family therapy approaches emphasize the function of symptoms within specific contexts, (e.g., Functional Family Therapy: Alexander & Parsons, 1982; Strategic Family Therapy: Madanes, 1981) and have demonstrated successful strategies for intervening across multiple systems (e.g., Multi-Systemic Therapy: Henggeler, Melton, & Smith, 1992; Multi-Dimensional Family Therapy: Liddle, 1995). These models advocate for collaboration and linkage between individuals and families and the multiple systems within which they are embedded. Relative to youth, these approaches often aim to increase pro-social behavior (e.g., decreasing youth association with deviant peers), engage youth in pro-social recreational activities, and help families develop support networks within the community (Alexander & Parsons, 1982; Aponte, 1976; Becker & Liddle, 2001; Coatsworth, Pantin, & Szapocznik, 2002). These eco-and multiple systems perspectives are foundational to the analysis of how social influence and material resources (including how problems are defined and the type of help offered to solve problems) are bartered over time.

Using a critical contextual lens is in keeping with those who have argued that helping families includes raising social awareness and supporting social equity (Almeida & Durkin, 1999; Falicov, 2003; Korin, 1994; Martín-Baró, 1994.) We agree with the importance of empowerment when clients are "othered" relative to the multiple systems in which they are embedded (Falicov, 1998) and the necessity of helping clients decipher how these relationships work within the constraints of power and privilege. Collaboration between families and other social systems may not be effective, or even feasible, if a family is not prepared to understand and manage the inherent power differences between systems.

A critical contextual lens is relevant across social classes and personal to all of us as evidenced by our daily decisions (e.g., whom we associate with and attempt to please, whom we feel relatively comfortable dismissing, how we dress and act in various contexts, our occupational and financial goals). Without action, a critical contextual perspective at best merely contributes to an understanding of how "the rich get richer and the poor get poorer." We believe, however, that when this approach informs attempts to support social equity, it can provide a framework for holding ourselves accountable and helping individuals and families responsibly secure the social influences and resources necessary to solve problems and promote positive mental health. Applying a critical contextual perspective requires therapists to maintain a multi-ocular lens that considers broad social, political, and historical realities simultaneously with individual, family, and local context dynamics. Understanding processes for gaining and losing social capital is crucial for intervening in these complex dynamics.

SOCIAL CAPITAL: ACCESS TO CLASS-BASED RESOURCES

Bourdieu (1986) defined social capital as the total resources linked to relationships with others, be it institutions or persons, which provide the "backing" of belonging to a group that has an accumulation of collectively owned capital. Stanton-Salazar (2001) developed a social capital framework that considers how experience and attempts to conform to the majority in a particular context are driven by exchanges of institutional resources. "This is to say that people make their way in the world by constantly negotiating both the constraints placed on them and the opportunities afforded them, by way of the social webs of which they are a part" (Stanton-Salazar, 2001, p. 18). The reproduction and accumulation of social capital assumes that social exchanges will be driven by affirmation and acceptance rather than discrimination and rejection; "the reproduction of social capital presupposes an unceasing effort of sociability, a continuous series of exchanges in which recognition is endlessly affirmed and reaffirmed" (Bourdieu, 1986, p. 250). Exchanges between individuals and their contexts should theoretically result in the accumulation of resources, such as increases in contacts, knowledge, and opportunities. However, accumulation of social capital is most available to those who belong or are "insiders" in the social webs of dominant groups. For example, a wealthy suburban mother is less likely to experience the same sense of invisibility that a low-income inner-city mother might when she walks into the principal's office. The wealthy mother is more likely than the poor mother to be admitted to join in an exchange of resources (such as more opportunities for her child to achieve academically and socially).

In order to gather social capital, it is necessary to become an insider to social webs that allow access to class-based resources. Dominant culture ideological messages may have adverse effects on members of traditionally marginalized groups as they struggle to maintain contrasting life worlds and/or become insiders without the appropriate "tools" to make this integration possible (Stanton-Salazar, 2001). In other words, those not centered in society may not choose or have the resources to be able to adapt to values and traits developed by and for those who have the greatest access to institutional resources (e.g., adequate housing, access to transportation, employment, association with those with economic stability).

Stanton-Salazar (2001) critically examined the influence of multiple community contexts on the lives of low-status Latino adolescents and found that the function of a particular social web shapes the way differences are viewed, managed, and labeled. For example, according to Stanton-Salazar, school systems view their function as one of socializing students into conforming to majority cultural beliefs, norms, and practices. He argued that school and government agents are not promoting values and traits that are "universal and rational," but supporting the culture and norms of particularly powerful groups in society that organize themselves on the basis of shared attributes of race, ethnicity, and social location. The system offers information that can only be assimilated by those who are familiar with what is being referenced due to their historical location in the dominant society (Bourdieu, 1986). This is an important consideration in the lives of low-status youth of color as they are rarely recognized and affirmed as belonging to the collective majority. Instead, they may experience discrimination and perceive society as closed to them, further impacting their psychological development, academic performance, behavior, and self-esteem (Degarmo & Martinez, 2006; Vega, Khoury, Zimmerman, & Gil, 1995; Wong, Eccles, & Sameroff, 2003). As individuals attempt to integrate themselves into cultures that are not congruent with their realities, they are most often unsuccessful. Consequently, they may be labeled by therapists, educators, and officers of the court as deviant or dysfunctional due to their failure to conform and responsibility for nonconformity placed on themselves and their families.

THE PROBLEM OF DIMINISHING SOCIAL CAPITAL

Bourdieu (1986) argued that individuals participate in social exchanges because they are profitable and likely to ensure an increase in social capital. Hence, an accumulation or at least the preservation of social capital is the foundation for willingness to participate in social exchanges. While all families can find themselves in situations that diminish their social capital (e.g., loss of income, legal problems, illnesses), it is more likely that low-status families will experience ongoing social exchanges that are diminishing and/or unproductive. Signifiers such as particular behaviors, language, and appearance are expressed through social exchanges and serve to affirm or allow individuals access to particular social webs. Those from traditionally marginalized groups are often at a disadvantage in exchanges relative to dominant cultural groups. Furthermore, membership in dominant cultural groups may require accommodating, or giving up, nondominant values, beliefs, and attitudes. For example, the value for an Asian Indian American of thinking collectively—acting for the good of the group—may be challenged when he or she faces those from the majority culture who have learned to thrive through practicing individualism. When a Latino adolescent boy gets caught doing something wrong, it is likely that the unwritten rule within the community or family would support not "ratting" on him. In the school system, however, the dominant voice insists that in order to stay out of trouble, you must report others to the authorities. Members of marginalized groups may attempt to conform, hoping to gain social capital. However, conformity is often short lived as it is not single acts that provide insider status but an extensive series of behaviors and customs that have been inherited through generations of insiders.

Bourdieu (1986) pointed out that the dominant majority, in most cases, will ascend the economic hierarchy during their lifetime. However, this phenomenon progresses differently for the minority; the lower they find themselves in the economic hierarchy, the more likely they are to descend rather than ascend the hierarchy during their lifetime. Portes (1998) discussed the notion of "downward leveling of norms," which occurs in marginalized groups to keep members in place when faced with outside discrimination. This phenomenon results from the group's cohesive opposition to the majority's subordination, hence creating diminishing social capital as the group's opposition is met in ways that continually reproduce a reduction in sources of socioeconomic ascent and development.

Each social web is organized around particular sets of values, beliefs, and practices, which are often in conflict with those in other contexts (e.g., family and peers), creating potential for lost capital when what is valued in one context is devalued in another. For example, a downward spiral of lost capital is evident when a low-income man's attempt to be a good father by missing work to be present for his adolescent's court hearing results in his being seen as a bad employee and losing his job.

EMBEDDEDNESS, SOCIAL SUPPORT, AND DEVELOPMENT

Children, adolescents, and adults need to be embedded in multiple social webs organized for their well-being, empowerment, and successful lifelong development (Bandura, 1969). In the context of these (optimal) nurturing webs, we are able to actively participate in social life, and in doing so, regularly seek help through diversified social relationships with capable people willing to provide or negotiate access to multiple forms of social support and institutional resources. Healthy development and social standing in contemporary society rest squarely on forms of embeddedness that generate and transmit vital resources and institutional support that enable all of us to become effective participants within mainstream institutional spheres (e.g., school systems, workplaces). Low-status families are embedded in different contexts than their counterparts who belong to more privileged groups and are assigned more advantages based on class, race, ethnicity, gender, family structure, fit of personality/social styles with dominant culture, and community location (Stanton-Salazar, 2001). When lower and higher status individuals are embedded in the same contexts, how they are embedded and their relative privilege are likewise impacted. For example, a first-generation Vietnamese adolescent may experience less privilege when negotiating power in school due to his lack of access to resources, including parents who can afford to take time off work to come to the school or a family that knows how to navigate the system and call in higher authorities for help. Consequently, this adolescent will not be embedded in the dominant structure in the same way as an adolescent whose parents are able to more effectively advocate for him. These group memberships and identities influence values, attitudes, beliefs, and styles of interaction in ways that in turn further increase and/or decrease access to advantages associated with membership in the dominant culture. Being "locked out" of socially sanctioned avenues for meeting personal, social, and material needs often leads to finding alternatives that increase the risk of being socially disenfranchised (Sanchez-Jankowski, 1991; Totten, 2000; Vigil, 1988).

MAPPING SOCIAL CAPITAL: A THERAPEUTIC TOOL

Within a critical contextual perspective, social capital is an important determinant of the interaction among multiple systems. The first step is to critically analyze the multiple intersecting systems and to acknowledge how each system is structured to maintain and legitimize economic, social, and political systems of the more privileged. The unequal distribution of social capital between the interacting parties places the party with the least amount of social capital in a less influential position to negotiate how the relationship will develop. In order to advocate for collaboration that benefits low-status families, the social capital of these families must be maximized to reach more equal standing with more privileged systems. Therapeutic interventions are refocused to work with the system at different levels in order to create a more egalitarian exchange of power and resources. The main idea is to balance interventions between increasing social capital to change the problem and changing the problem to increase social capital. As therapists and clients become aware of the dynamics of social forces and related social capital in clients' lives, they can map these influences to track areas of marginalization, spaces of opportunity, and connections to those with access to capital in order to identify constraints and opportunities.

As noted above, mapping social capital can be helpful in identifying possibilities and reflecting on choices about which contexts to participate in and how. Clients and therapists can consider the cost of various actions within specific systems as well as what can be gained or lost by (even temporarily) conforming versus resisting contextual demands. The map can thereby be used to optimize opportunities and challenge constraints in ways that lead to increased overall capital. For example, constraints for low-status youth of color often include internalized racism and classism since members of minority and lower class groups are typically exposed to myriad messages describing their deficiency and deviancy. Additionally, families from disadvantaged positions are often fighting to meet basic needs of food, shelter, and health care and may not be readily able to take empowered action. Building resilience by identifying historical antecedents and cultural strengths can alleviate some of the stressors associated with continual focus on acquisition of basic needs and internalized racism and classism. Learning to value others from the same culture, trust one's own experience, redefine one's identity, appreciate values, and identify personal and cultural strengths are important steps to maximize choices and potential in all contexts (Worrel & Remer, 1992).

The process of mapping social capital in order to raise social awareness, maximize potential, and challenge constraints through more informed, critical decision making and action (Freire, 1970) moves continuously and fluidly between dialogue, validation, reflection, awareness, and action. The map allows therapists and clients to identify behaviors and attitudes that may seem deviant at first glance, but in fact may be attempts to resist oppression. For example, when low-status adolescents act out, we typically recognize the potential for long-term negative consequences and invest ourselves in deterring such actions. We rarely entertain the possibility that acting out in some cases may constitute resistance to oppressive social dynamics. Identifying clients' intentions to resist injustice is a first step to helping them build a sophisticated repertoire of actions that can be used to build lasting social capital. Decisions can be made about the most beneficial forms of resistance, with therapists acting as allies or advocates. While not specifically noted on the map in Figure 20.1, we assume that class, gender, and culture are contributing factors in each context.

In the sections that follow, we offer a case example of Pepe and his family to demonstrate how analyzing social capital can be helpful in therapeutic work. We include several ideas for how to use mapping to guide interventions, including (a) analyzing multiple systems

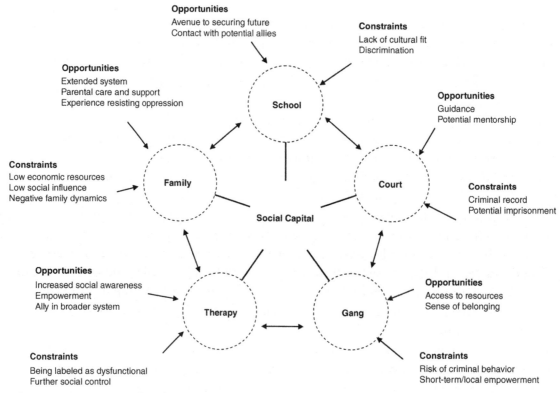

Opportunities
Avenue to securing future
Contact with potential allies

Constraints
Lack of cultural fit
Discrimination

Opportunities
Extended system
Parental care and support
Experience resisting oppression

Opportunities
Guidance
Potential mentorship

School

Constraints
Low economic resources
Low social influence
Negative family dynamics

Family

Court

Social Capital

Constraints
Criminal record
Potential imprisonment

Opportunities
Increased social awareness
Empowerment
Ally in broader system

Therapy

Gang

Opportunities
Access to resources
Sense of belonging

Constraints
Being labeled as dysfunctional
Further social control

Constraints
Risk of criminal behavior
Short-term/local empowerment

Figure 20.1. *Examples of constraints and opportunities relative to social capital.*

to determine those most relevant in clients' lives and the relationships between systems, (b) considering the dynamics of crossing boundaries, (c) recognizing and optimizing resistance to oppression, (d) finding ways to limit constraints and optimize opportunities within and across contexts, and (e) developing a web of allies to support family functioning and access to resources. Therapists must become as knowledgeable as possible about the social dynamics surrounding each client's life. To this end, we integrate literature on low-status families and Latino youth throughout the discussion of our case example.

CASE EXAMPLE: USING A SOCIAL CAPITAL FRAMEWORK TO INFORM INTERVENTIONS

Pepe is locked up in a cell at the juvenile detention center until the courts can have him admitted to a residential treatment facility. Pepe is a 13-year-old third-generation Puerto Rican American male. He is one of the most charismatic, caring, respectful, and social people I (Marisol) know. His world is defined by multiple and intersecting contexts (school, juvenile court, gangs, family, etc.) Pepe's struggle is to find ways to successfully navigate among each of these contexts.

I met Pepe and his family while working at a child guidance clinic. The agency's approach expected me to work with the multiple systems involved in Pepe's life (e.g., court and school). Pepe was referred to the clinic by the juvenile court after an outburst at his elementary school. As a family therapist, my (Marisol's) task was to decrease Pepe's "dysfunctional" behaviors. It rapidly became apparent, however, that his behaviors, and how they were labeled, changed given each context in which he participated. I began to question how Pepe managed these many worlds that privileged different rules, values, behaviors, and interactions. What was labeled as dysfunctional behavior in one context seemed to be protective in another. For example, if someone were to say something disrespectful to Pepe, he would fight to ensure respect. This behavior was functional in his family and community environments, but Pepe needed to learn a new way of fighting back in order to stay in school. Pepe's behavior took on a different meaning when viewed through a lens that focuses on how multiple social contexts mutually influence the wellbeing of individuals and families (Brofenbrenner, 1979; Phelan, Yu, & Davidson, 1994; Stanton-Salazar, 2001). Pepe's ability to competently move among worlds was essential, yet like many adolescents, he was left to manage these transitions and the consequences of his behaviors across contexts without assistance.

Analyzing Multiple Intersecting Systems

The constraints and opportunities shown in the social capital map in Figure 20.1 serve as examples of the many constraints and opportunities that might be identified relative to our case example. The map can be used as a starting place to ask questions, gather information, validate experiences and feelings, encourage reflection, and collaborate on specific actions. Areas of consideration might include how boundary crossing is negotiated, what resources can be accessed and what restraints must be overcome, the cost of resistance and noncompliance across contexts, the level of dissonance between contexts, and the development of a web of allies who can protect and enhance the family's future. Note that the map in Figure 20.1 suggests a rather static view where in reality the process of negotiating social capital is multidirectional, fluid, dynamic, and situational.

Crossing Boundaries

Most of us are involved in numerous social contexts (e.g., home, work, school, faith institutions, and friendships). These contexts have generally been treated as distinct entities without close examination of how they are interrelated (Phelan et al., 1994; Stanton-Salazar,

2001). When there is a high level of agreement between contexts relative to expected behaviors, attitudes, values, and beliefs, we are likely to move smoothly across contexts, carrying successes in one milieu to enhance successes in another. For example, if a child of well-educated middle-class parents plays an instrument in the band and gets good grades in school, these contexts are likely to be mutually enhancing. However, for some, one or more milieus may include conflicting values and norms, creating significant stress and dissonance as they move from one context to another (Phelan et al., 1994). For example, someone who belongs to both a nongayaffirming faith institution and a gay/lesbian community is likely to experience distress moving between these contexts and identities.

Phelan, Davidson, and Cao (1991) identified several ways in which adolescents manage the task of boundary crossing. Of the four types they identified, two are of particular concern: hazardous and impenetrable and insurmountable. Hazardous boundary crossing is evident when home, school, and peer contexts are oppositional in terms of norms and values. Boundary crossing is possible only under particular conditions and causes friction and unease. The pattern often includes adolescents vacillating between "success and failure, involvement and disengagement, commitment and apathy" (Phelan et al., 1991, p. 237). Impenetrable and insurmountable boundary crossing is evident when values and norms are so discordant across contexts and border crossing is so painful that, over time, adolescents develop coping mechanisms or rationales to protect themselves against further distress. These adolescents feel alienated as outsiders, experiencing anger, hopelessness, and lower self-esteem (Arunkumar & Midgley, 1999; Phelan et al., 1994). Low-status youth are likely to be involved in highly discordant groups (e.g., church and gangs), increasing the likelihood they will engage in hazardous and/or insurmountable boundary crossing. The discrimination they are likely to face exacerbates this situation. In fact, Phelan et al. (1994) found that 70% of adolescent students facing insurmountable boundary crossing reported difficulties with at least one or two teachers as a result of being "picked on" for reasons of "ethnicity, gender, behavior, values and beliefs, and/or personal attributes" (p. 430).

Identifying and Supporting Effective Resistance

I (Marisol) was called to Pepe's school when he became what school personnel described as "out of control" and threatened to kill himself. Pepe had been having many problems in the school perhaps in part because he was a 12-year-old in a fourth-grade classroom. When I arrived, Pepe was sitting in a corner huddled up while the vice principal, social worker, and teacher all issued him lectures regarding how he must learn to follow rules and respect his elders. Pepe repeated, "I just want to be dead." I asked everyone to step out so that I could talk to Pepe. "Will you be ok?" they asked. (Did they think Pepe would pose a danger?) When I asked Pepe what had happened, he told me that the day before he had asked the teacher if he could go to the bathroom and the teacher refused. Pepe, who was on medication, urinated on himself. Pepe told me he had not wanted to go back to school after this incident. When he did, his teacher asked in the midst of a class session, among all his peers, "Pepe, how is your bladder problem today, ha, ha!"

Falicov (1998) argued that school is often where problems begin or intensify for Latino children. Many youth of color report incidents of discrimination at school that leave them feeling dehumanized. They further may not want to jeopardize inclusion in contexts that are accepting of them (e.g., peers and gangs) to be included in contexts that they have found to be rejecting (e.g., school; Phelan et al., 1994). Stanton-Salazar (2001) used a social capital framework to examine how schools are organized to reproduce social inequality in low-income families. When schools offer their help and guidance it is with the expectation that students will adhere to middle-class rules and values. However, low-status adolescents may not possess the tools (language, education, socioeconomic stability, available parents, safety, etc.) to be able to conform to the school's agenda. In response to their inability to conform, the school answers their differences with actions (e.g., special education, social workers) that attempt to encourage conformance and performance. Adolescents must not only manage school contexts, but also they must do so while managing other environments. When navigating from the context of the neighborhood to the school, they may be placed in a position of trading social capital resources in one context (e.g., being tough) in order to increase social capital in another (e.g., complying with school rules). The results of these negotiations may be bitter for low-status youth as they often result in diminished social capital and pain from hazardous and insurmountable boundary crossing. For example, through meetings with school personnel and Pepe's family, I (Marisol) observed the school's insistence that Pepe conform to rules made for nine-year-olds. Pepe, on the other hand, expressed frustration and anger to me when he was forced to follow these mandates in a climate that marginalized his life experience. Pepe related to me his struggles to integrate what was important in his community environment (e.g., respect) and the school's demand that he follow rules that were disrespectful and humiliating, such as not being allowed to go to the bathroom or having to take the bus home with much younger children. At the same time, Pepe's street peers demanded that he act tough and not give in to teachers. These messages were divergent and placed stress on Pepe, his family, and the school personnel. Each system was invested in promoting a particular set of beliefs and values, believing they were doing the best for Pepe.

The immediate intervention I (Marisol) used when Pepe was in the principal's office with me was to recognize his behavior as an act of resistance. He needed to be validated for having resisted an act of oppression. However, he had not chosen the particular form of resistance that would be most beneficial for him at this moment. Consequently, I validated his behavior and provided other alternatives to resist, given the situation. Pepe and I talked about how he could get what he wanted at that moment. He wanted to go home and have everyone leave him alone. I helped Pepe decide to resist by yielding (McDowell, 2004), that is, to do what was being asked of him in the present situation while not forgetting or dismissing the incident. Pepe was momentarily conforming, but we needed to go back to talk about this and consider taking action when we had more time and resources.

Later, Pepe and Celinez (his mother) could aid in mapping their social capital in order to react to this act of discrimination in a way that gave Pepe back some pride. The therapist could begin by asking which people in their family or community saw Pepe as a person with potential, or by asking who they would go to if they had a problem. The therapist would include himself or herself as a contributor to social capital. The behavior apparent at school would be seen within the context of opportunities and constraints. Given this mapping, the family could decide to speak up against the school and the teacher with the support of numerous parties (e.g., therapist, social worker, priest).

Optimizing Opportunities / Challenging Constraints

Celinez was very agitated when she told me (Marisol) that gang members had come to her house looking for Pepe. They were carrying bats and guns, claiming Pepe had stolen a cell phone from them and sold it to someone else for $50.00. They threatened to kill Pepe if he did not return the cell phone and pay back the money. Celinez had to send Pepe to her sister's house as she packed the rest of the family's belongings to join him. I encouraged her to tell the courts so that they could protect Pepe. Celinez refused, stating that it would make matters worse.

Forty percent of all U.S. gang members are urban Latinos (Arfaniarromo, 2001). Arfaniarromo argued that difficulties crossing boundaries and integrating into school contexts have forced adolescents to look at other contexts in which they can engage with more ease (e.g., gangs). Adolescents find power, protection, and validation through gang membership (Totten, 2000,). Furthermore, those individuals who are most alienated from public institutions are most likely to become gang members because gangs replace institutions as a source of emulation and identification (Vigil, 1988). Gangs resocialize members to internalize and adhere to specific intragroup norms and modes of behavior. Patterns of gang behavior play a significant role in helping members acquire a sense of importance, self-esteem, and self-identity. In short, rather than feeling neglected and remaining culturally and institutionally marginalized, gang members are provided with a way to participate in public life. Sanchez-Jankowski (1991) found that most members reported joining a gang because it would increase their chances of securing money, protection, and/or aid in times of trouble. They also stated they wanted to make contact with individuals who may eventually help them financially or do favors for them. In these ways, gangs offer advantages to members who may not have the necessary social capital to "legitimately" access resources through socially sanctioned institutions. Members also stated that they used gangs as a place for recreation and refuge. Finally, some felt they had an obligation to join as the gang represented the community and its legacy.

Low-income areas are organized around an intense competition and conflict over the scarce resources that exist in these communities. This leads to the development of an alternative social order. Gangs emerge as one organizational response to improve the competitive advantage of its members in obtaining an increase in material resources. Gang members believe that through the business dealings of the gang, or the contacts they are able to establish through gang membership, they will be able to improve the quality of their lives (social capital). Arfaniarromo (2001) argued that low-income Latino adolescents are left in a state of anomie where they are eager to obtain socially encouraged goals but do not have the means to achieve these goals. These adolescents are surrounded by those who are struggling to survive, and their only means to attain the goals of a capitalist society are to adopt a predatory model of acquiring material benefits (Sanchez-Jankowski, 1991). Coping and surviving, for these youths, become a principal life activity.

It is unclear whether Pepe was actually a gang member as this incidence occurred the last day of treatment with this family, but Pepe was frequently found at the gang's meeting place. Regardless, Pepe's life and that of his family were strongly influenced by the presence of gangs, and they had to find ways to live among them. My (Marisol's) response was to talk about the different options they had available to them. The act of sharing the current situation with the courts was analyzed in terms of whether it would increase opportunities or decrease constraints. The repercussions of providing information about the gang would place the family in danger (decreasing social capital as far as community resources) and would not contribute to any gains in social capital (such as protection). Celinez decided that it would not be to her benefit to share any of this information.

Gathering a Web of Allies

Pepe was placed on house arrest by the judge. I (Marisol) asked that he be allowed to continue to go and help his priest at the church, as I saw this as a positive opportunity. The permission was denied until Pepe could prove that he was willing to follow rules. He needed to be in his house at all times during two long and hot summer weeks. The following day, Celinez called crying, reporting she had lost her job after taking the whole day off work for Pepe's court date. It had been the second court day in two months in addition to leaving work for all the calls from Pepe's school. Had she not gone to these court dates or picked up her son from school, she would have been reported to family services. Pepe broke house arrest, went to his neighbor's house, and did not come home until 12:00 a.m.

According to Becker and Liddle (2001), the dire economic situation of the growing population of single mothers accounts for the feminization of poverty (Sands & Nuccio, 1989). Single women head 49% of Latino families. Pepe's mother found herself without work, with little influence or social capital relative to institutional systems, and few material resources to find alternative solutions. Their resources within each system determined Celinez and Pepe's social capital as a family. Auerswald's (1968) ecological and Aponte's (1976) eco-structural approach emphasized the importance of collaboration among professionals who are involved with the same family. In this case, majority culture institutions established to provide both social control and support (e.g., the courts and family services) created greater stress on Celinez and Pepe by failing to coordinate with each other to develop reasonable expectations that were respectful of the family's situation (e.g., requiring a single mother to be in court during work hours). Furthermore, if Celinez were to resist the social control of the courts and family services in order to maintain her family's livelihood, she would have faced an increase in their involvement and control over her life.

Celinez was also in the agonizing position of having to call the probation officer and "rat" on her son. She struggled with this in therapy, indicating that this action was against her cultural and community values. Celinez wanted help for her son but in a manner that would increase her power, not compromise it. If Celinez were to call the probation officer, she would lose social capital in the family and community without being guaranteed any gain by further involving her son in the correctional system. Celinez talked with me (Marisol) about how she could show she was a good mother. Reporting Pepe might have sent a message to court and mental health systems that Celinez was a competent mother because she was placing consequences on his behavior. However, her drive to protect him (also being a good mother) made the decision agonizing. It seemed apparent in therapy that Celinez's struggles in navigating among these differing and conflicting environments resulted in desperation, pain, frustration, and anger as she herself did not possess the resources to manage the crossing of boundaries in a nonhazardous manner.

Mapping social capital can inform our efforts to help families secure a web of allies who will advocate for and protect them. The therapist can be a key member of this network as someone who has the societal authority to challenge stories that have scripted clients as problematic, dysfunctional, or dangerous. Therapists can normalize behavior, reframe dysfunctions, validate choices their clients make, and create space for voices to be heard. They can also play key roles in helping to secure additional allies.

Allies may be found in immediate and extended families, the community, social service agencies, schools, courts, and so on. Tracking opportunities in terms of allies can guide family and clinical decisions about who to include in therapy, who to seek out in solving family problems, which relationships to nurture, and who can provide solidarity by guiding and supporting positive acts of resistance. Social webs that have proven to be supportive can be further accessed in the best interest of the family, keeping in mind that in social relationships what counts is not so much the number of resources actors have at their disposal, but the relationship between the resources and the actors, that is, which actor can bring more resources to bear in each case and situation. This web of allies should include the collective history of groups that have found ways to successfully resist oppression, including facing the consequences of these acts with strength and purpose (e.g., actors in the civil rights movement).

I (Marisol) intervened by helping Celinez reflect on whether she had to define either reaction (reporting her son or not) in terms of being a good parent, but rather in terms of what would increase her power and advantage in this situation. I encouraged Celinez to consider who she wanted to include in her web of allies relative to this particular situation. She decided not to include the juvenile courts. Instead, she called upon Pepe's father and the priest for help. The priest was asked to monitor Pepe's behavior on a more permanent and continual basis, and Pepe's father agreed to take him more often and teach him how to be a man in terms of protection and resistance based on his own life experiences.

ROLE AND SELF OF THE THERAPIST

By nature of our role in society as therapists, we are assigned significant social capital and privilege that we must use responsibly. When we advocate for clients, we lend them capital and/or make space in the social fabric for them to increase their own capital. We may do this by going with families to school meetings, writing letters to family services on the behalf of clients, and testifying in court. These remain important avenues for supporting low-status families; however, we must be careful that advocating is done with and not for families to avoid thoughtlessly contributing to existing social inequities. Furthermore, we can expand our support in important ways by assuming positions as allies when families resist oppressive social forces.

Those family therapists who have experienced oppression due to race, class, nation of origin, sexual orientation, or other socially located identities may be more skilled at identifying and strategizing successful interventions that target social inequities. Others who have more consistently held privilege may rely on single forms of challenging injustices. For example, if we have adequate capital (e.g., white, middle/upper-middle class, and secure employment), we might teach our children to speak out directly when faced with unfair situations, knowing at some level that we can support them when they take these risks.

It may not occur to us that for some people and for all of us in some situations, direct challenges might at best fail to make a difference and at worst create further oppression and/or danger. We need to carefully consider how our own experiences of privilege and oppression might hinder or help us strategize ways to resist that do not compromise clients or risk their chances of securing resources. To do this, we need to develop sophisticated understandings of the many forms of resistance, including withdrawing or staying silent, taking collective action, yielding to pressures, and directly challenging (McDowell, 2004).

Authentic participation on the part of therapists is crucial in order for us to reflect on our own attitudes and contributions to relational dynamics. As therapists, we must carefully consider our role as both mediator and participant within and across systems. It is important for us to examine personal biases toward other providers (e.g., school, psychiatrists, family services) in order to access all of those who have the family's best interests in mind. Therapists should be hesitant to assume a position of being the only one willing to help or capable of helping. The goal is to strive for collective understanding and action in order to obtain the optimum resources for the individual and family. Finally, it is important to note that we are all at different levels of critical awareness. Ongoing dialogue and reflection among allies can increase collective and individual social awareness and effectiveness in supporting families.

CONCLUSION

In this article, we argued that a broad understanding of power, privilege, and oppression along with a stance of care and advocacy are not adequate to effectively and ethically work with low-status families. We introduced how the concept of social capital might inform our therapeutic work by offering a way of thinking about how privilege is lost or gained in response to both constraints and opportunities in local contexts, including therapy. We suggested that a critical contextual lens that systemically tracks the flow of social capital can help us work collaboratively with clients to raise social awareness and act as allies in promoting social justice.

Analyzing class and social capital can help therapists avoid common pitfalls of "rescuing" clients, siding with institutions of control, or situating problems solely within the family. Further, it can enhance our abilities to challenge systems that impose dominant values and behaviors, and to help those with whom we work navigate complex and competing social terrains necessary to protect, sustain, and improve their lives. By engaging in an analysis of their own lives, clients are able to raise their consciousness of the dynamics of power and social capital in order to take action on their own behalf (Freire, 1970; Korin, 1994; Martín-Baró, 1994).

We are deeply grateful to Pepe and Celinez for guiding our developing understanding of the lives of many low-status Latino youth and offering us an opportunity to further develop our ideas.

REFERENCES

Alexander, J., & Parsons, B. (1982). *Functional family therapy: Principles and procedures. Carmel*, CA: Brooks & Cole.

Almeida, R., & Durkin, T. (1999). The cultural context model: Therapy for couples with domestic violence. *Journal of Marital and Family Therapy*, 25, 313–324.

Aponte, H. (1976). The family-school interview: An eco-structural approach. *Family Process*, 15, 303–311.

Arfaniarromo, A. (2001). Toward a psychosocial and sociocultural understanding of achievement motivation among Latino gang members in U.S. schools. *Journal of Instructional Psychology*, 28(3), 123–136.

Arunkumar, R., & Midgley, C. (1999). Perceiving high or low home-school dissonance: Longitudinal effects on adolescent emotional and academic well-being. *Journal of Research on Adolescence*, 9, 441–466.

Auerswald, E. H. (1968). Interdisciplinary versus ecological approach. *Family Process*, 7, 299–303.

Bandura, A. (1969). Social learning of moral judgments. *Journal of Personality and Social Psychology*, 11, 275–279.

Becker, D., & Liddle, H. (2001). Family therapy with unmarried African American mothers and their adolescents. *Family Process*, 40, 413–424.

Bourdieu, P. (1986). The forms of capital. In J. G. Richardson (Ed.), *Handbook of theory and research for the sociology of education* (pp. 241–258). New York: Greenwood Press.

Boyd-Franklin, N. (1989). Black families in therapy: *A multisystems approach*. New York: Guilford Press.

Brofenbrenner, V. (1977). Toward an experimental ecology of human development. *American Psychologist*, 513–531.

Brofenbrenner, U. (1979). *The ecology of human development: Experiments by nature and design*. Cambridge, MA: Harvard University Press.

Coatsworth, D., Pantin, H., & Szapocznik, J. (2002). Familias Unidas: A family-centered ecodevelopmental intervention to reduce risk for problem behavior among Hispanic adolescents. *Clinical Child and Family Psychology Review*, 5(2), 113–132.

Degarmo, D., & Martinez, C. (2006). A culturally informed model of academic well-being for Latino youth: The importance of discriminatory experiences and social support. *Family Relations*, 55, 267–278.

Falicov, C. (1998). *Latino families in therapy: A guide to multicultural practice*. New York: Guilford Press.

Falicov, C. (2003). Culture in family therapy: New variations on a fundamental theme. In T. Sexton, G. Weeks, & M. Robbins (Eds.), *Handbook of family therapy: The science and practice of working with families and couples* (pp. 37–55). New York: Brunner-Routledge.

Freire, P. (1970). *Pedagogy of the oppressed*. New York: Continuum.

Henggeler, S., Melton, G., & Smith, L. (1992). Family preservation using multisystemic therapy: An effective alternative to incarcerating serious juvenile offenders. *Journal of Consulting and Clinical Psychology*, 60, 953–961.

Korin, E. C. (1994). Social inequalities and therapeutic relationships: Applying Freire's ideas to clinical practice. *Journal of Feminist Family Therapy*, 5(3/4), 75–98.

Liddle, H. (1995). Conceptual and clinical dimensions of a multidimensional, multisystems engagement strategy in family-based adolescent treatment. *Psychotherapy: Theory, Research, Practice, Training*, 32(1), 39–58.

Madanes, C. (1981). *Strategic family therapy*. San Francisco: Jossey-Bass.

Martín-Baró, I. (1994). *Writings for a liberatorion psychology*. Cambridge, MA: Harvard University.

McDowell, T. (2004). Listening to the racial experiences of graduate trainees: A critical race theory perspective. *The American Journal of Family Therapy*, 32, 305–324.

McDowell, T., Fang, S., Griggs, J., Speirs, K., Perumbilly, S., & Kublay, A. (2006). International dialogue: Our experience in a family therapy program. *Journal of Systemic Therapy*, 25(1), 1–15.

Phelan, P., Davidson, A., & Cao, H. (1991). Student's multiple worlds: Negotiating the boundaries of family, peer, and school cultures. *Anthropology and Education Quarterly*, 22, 224–250.

Phelan, P., Yu, H., & Davidson, A. (1994). Navigating the psychosocial pressures of adolescence: The voices and experiences of high school youth. *American Educational Research Journal*, 31, 415–447.

Portes, A. (1998). Social capital: Its origins and applications in modern sociology. *Annual Review of Sociology*, 24, 1–24.

Sanchez-Jankowski, M. (1991). *Islands in the street*. Berkeley: University of California Press.

Sands, R., & Nuccio, K. (1989). Mother headed single-parent families: A feminist perspective. *Affilia*, 4(3), 25–41.

Stanton-Salazar, R. (2001). *Manufacturing hope and despair*. New York: Teachers College Press.

Totten, M. (2000). *Gays, Gangs, and Girlfriend Abuse*. Peterborough, Ontario, Canada: Broadview.

Vega, W., Khoury, E., Zimmerman, R., & Gil, A. (1995). Cultural conflicts and problem behaviors of Latino adolescents in home and school environments. *Journal of Community Psychology*, 23, 167–179.

Vigil, J. (1988). *Barrio gangs: Street life and identity in Southern California*. Austin: University of Texas Press.

Wong, C., Eccles, J., & Sameroff, A. (2003). The influence of ethnic discrimination and ethnic identification on African American adolescents' school and socioemotional adjustment. *Journal of Personality*, 71, 1197–1232.

Worrel, J., & Remer, P. (1992). *Feminist perspectives in therapy: An empowerment model for women*. New York: John Wiley & Sons.

SHOULD THE GOVERNMENT PROMOTE MARRIAGE?

By Andrew J. Cherlin

I s getting parents to marry the answer to the difficulties that children in single-parent families face? This question became a focus of debate when the Bush administration proposed in 2002 to include funds for promoting marriage in legislation extending the welfare reform act. As of this writing, it appears that the proposal will succeed. Although the marriage promotion fund (about $300 million per year) is relatively modest compared to the total cost of welfare, the proposal generated more controversy per dollar than any other part of the bill. The strong opinions on both sides reveal the high stakes of the debate.

On one side is the "marriage movement"—a loose group of conservative and centrist activists, religious leaders, and social scientists who want to strengthen the institution of marriage. Some of them advocate marriage because they are morally certain that it provides the best kind of family. Others, including most of the social scientists in this camp, favor it because they believe children's well-being would improve if more of their parents were married.

On the other side are "diversity defenders"—liberal activists, feminists, and sympathetic social scientists who argue that single-parent families can be just as good for children if they receive the support they need. The marriage movement favors public policies that encourage marriage. The diversity defenders favor policies that provide services and economic opportunities to low-income parents, whether married or not, and their children. In the end, the evidence suggests that the benefits of marriage promotion would be marginal. But the real debate may be far more about symbols than substance.

Cherlin, A. (2008). Should the government promote marriage?. In J. Goodwin & J. M. Jasper (Eds.), *The Contexts Reader* (pp. 55–61). W. W. Norton & Company, Inc.

THE DECLINE OF MARRIAGE

Most observers on both sides agree that the social institution of marriage is substantially weaker than it was 50 years ago. In mid-twentieth-century America, marriage was the only acceptable context for having a sexual relationship and for bearing and raising children. In 1950, just 4 percent of children were born to unmarried women. (Fifty years later, the figure was 33 percent.) Most women, and

> Some families have pre-existing problems, such as genetic predispositions to depression, that raise the probability that parents will divorce and the probability that their children will have mental health problems. In these cases, the divorce would not be the reason for the children's misfortunes.

many men, abstained from sexual intercourse until they were engaged to be married. When an unmarried woman became pregnant, relatives pressured her and her partner to agree to a "shotgun wedding." Once married, couples were less likely to divorce— approximately one in three marriages begun in the 1950s ended in divorce, compared to one in two today. Consequently, even among the poor, most families had two parents.

In the ensuing decades, however, the likelihood that a child would spend a substantial portion of time in a single-parent family grew. More adults had children outside of marriage, choosing either to remain single or live with their partners without marrying. Divorce became more common. As a result, about half of all children are projected to spend some time in a single-parent family while growing up. Although these trends cut across class, racial, and ethnic lines, poor children and black children are more likely to be raised in single-parent families than are middle-class children and white children, respectively.

STATISTICS AND POLITICS

Although the marriage movement and the diversity defenders tend to agree that the institution of marriage is weaker, they disagree about the consequences that has for society. Their debates have two levels, the statistical and the political. The statistical debate concerns whether the findings of social scientific research, most of it analyses of survey data, show marriage to be beneficial, and divorce and childbearing outside of marriage detrimental to children. While such research shapes the debates by providing facts for policy makers, those who dispute the numbers often skate on the surface of the subject. A deeper, political dispute lies beneath the statistical arguments, reflecting basic disagreement about whether the government should favor one model of family life above all others.

The Statistical Debate

Most social scientists would agree that, on average, children who grow up in a one-parent family are more disadvantaged than children who grow up with two parents. As Sara McLanahan wrote in the spring 2002 issue of *Contexts:*

They are more likely to drop out of high school, less likely to attend college, and less likely to graduate from college than children raised by both biological parents. Girls from father-absent families are more likely to become sexually active at a younger age and to have a child outside of marriage. Boys who grow up without their fathers are more likely to have trouble finding (and keeping) a job in young adulthood. Young adult men and women from one-parent families tend to work at low-paying jobs.

But we cannot conclude from these differences that growing up in a single-parent family causes these unwanted outcomes. Both conditions—the number of parents in the home while growing up and problems in adulthood—could be caused by other factors. For example, poverty could cause parents to divorce and also prevent their children from attending college. Research by McLanahan and Gary Sandefur suggests that as much as half of the apparent disadvantage of growing up in a single-parent family is due to the lower incomes these families typically have.

> The politics of single parenting involve not simply disagreements about data, but about how Americans view the autonomy of women, the authority of men, and the imposition of a particular moral view of family life on those who choose other lifestyles.

In addition, some families have pre-existing problems, such as genetic predispositions to depression, that raise the probability that parents will divorce and the probability that their children will have mental health problems. In these cases, the divorce would not be the reason for the children's misfortunes. Several colleagues and I examined an extensive British study that followed individuals from birth to adulthood. As expected, we found that people whose parents had been divorced had poorer mental health as adults. But by looking at records of their childhood, we found that some portion, although not all, of their difficulties could be accounted for by behavior problems and psychological distress that were visible early in their lives, before their parents had divorced. Our study and others like it suggest that being short a parent in the home is not responsible for all the ills these children show. Therefore, a policy aimed at reducing single-parent families and increasing two-parent families would most likely not eliminate such problems.

Nevertheless, family structure has something to do with the difficulties children experience. Our study and others do find some differences that could be due to divorce or birth outside of marriage. Only a minority of children in single-parent families actually experience problems later, but divorce and child-bearing outside of marriage are so common that this minority still represents a large number of children. Taken together, all of these findings suggest that while the number of parents matters, it matters less than most people think; and it matters less than many other factors for how children fare.

The Political Debate

If the debate ended with social scientific studies and statistics, marriage promotion policies would not be so contentious. But there is a deeper level to the controversy. The politics of single parenting involve not simply disagreements about data, but about how Americans view the autonomy of women, the authority of men, and the imposition of a particular moral view of family life on those who choose other lifestyles. Until the mid-twentieth century, marriage was taken for granted as the central institution of family life. Men held considerable power in marriages because of social norms and because they typically earned more money. In the stereotypical mid-twentieth-century marriage, women restricted themselves to home and family. As recently as 1977, two-thirds of those interviewed in the General Social Survey—a national sample of adults repeated every year or two—agreed that "It is much better for everyone involved if the man is the achiever outside the home and the woman takes care of the home and family." By 1998, just one-third agreed with the same statement.

> Marriage, it would seem, is valued as long as it is consistent with the expressive individualism that Americans hold most dear. That is why pro-marriage policies that seem to interfere with individual decisions and self-expression are not broadly popular.

Since mid-century, new options have made it possible for women to live full lives outside of marriage. New job opportunities provide independent income and welfare provides an income floor (although the recent welfare reform now limits reliance on that floor to five years). The birth control pill allows for sexual activity without unwanted pregnancies, and the greater acceptability of raising a child outside of marriage allows single women to have children if they want. At the same time, the economic fortunes of men without college educations have diminished, reducing the attractiveness of marriage for many women. All told, alternative paths to parenthood other than long-term marriage are more feasible and more attractive.

Feminists fought for these gains in women's autonomy, and many of them see the pro-marriage movement as an attempt to reassert men's control over women's lives. Being a single parent may not be easy, but it is a more viable alternative than it used to be and many feminists defend women's freedom to follow this path. Other liberals argue that gay and lesbian parents, whether single or partnered, should receive the same acceptance and support as heterosexual parents. These diversity defenders argue for public policies that would provide more income support, child care options, and flexible work arrangements for single-parent families to minimize any remaining disadvantages of these non-marital choices.

But it can be difficult to disentangle the political debate from the statistical debate. Often the political debate constitutes the unspoken subtext of a seemingly statistical argument. In an influential 1972 book, *The Future of Marriage*, Jessie Bernard argued that men get most of the rewards in marriage because women do most of the work in the home while being denied (at least in the 1950s and 1960s) the opportunity to work outside the home. Bernard claimed, for

> Even the Bush administration acknowledges that not all marriages are equally good for children. Its officials state that they, too, are only interested in promoting healthy marriages. The problem is that it is hard to support healthy marriages without concurrently supporting unhealthy marriages.

example, that married women are more depressed than single women, whereas married men are less depressed than single men. The subtext is that marriage, at least in its current form, oppresses women, and that policies that promote marriage should be resisted by feminists. More recently, Linda J. Waite and journalist Maggie Gallagher argued in their book, *The Case for Marriage: Why Married People Are Happier, Healthier, and Better Off Financially*, that marriage is just as beneficial for women as it is for men. The subtext here is that because marriage is not an oppressive institution, opposition to pro-marriage policies is misguided. Although Waite and Gallagher persuasively demonstrate that marriage is not all bad for women, their attempt to show that it benefits women as much as men is less convincing.

MARRIAGE AND MORALITY

In some writing on marriage, the political and moral claims are in plain view. Consider *The Marriage Problem: How Our Culture Has Weakened Families*, a recent book by political scientist James Q. Wilson. He endorses an evolutionary model in which men are by nature promiscuous and women are by nature more interested in raising children. Marriage, he argues, is the cultural invention that restrains men and provides mothers and children with support and protection. Wilson concludes that more women need to emphasize marriage over career, even though this may limit their autonomy. He offers sympathy, but little more, for the difficulty of this choice. Postponing marriage, Wilson writes, is risky: "Older women lose out in the marriage race much faster than do men. It may be unfair, but that is the way the world works" (p. 12). Women's lot in life, the book implies, is to make the selfless choice to marry for the good of their children.

Even if one agreed with Wilson's view of the need for marriage, his exhortations are increasingly out of step with Americans' moral views. Although most Americans still value marriage, they hesitate to impose their preferences on others. Rather, the American philosophy, Alan Wolfe argues, is "moral freedom": Each person should be freedom decide what is a good and virtuous life. Each is free, in other words, to choose his or her own morality. For example, Americans view divorce as a serious and unwelcome step. But they tend to believe that each person should be allowed to decide when a marriage no longer works. As Grace Floro, a Dayton housewife and one of Wolfe's interview subjects said: "How loyal can you be if somebody's wronged you? When is loyalty appropriate and when isn't it? You can be loyal to a fault just like you can be honest to a fault. That's what makes life so difficult. Nothing is black and white and every circumstance merits its own judgment" (p. 55).

Americans' view of marriage was also apparent in a 1999 *New York Times* national survey. Respondents were presented with a list of values and asked how important each was to them. After the replies were tallied, the values were ranked by the percentage of people who said each was "very important." The top-ranking values largely reflected self-reliance ("Being responsible for your own actions," "Being able to stand up for yourself") and self-expression ("Being able to communicate your feelings"). "Having children" came in sixth. "Being married" ranked tenth—below "Being a good neighbor." Marriage, it would seem, is valued as long as it is consistent with the expressive individualism that Americans hold most dear. That is why pro-marriage policies that seem to interfere with individual decisions and self-expression are not broadly popular.

BUT DO THEY WORK?

In addition, the effectiveness of pro-marriage policies is an open question. The best case for such programs has been made by Theodora Ooms of the Center for Law and Social Policy, who advocates support for "healthy marriages" (those that are relatively conflict-free and provide good parenting to their children), but not to the exclusion of helping single parents. Ooms argues for programs that provide young adults who wish to marry with "soft services" such as communication and conflict resolution skills, along with more traditionally liberal programs such as greater income support for the working poor. But soft-service interventions such as teaching relationship skills are based on programs developed for middle-class couples;

whether they can be adapted to help the poor and near-poor has yet to be determined. Before trying to institute them nationwide, some small-scale pilot projects ought to be attempted.

It is also questionable whether all unmarried mothers should be encouraged to marry. Consider a study several collaborators and I conducted with more than 2,000 low-income children and their mothers in Boston, Chicago and San Antonio. We followed the families over a one-and-a-half-year period and found that more of the mothers were married by the end than had been at the beginning. But very few of the new wives' marriages involved the fathers of their children. Unfortunately, the research literature shows that children in step-families fare no better than children in single-parent families. The addition of a stepfather to the household usually brings an increase in income, but it also complicates the family situation. The role of the stepfather is often unclear, and teenagers may reject his presence as they cope with the typical issues of adolescence. Moreover, the marriages of the mothers in our sample broke up at a faster rate than the already high national rates would predict, thus exposing their children to much family change—a father moved out, for example, or a stepfather moved in. Studies suggest that experiencing several such family changes may in itself harm children's well-being. We concluded that encouraging poor, single mothers to marry may not benefit as many children as pro-marriage boosters would think.

Even the Bush administration acknowledges that not all marriages are equally good for children. Its officials state that they, too, are only interested in promoting healthy marriages, although that phrase is never defined. The problem is that it is hard to support healthy marriages without concurrently supporting unhealthy marriages. Consider West Virginia, which now gives women who are receiving welfare a bonus of $100 per month if they marry. There may be good reasons why some mothers have not married the fathers of their children (e.g., violence, drug addiction), but they may be tempted to do so by the promise of an additional $100 per month. It is not clear that, on balance, children benefit from the marriages this policy encourages.

SYMBOLS AND PRACTICES

Despite the attention paid to social science research, the debate over marriage promotion is, at heart, a debate over symbolism more than statistics. Should our government state symbolically that marriage is preferred over other family forms, as the marriage movement urges, or should it make the symbolic statement that individuals should be free to choose any form, as the diversity defenders desire? The marriage-promotion provision in the welfare reauthorization bill may be more important as a statement of how our government thinks family life should be lived than as a source of funds for particular programs.

Such statements may influence the way people view marriage and family life, even if they never participate in a federally funded marriage enrichment course. Interested groups are fighting hard to have their symbolic perspective prevail. The likely inclusion of marriage-promotion funds signals the renewed strength of the pro-marriage view; their rejection would have signaled the continued strength of the family pluralists.

But symbolism does not justify major new legislation. A new initiative should have the promise of efficiently meeting its goals, and the proposed marriage promotion policy fails this test. If low-income single mothers are urged to marry, the kinds of families that would be formed often would not match the healthy, two-biological parent, steady-breadwinner model that policymakers envision. Effective programs for promoting marriage among the poor do not yet exist. Even if they could be developed, fewer children would benefit from them than their supporters suggest. And if overdone, they could hurt some of the children they intend to help.

RECOMMENDED RESOURCES

Jesse Bernard. *The Future of Marriage* (Bantam, 1972).

   An influential book that argues marriage is good for men but bad for women.

Andrew J. Cherlin, P. Lindsay Chase-Lansdale, and Christine McRae. "Effects of Parental Divorce on Mental Health throughout the Life Course." *American Sociological Review* 63 (1998): 239–49.

   Suggests some of the apparent effects of parental divorce on mental health were visible before the parents divorced.

Andrew J. Cherlin and Paula Fomby. "A Closer Look at Children's Living Arrangements in Low-Income Families." Policy Brief 02–03, Welfare, Children, and Families Study, 2002. Online, http://www.jhu.edu/~welfare/19837BriefLivingArrang.pdf.

   A report on changes in family structure among a sample of low-income, urban families. It finds an increase in families composed of a mother, her children, and a man other than the father of the children.

Theodora Ooms. "Marriage and Government: Strange Bedfellows?" 2002. Washington D.C.: Center for Law and Social Policy. Online, http://www.clasp.org/DMS/Documents/1028563059.86/MarriageBrief1.pdf.

A policy brief that argues for marriage promotion programs from a liberal perspective.

Linda J. Waite and Maggie Gallagher. *The Case for Marriage: Why Married People are Happier, Healthier, and Better Off Financially* (Doubleday, 2000).

Waite and Gallagher argue that marriage benefits both women and men equally.

James Q. Wilson. The Marriage Problem: How Our Culture Has Weakened Families (HarperCollins, 2002).

Contends that the decline in marriage has been detrimental to society and suggests that women should place a higher priority on marriage and child-rearing.

Alan Wolfe. *Moral Freedom: The Search for Virtue in a World of Choice* (W. W. Norton, 2001).

Maintains that the American philosophy is "moral freedom," in which each person is free to decide what is a good and virtuous life.

REVIEW QUESTIONS

1. Compare the positions of the "marriage movement" and the "diversity defenders" Which do you find more compelling?
2. According to this essay, why can you not make the following assumption: As compared to a child who is raised by both biological parents, being raised in a single-parent home increases the chances of that child dropping out of college and decreases the chances of enrollment?
3. The debate surrounding marriage is a difficult one, with multiple dynamics at play. Do you think the same factors that affect marriage between heterosexuals affect gay marriages? Discuss those issues, and consider how they might differ.

Family

Sorting Out the Pushes and Pulls

Families are considered the primary agent of socialization since society expects the "family" to be the setting in which children learn what is expected of them as well as how they are to behave in society. We encourage readers to consider their own biases, the possible preconceptions of the author(s), and the norms of society today when examining the information presented.

Family dynamics include things such as how members relate to one another, learn their status within the family, and cope with conflict. Families are impacted by forces within the family as well as externally. The article "Family Patterns of Gender Role Attitudes" explores the attitudes associated with traditional gender roles and egalitarian gender roles and their impact on the family. The authors conclude that "gender role attitudes are connected to aspects of family life" in many different ways.

Many times, we have heard students or clients comment, "I am not simply a statistic," or that they do not want to be. What we believe they are expressing is that while there may be aspects of their life that resemble others in similar situations, they will not become what research and the news depict as the general trajectory for them. We have included an essay by O'Neal (2014) for this very reason. Despite the surmounting stressors and family dynamics she is faced with, she remains committed to not being a simple result of her circumstance. In light of her narrative, we ask the reader to think about what values (see Chapter 2) are apparent not only from O'Neal, but the societal values that have impacted this family. What connections can one draw to the article by Marks, Bun, and McHale (2009)?

Faure (2000) applies a feminist perspective to child sexual abuse in her discussion of a specific family case study, "Carol, Anna, and Khadia: Work with a Three Generation Black Family." This perspective is applied when considering the dynamics of the family and how the child was socialized or "groomed" for the abuse that occurred. Faure also introduces and evaluates interventions used to address the abuse in this family constellation. While this article is quite different from many of the articles selected for this book, we believe it can elicit dialogue as well as provide an example of practice in the helping professions and of how critical and creative thinking can be applied in this context.

Questions for Consideration:

1. Based on these three articles about family, what are some ways you can apply Bernacki's attributes for "thinking outside the box" (addressed at the beginning of chapter 3 of this book) in terms of your family or upbringing?
2. Review Sweet, Blythe, and Carpenter's nine teaching-learning skills of creative thinking presented in article 3 of this book. How might you apply these to challenge or support any of the positions taken in the article "Family Patterns of Gender Role Attitudes"?

twenty one

FAMILY PATTERNS OF GENDER ROLE ATTITUDES

By Jaime Marks, Lam Chun Bun, and Susan McHale

INTRODUCTION

Although the importance of gender role attitudes in family dynamics has been of interest to researchers for several decades (e.g., Benin & Agostinelli, 1988; Ruble, Martin, & Berenbaum, 2006; Thompson & Walker, 1989), the gender role attitudes of family members—mothers, fathers, sisters and brothers—are typically studied in adults and children separately, or within single (i.e., marital or parent-child) dyads. This approach is likely to limit our understanding of the way in which family members' gender characteristics are connected. As proposed within a family systems perspective, families are composed of subsystems that are interrelated (Cox & Paley, 1997; Minuchin, 1985) and, as such, understanding of one subsystem in the family is incomplete if the processes that operate in other subsystems are not considered. The present study was intended to fill a gap in the literature on gender role attitudes and family dynamics. Using interview data on US families, we aimed: (1) to identify distinct *family patterns* of gender role attitudes of mothers, fathers, and two adolescent siblings using cluster analysis; (2) to explore the conditions under which different family patterns emerged, including family socioeconomic status (SES), parents' time spent on gendered household tasks, parents' time spent with children, and the sex constellation of sibling dyads; and (3) to assess the implications of family patterns of gender role attitudes for conflict between family members. We focused on gender role attitudes because of the extensive changes in gender ideologies within the US in recent decades (Fortin, 2005). We reasoned that sustained social change may differentially affect families and family members and thus

Marks, J. L., Lam, C. B., & McHale, S. M. (2009). Family patterns of gender role attitudes. *Sex roles, 61*(3-4), 221-234.

give rise to distinct family patterns of gender role attitudes, with some families exhibiting more traditional attitudes, some exhibiting more egalitarian attitudes, some exhibiting similarity in attitudes within the family, and some exhibiting differences in attitudes within the family.

GENDER ROLES ATTITUDES OF FAMILY MEMBERS: CONGRUENCE AND INCONGRUENCE

Our first goal was to identify family patterns of gender role attitudes. We used a cluster analysis approach which involves grouping units (families in our case) based on their similarities in multiple measures and which produces subgroups that maximize within-group similarities and between-group differences (Henry, Tolan, & Gorman-Smith, 2005). This pattern-analytic technique is exploratory in nature and involves few a priori assumptions about the structure of the resultant patterns (Whiteman & Loken, 2006). Within the family literature, efforts to identify types of families based on similarity and differences between family members are rare, and we found no prior research that explored family patterns of gender role attitudes. Thus we had no data to guide our predictions on what types of families would emerge. However, as we describe below, a review of literature on gender role attitudes and family systems theory, in general, suggested that, whereas some families may be characterized by congruence in attitudes across family members (e.g., all members are traditional or all are egalitarian), other families may be characterized by incongruence (i.e., some members are traditional and some are egalitarian).

Congruence and Incongruence between Wives and Husbands—One line of studies grounded in the assortive mating theory (Crow & Felsenstein, 1968) predicts that individuals will tend to choose mates with attributes similar to themselves, and thus that wives and husbands will be more similar than unrelated women and men. Empirical findings support this perspective in showing that married couples, as compared to randomly paired couples, are more similar on demographics, values, attitudes, personality, and psychological outcomes (Luo & Klohnen, 2005). From this perspective, wives' and husbands' gender role attitudes should be similar.

A family systems perspective, in contrast, posits that families are complex units composed of individuals with different experiences and needs (Cox & Paley, 1997; Minuchin, 1985). As integrated units, families self-organize in response to both external and internal forces. Across the course of family development, some components of the family may change more rapidly than others (Ross, Mirowsky, & Huber, 1983). Spouses' gender role attitudes, for example, may develop and change at different rates. Studies based on nationally representative samples of U.S. couples found that husbands hold more traditional gender role attitudes than their wives (Bolzendahl & Myers, 2004; Zuo & Tang, 2000). This is not surprising, given that concepts of male privilege and dominance are inherent in traditional views of gender roles (Ferree, 1990). Further evidence suggests that the effects of assortive mating are stronger for demographic characteristics than for psychosocial traits: Although spousal correlations for psychosocial traits are statistically significant, the effect sizes typically range from low to moderate (Epstein & Guttman, 1984). Taken together, theory and findings on attitude congruence in marital dyads may mean that some couples exhibit similar views on gender roles, but others do not.

Congruence and Incongruence between Parents and Children—A socialization perspective highlights parents' roles as instructors, reinforcers, and models of children's gender role attitudes (Lytton & Romney, 1991). Specifically, parents directly communicate their beliefs about gender by providing instruction, guidance, and training to their children (Eccles, 1994). They also reinforce sex-typed behaviors by encouraging their children's involvement in gender-stereotypical activities (Lytton & Romney, 1991). In addition, gender socialization messages are indirectly transmitted through parents' modeling of sex-typed behaviors (Collins & Russell, 1991). For example, children learn that women and men (should) act differently when they observe that mothers spend more time on care-giving and fathers, on leisure activities with their children. From this perspective, parents should pass their attitudes about gender roles to their children, resulting in congruence between parents' and children's gender role attitudes.

A gender schema perspective, in contrast, emphasizes the importance of cognitive processes in gender development. Across childhood and adolescence, youth build schemas about gender-appropriate roles and behaviors (Martin & Ruble, 2004). Through the cognitive processes of identification and categorization, youth continually integrate novel ideas about gender into their schemas. These processes are based upon the unique learning contexts in which youth develop, including family and non-family contexts (Serbin, Powlishtak, & Gulko, 1993). Therefore, although a gender schema perspective also acknowledges parents as key socializing agents, from this perspective, youth act as producers of their own development (Martin, Ruble, Szkrybalo, 2002), meaning that youth's gender role attitudes are informed, but not determined, by parental practices and the larger social world. In fact, empirical studies show only modest and sometimes nonsignificant associations between parents' and children's gender role attitudes (Crouter, Whiteman, McHale, & Osgood, 2007; Tenenbaum & Leaper, 2002). These findings suggest that, whereas some children model their parents' views on gender roles, others do not.

Congruence and Incongruence between Siblings—We know much less about similarities and differences between siblings' gender role orientations than we do about those of marital and parent-child dyads. The larger literature on siblings, however, highlights the role of siblings as models, companions, and sources of advice and reinforcement, particularly in adolescence, when parents may be seen as less knowledgeable about peer and school social norms and activities (McHale, Kim, & Whiteman, 2006). From a social learning perspective, influence processes should operate to produce similarities between siblings' gender role attitudes. Indeed, consistent with social learning tenets, one study found that the gender attitudes of older siblings predicted changes in the attitudes of younger siblings over a two year period (McHale, Updegraff, Helms-Erikson, & Crouter, 2001): When older siblings reported more egalitarian attitudes, younger siblings' egalitarianism increased more over time.

In this study, however, evidence for a competing sibling influence process, termed de-identification, also emerged: When younger siblings reported more egalitarian attitudes, older brothers' attitudes became more traditional over time (McHale et al., 2001). Findings also revealed that sisters' attitudes were more egalitarian than brothers, on average, and longitudinal analyses indicated that the attitudes of sisters with younger brothers became more egalitarian over time. Findings of divergence between siblings are consistent with Alfred Adler's Theory of Individual Psychology (Ansbacher & Ansbacher, 1956) which holds that siblings de-identify with one another during the course of their development, choosing distinct niches in their families in an effort to reduce competition and garner unique family resources. In sum, although empirical data are limited, there is reason to expect both similarities and differences between siblings' gender role attitudes.

Taken together, although it is likely to observe congruence in gender role attitudes across family members in the same family, developmental and family dynamics may also operate to make family members different. As noted, the latter is consistent with the family systems perspective that highlights the potential for divergent experiences and points of view among different family members (Cox & Paley, 1997; Minuchin, 1985). Our first study goal was using cluster analysis to identify distinct and meaningful patterns based on the gender roles attitudes of four family members—wives, husbands, and two adolescents—from the same families.

CONDITIONS UNDERLYING FAMILY PATTERNS OF GENDER ROLES ATTITUDES

Our second goal was to explore the conditions under which family patterns of gender role attitudes emerged. Given that the purpose of cluster analysis is to discover rather than enforce a predetermined structure on the data (Whiteman & Loken, 2006), we could not precisely predict how many subgroups would be found, nor how these subgroups would be linked to other family conditions. However, previous literature targets some family conditions that are related to gender traditionality of parents and children: If we were successful in identifying subgroups of more and less traditional families, we would then expect significant differences between these subgroups in family factors, including SES, parents' time spent on gendered household tasks, parents' time with children, and the sex constellation of sibling dyads.

Family SES—Evidence that socioeconomic factors may affect family gender role attitudes includes findings that women and men who have higher educational attainment and income express more egalitarian gender role orientations (e.g., Crompton & Lyonette, 2005; Lackey, 1989). Within the educational system in the US, students are exposed to egalitarian ideas and both female and male role models, and are taught to identify gender myths and stereotypes (Brooks & Bolzendahl, 2004; Cassidy & Warren, 1996). In addition, higher education levels provide both women and men with training and credentials for higher paying jobs and, in turn, the ability to contribute to the family economy (Raley, Mattingly, & Bianchi, 2006). Longitudinal studies based on nationally representative samples in the US have shown that wives tend to be more egalitarian when they contribute more to the total family income (Zou & Tang, 2000). Consistent with a social learning perspective, children from more economically advantaged family backgrounds also have more egalitarian gender attitudes (e.g., Antill, Cunningham, & Cotton, 2003; Kulik, 2002).

Parents' Time Spent on Gendered Household Tasks—As noted, children learn about gender appropriate behaviors by observing the behaviors of their parents. Over time, their knowledge consolidates to form cognitive schema which later organize new knowledge about gender and channel gendered behaviors (Martin & Ruble, 2004). Based on data from a 31-year panel study of US families, Cunningham (2001) found that parents' division of housework, measured when children were about one year of age, predicted children's later participation in household tasks in their own marriages. Specifically, fathers' contribution to stereotypically feminine housework predicted sons' involvement in the same type of work in adulthood. Cunningham's findings, along with other studies on household task division (e.g., Blair, 1992; White & Brinkerhoff, 1981), point to the importance of parents' time spent on housework in children's gender role development: Non-traditional allocation of housework is likely to promote egalitarian attitudes within the family.

Parents' Time with Children—Another family process that may affect children's gender role attitudes is fathers' temporal involvement (Risman & Myers, 1997). Child care is a stereotypically feminine activity, and marks a less traditional family role for fathers. This may be especially the case when fathers spend time with daughters. On the other hand, within-family comparisons have shown that fathers are more inclined toward sex-typed activities with children (especially boys) than are mothers (Harris & Morgan, 1991; Crouter,

McHale, & Bartko, 1993). As reviewed by Maccoby (2003), fathers-son dyads engaged in almost twice as much rough-and-tumble play as mother-son dyads in experimental settings. Fathers also react more negatively to crying, fearfulness, or signs of feebleness in sons than in daughters. These data suggest that, although fathers' involvement with children, generally, reflects a more egalitarian gender role orientation, high level of paternal involvement selectively with sons may reinforce a more traditional gender ideology.

Sex Constellation of Sibling Dyads—A family systems perspective emphasizes the bidirectional influences between parents and children, and previous research suggests that children may influence parents in some of the same ways that parents influence children. McHale and Crouter (2003) have shown, for example, that the sex constellation of sibling dyads shapes gendered patterns of family activities. Studying two-parent US families with at least two children in middle childhood, they found that mothers spent more time with children than did fathers in families with two daughters, whereas fathers spent more time with children than did mothers in families with two sons. That is, parents' greater involvement was predicted by having not one, but two children of their same gender. Given that fathers are more concerned about the gender typicality of boys (Maccoby, 2003) and that brother-brother sibling dyads tend to spend more time with their fathers, we may find that they have more traditional gender role attitudes when compared to sister-sister dyads. Findings from McHale and Crouter's (2003) study also showed that children's involvement in household tasks varied as a function of the sibling dyad sex constellation. Older siblings generally performed more housework than younger siblings, but this difference was most pronounced in older-sister-younger-brother dyads. Further, in older-brother-younger-sister dyads, younger girls did more housework than their older brothers. These findings suggest that the presence of a boy and a girl in the same family affords an opportunity for parents to reinforce traditional gender role orientations. As such, families with mixed-sex sibling dyads may have more traditional gender role patterns, particularly as compared to families with sister-sister sibling dyads.

GENDER ROLE ATTITUDES AND FAMILY CONFLICT

Our third aim was to assess the implications of the family patterns of gender role attitudes for the quality of family relationships. As mentioned, unlike a priori methods, cluster analysis does not allow us to make precise predictions about the underlying latent patterns, nor about how the derived patterns would be related to other constructs (Whiteman & Loken, 2006). However, previous literature suggests that family members with divergent attitudes are less satisfied with their family relationships. If we proved successful in identifying subgroups of families that are characterized by congruence and incongruence among family members' attitudes, the literature generally suggests that there would be more conflict in families marked by incongruence.

Marital Conflict—Marital quality has been found to be related to spousal similarity. Couples who are similar in values, leisure interests, role preferences, and cognitive skills tend to be more satisfied with their marriages than those who are dissimilar in these aspects (e.g., Burleson & Denton, 1992; Ickes, 1993; Kaslow & Robison, 1996). Furthermore, based on nationally representative samples of US couples, Lye and Biblarz (1993) found that when couples disagree with respect to gender role attitudes (i.e., housework division), both wives and husbands report higher levels of marital tension and conflict. As Cook and Jones (1963) observed, couples with different values and attitudes may have difficulty in their relationships because they appraise events from different perspectives. Dissimilar wives and husbands may have to constantly negotiate and redefine their marital roles—a process that may generate new sources of disagreement and problems.

Parent-Child Conflict—Only few studies examined intergenerational incongruence in attitudes and its links to parent-child relationships. For example, a limited body of research on acculturation has documented the existence of intergenerational conflicts due to differential acculturation of immigrant parents and their children (e.g., Atzaba-Poria & Pike, 2007; Tsai-Chae & Nagata, 2008; Ying & Han, 2007). Overall, findings suggest that when parents and children show marked discrepancies in cultural values and attitudes, they report more conflict and poorer relationship quality. Comparable consequences may occur when parents and children have different views on gender roles. Like dissimilar couples, dissimilar parents and children may need to negotiate and redefine their roles in the family, which may, in turn, compromise parent-child relationships. However, it is important to recognize that in some instances children's divergence from their parents' attitudes is encouraged by parents (Acock, 1984), and thus incongruence may not always result in problematic relationships.

Sibling Conflict—Our review of the literature found no studies linking sibling attitude similarity with sibling conflict, and from a theoretical perspective, predictions are inconsistent. Social learning theories highlight the role of a model's warm and nurturant behavior in observational learning (Bandura, 1977), and indeed, some research shows that siblings with closer relationships exhibit more similarity in their behaviors (McHale et al., 2006). On the other hand, sibling differentiation theory suggests that siblings pick different niches in their families in an effort to reduce sibling rivalry (Ansbacher & Ansbacher, 1956). From this perspective, sibling conflict should be lower when siblings exhibit larger differences in their gender role attitudes.

STUDY OBJECTIVES AND HYPOTHESES

The present study was designed to address three research goals. Our first aim was using mothers, fathers, and first- and second-born siblings' reports on gender role attitudes as clustering variables to identify groups of families that differ in their family-wide patterns of gender role attitudes. We followed recent studies (e.g., Allen & Olson, 2001; Fisher & Ransom, 1995; Fowers & Olson, 1992), and took a two-step approach of cluster analysis. First, a hierarchical cluster analysis using a cosine index of similarity with average linkage was conducted. Families were successively paired until all units were grouped into a common cluster. Hierarchical clustering was used here because nonlinear methods cannot represent nested structures within multivariate data (Henry et al., 2005). Solutions with different numbers of clusters were compared based on several stopping criteria, including dendrogram patterns, interpretability, and cell size (Blashfield & Aldenderfer, 1988). Second, a confirmatory factor analysis using the K-means method was conducted. The additional cluster analysis determined whether the chosen cluster structure derived from the hierarchical cluster analysis was replicable (see Whiteman & Loken, 2006, for a detailed discussion of the procedure and advantages of this two-step approach). To further test our hypothesis regarding gender role attitude patterns, we conducted a mixed model analyses of variance (ANOVA) to examine the between- (cluster) and within-group (family member) differences in the clustering variables.

Our second aim was to explore the conditions under which different patterns of gender role attitudes emerged by comparing family clusters in terms of SES, parents' time spent on gendered household tasks, parents' time with children, and the sex constellation of sibling dyads. Here we conducted a series of mixed model ANOVAs and chi-square analysis to examine the between- (cluster) and within-group (family member) differences in these factors.

Our third aim was to assess the potential implications of family patterns for family conflict by comparing family clusters in terms of marital, parent-child, and sibling conflict. Toward this end, we also conducted mixed model ANOVAs to examine the between- (cluster) and within-group (family member) differences in family conflicts.

We tested the following hypotheses.

1. Cluster analyses will identify family patterns characterized by congruence and incongruence among family members' gender role attitudes.
2(a) In families characterized by more traditional gender role attitudes, parents will have lower SES (i.e., lower education and income levels).
2(b) In families characterized by more traditional gender role attitudes, parents will have a more traditional division of household labor.

2(c) In families characterized by more traditional gender role attitudes, fathers will spend more time with sons.

2(d) The group of families with more egalitarian gender role attitude patterns will include more families with girl-girl sibling dyads as compared to boy-boy or mixed-sex sibling dyads.

3. Families characterized by incongruent gender role attitudes across family members will have higher levels of marital, parent-child, and sibling conflict compared to families characterized by congruent gender role attitudes across family members.

METHOD

Participants

Participants were 358 two-parent families from two cohorts of a longitudinal study of family relationships. One cohort included a firstborn and a secondborn sibling who were in middle childhood when they first entered the study, and the second cohort included a firstborn and a secondborn sibling who were in adolescence when they first entered the study. Recruitment letters were sent home to all families with children of the targeted age within school districts of a northeastern state. The letters explained the purpose of the research project, and described the criteria for participation. Families were given postcards to fill out and return if they were interested in participating. Families were eligible if the couple was married, both parents were working, and they had at least two children in middle childhood or adolescence who were not more than four years apart in age. Over 90% of families that returned postcards were eligible and eventually participated. For the present analyses, we only used data from one occasion for each cohort in which (a) data on gender attitudes of both parents and children were collected and; (b) children were in early (younger siblings) and middle (older siblings) adolescence.

This study included an exclusively White working- and middle-class sample. The average income was $24,756 ($SD = 17,733$) for mothers and $48,747 ($SD = 28,158$) for fathers. The average level of education was 14.66 years ($SD = 2.19$) for mothers and 14.60 years ($SD = 2.39$) for fathers, where a score of 12 signified a high school graduate and 16 a college graduate. The average age was 42.05 years ($SD = 3.95$) for mothers, 44.17 years ($SD = 4.70$) for fathers, 16.72 ($SD = .80$) for firstborn siblings, and 14.20 years ($SD = 1.12$) for secondborn siblings.

Procedure

We collected data through home and phone interviews. Trained interviewers visited families to conduct individual home interviews. At the beginning of the interview, informed consent was obtained, and the family received a $100 or $200 honorarium depending on the study phase. Family members were then interviewed individually. In the interviews, family members reported on measures of development, adjustment, and family relationships.

In the two to three weeks following the home interviews, parents and children respectively completed four (3 weekdays, 1 weekend day) and seven (5 weekdays, 2 weekend days) nightly phone interviews. Trained interviewers called family members in their homes, mostly during the evening hours. Each family member completed their portion of calls individually. The interviewer guided each parent and child through a list of activities and probed for the context of any completed activities, including the type of activities, how long they lasted, and with whom they engaged in the activities. Youth reported on activities, including household tasks, personal activities, sports participation, and hobbies. Parents reported on all of their own household tasks, as well as any activities they did with either child, using the provided list of activities. The two children participated in all seven phone calls and parents participated in four calls each. Phone interviews lasted between 30 to 45 minutes per call.

Measures

Background characteristics—We collected information on family members' ages and parents' education level and income during home interviews with parents.

Parents' gender role attitudes—Parents completed the 15-item Attitudes Towards Women (ATW) Scale (Spence & Helmreich, 1972). A sample item was "In general, the father should have greater authority than the mother in making decisions about raising children." Responses ranged from 1 (*strongly agree*) to 4 (*strongly disagree*). The parents' attitudes scores were computed by summing the scores for all 15 items, with higher scores indicating more traditional views on gender roles. Cronbach's alphas were .80 for mothers and .77 for fathers.

Youth's gender role attitudes—Youth completed either the Attitudes Towards Women Scale (Spence & Helmreich, 1972) or the Children's Attitudes Towards Women Scale (Antill, Cotton, Goodnow, & Russell, 1993). Different scales were used for the two cohorts because the children entered our longitudinal study at different age. Given that different measures were used, youth's scores on each scale were standardized within cohort and birth order. The Attitudes Towards Women Scale, completed by youth who entered the study as adolescents, was the same measure as described above for parents. Cronbach's alpha was .80 for first- and .81 for secondborn siblings. The Children's Attitudes Towards Women Scale, completed by youth who entered the study in middle childhood, was a 19-item measure with responses ranging from 1 (*strongly agree*) to 4 (*strongly disagree*). A sample item was "Sons in a family should be given more help to go to college than daughters." Cronbach's alpha was .88 for first- and .83 for secondborn siblings. The youth's attitudes scores were computed by summing the scores for all 19 items, with higher scores indicating more traditional views on gender roles.

Parents' time spent on feminine household tasks—We assessed parents' participation in feminine household tasks via telephone interviews with parents. Specifically, mothers and fathers reported how much time they spend doing dishes, cooking meals, cleaning the house (e.g., dusting, washing floors), and doing laundry across the 4 days of time use data. These tasks were labeled as feminine tasks based upon prior theory and research (Atkinson & Huston, 1984). Additionally, a paired t-test showed that mothers in this sample reported spending significantly more time in these tasks than did fathers, $t(341) = 22.78, p < .01$. Reports of these activities were aggregated across the four calls each parent completed to construct measures of how much time mothers and fathers spent on stereotypically feminine household tasks. To correct for skewness, square root transformations of the total duration of time (minutes per 4 days) were used.

Parents' time with children—We assessed parent-child shared time via phone interviews with youth. Parent-child dyadic time (parent-child shared time with no one else present) was measured by summing the minutes each child reported spending alone with each parent across all activities and across the seven calls each child completed. To correct for skewness, square root transformations of the total duration of time (minutes per 7 days) were used.

Parents' marital conflict—Parents completed a 5-item scale developed by Braiker and Kelly (1979). A sample item was "How often do you feel angry or resentful toward your partner?" Responses ranged from 1 (*not at all*) to 9 (*very much*). Total marital conflict scores were computed by summing the score for each of the 5 items. Cronbach's alphas were .75 and .73 respectively for mothers' and fathers' reports on marital conflict.

Parent-child conflict—Youth completed an 11-item measure adapted from Smetana (1998). Youth reported on the frequency of conflict within 11 domains of daily life (e.g., chores, homework/schoolwork, social life, bedtime/curfew) respectively for mothers and fathers. Responses ranged from 1 (*not at all*) to 6 (*several times a day*). Total parent-child conflict scores were computed by summing the score for each of the 11 domains. A separate score was computed for each parent-child dyad (i.e., mother-firstborn, mother-secondborn, father-firstborn, father-secondborn). Cronbach's alpha coefficients ranged from .78 to .83.

Youth's conflict with siblings—Youth completed a 5-item scale developed by Stocker and McHale (1992). A sample item was, "How often do you feel mad or angry at your brother/sister?" Responses ranged from 1 (*not at all*) to 5 (*very much*). Total sibling conflict scores were computed by summing the score for each of the 5 items. Cronbach's alpha were .75 and .79 respectively for first- and second-born siblings' reports on sibling conflict.

Table 22.1 Means (and Standard Deviations) of all Variables Reported by Mothers, Fathers, and Youth

	Mothers	Fathers	Firstborns		Secondborns	
			Girls (N = 176)	Boys (N = 182)	Girls (N = 178)	Boys (N = 180)
Parents' Education	14.66 (2.19)[a]	14.60 (2.39)[a]	—	—	—	—
Parents' Income	24,756 (17,733)[a]	48,747 (28,158)[b]	—	—	—	—
Attitudes toward women	26.19 (6.05)[a]	28.11 (5.82)[b]	-.48 (.70)[a]	.45 (1.03)[b]	-.36 (.87)[a]	.35 (1.01)[b]
Parents' time on household tasks	18.07 (8.77)[a]	8.76 (5.13)[b]	—	—	—	—
Mothers' time with children	—	—	8.16 (5.44)[a]	4.46 (4.43)[b]	9.42 (5.49)[a]	6.42 (4.60)[b]
Fathers' time with children	—	—	4.87 (4.31)[a]	7.33 (5.78)[b]	6.30 (4.75)[a]	8.11 (6.01)[b]
Marital conflict	—	—	20.03 (6.28)[a]	18.28 (5.87)[b]	—	—
Mother-child conflict	—	—	23.53 (6.06)[a]	23.52 (5.94)[a]	24.43 (6.15)[a]	25.19 (7.06)[a]
Father-child conflict	—	—	21.97 (6.23)[a]	22.02 (6.12)[a]	22.22 (6.79)[a]	23.16 (6.54)[a]
Sibling conflict	—	—	18.85 (7.50)[a]	19.07 (7.23)[a]	19.42 (7.66)[a]	19.07 (7.33)[a]

Note. Mothers' and fathers' scores were compared using pair-sample t-tests. Girls' and boys' scores were compared separately for first- and secondborn siblings using independent sample t-tests; Scores for time variables represent square root transformations of number of minutes;

Scores for youth-reported gender role attitudes were standardized within cohort and birth order.

a, b, c Scores with different subscripts are significantly different, $p < .05$;

Table 22.2 Cross-Tabulation of Results of the Hierarchical and K-Means Clustering Techniques

Hierarchical	K-Means			
	Cluster 1	Cluster 2	Cluster 3	Total
Cluster 1	100	35	29	164
Cluster 2	0	108	18	126
Cluster 3	1	10	57	68
Total	101	153	104	358

RESULTS

Means and standard deviations of all variables in the study are shown in Table 22.1 separately for mothers, fathers, and female and male first- and secondborn siblings. Paired-sample t-tests showed that mothers had significantly lower income, $t(352) = -13.35, p < .01$, were more egalitarian, $t(357) = -5.18, p < .01$, spent more time on household tasks, $t(341) = 22.78, p < .01$, and reported higher levels of marital conflict compared to fathers, $t(353) = 5.28, p < .01$. Independent sample t-tests showed that first- and second-born girls were more egalitarian than firstborn, $t(356) = -9.95, p < .01$, and second-born boys, $t(356) = -7.09, p < .01$. Adolescents also spent more time with their same-sex parents: Whereas first- and second-born girls spent more time with mothers than did firstborn, $t(339) = 6.90, p < .01$, and second-born boys, $t(339) = 5.46, p < .01$, first- and second-born boys spent more time with fathers than did firstborn, $t(339) = -4.44, p < .01$, and second-born girls, $t(339) = -3.10, p < .01$.

Patterns of Gender Role Attitudes

Hypothesis (1) posited that cluster analyses would identify family patterns characterized by congruence and incongruence among family members' gender role attitudes. Prior to conducting the cluster analyses, all reports of attitudes were standardized so that variables with larger variances would not dominate the cluster solution. We compared several solutions with two-, three-, four- and five-cluster structures derived from hierarchical clustering. On the basis of several stopping criteria, including dendrogram patterns, interpretability, and cell size (Blashfield & Aldenderfer, 1988), we chose a three-cluster solution as the best characterization of the data. The solution was replicated by K-means clustering technique, $\chi^2(4) = 286.68, p < .01$ (see Table 22.2). Three patterns of families emerged were consistent with our expectation: A traditional group ($n = 164$), in which both parents

Table 22.3 Standardized Means (and Standard Deviations) of Clustering Variables by Family Types

	CLUSTER 1: TRADITIONAL	CLUSTER 2: EGALITARIAN	CLUSTER 3: DIVERGENT
Mother's Attitudes	.41 (1.01)[a, 1]	−.73 (.60)[b, 1]	.34 (.83)[a, 1]
Father's Attitudes	.18 (.91)[a, 2]	−.69 (.72)[b, 2]	.71 (.79)[c, .2]
Older Sibling's Attitudes	.57 (1.02)[a, 3, 4]	−.52 (.73)[b, 2]	−.45 (.57)[b, 3, 4]
Younger Sibling's Attitudes	.71 (.89)[a, 1, 3, 4]	−.57 (.69)[b, 1,2]	−.68 (.52)[b,1 3, 4]

Note.
[a,b,c] Scores with different subscripts within row are significantly different, $p < .05$;
[1,2,3,4] Scores with different subscripts within column are significantly different, $p < .05$.

and both siblings scored above the sample means on gender role attitude traditionality, an egalitarian group ($n = 126$), in which both parents and both siblings scored below the means on gender role traditionality, and a divergent group ($n = 68$), in which parents reported relatively more traditional, but siblings reported relatively less traditional attitudes (see Table 22.3 and Figure 22.1 for standardized means of the clustering variables).

To further test our hypothesis regarding the family patterns, we compared the clusters using a 3 (cluster) × 4 (family member) mixed model ANOVA, and found significant univariate effects for mothers', $F(2, 357) = 71.29$, $p < .01$, $\varepsilon = .53$, fathers' $F(2, 357) = 72.56$, $p < .01$, $\varepsilon = .53$, firstborns', $F(2, 357) = 65.70$, $p < .01$, $\varepsilon = .51$, and second-borns', $F(2, 357) = 131.12$, $p < .01$, $\varepsilon = .65$, gender role attitudes (see Table 22.3), as well as a

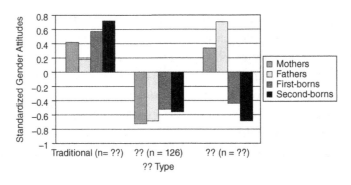

Figure 22.1. *Family Patterns of Gender Role Attitudes*

significant between groups effect of cluster, $F\ (2,\ 357) = 233.93,\ p < .01,\ \varepsilon = .75$, and a significant cluster × family member interaction, $F(2, 357) = 29.59, p < .01, \varepsilon = .37$.

Tukey follow-up tests for the univariate effects indicated that fathers in all groups were significantly different from each other in their gender role attitudes, with fathers in the divergent group reporting the most, and fathers in the egalitarian group reporting the least traditional attitudes. The results also showed that mothers in the egalitarian group were significantly different from mothers in both the traditional and divergent groups, but mothers in the traditional and divergent groups did not differ. Finally, both first- and second-born children in the traditional group were significantly different from those in the egalitarian and divergent groups, but there were no differences between the latter two groups.

To follow up the cluster × family member interaction, we examined difference scores between family members using Tukey follow-up tests. Beginning with mother-father

Table 22.4 Means (and Standard Deviations) of Demographic Variables, Parents' Household Tasks, and Parent-Child Shared Time by Family Types

	CLUSTER1: TRADITIONAL	CLUSTER2: EGALITARIAN	CLUSTER3: DIVERGENT
Control Variables			
Mothers' Education	14.31 (2.10)[a]	15.42 (2.20)[b]	14.07 (2.02)[a]
Fathers' Education	14.10 (2.22)[a]	15.43 (2.44)[b]	14.26 (2.32)[a]
Mothers' Income	22,666 (14,319)[a]	28,746 (28,478)[b]	21,632 (22,601)[a]
Fathers' Income	47,570 (27,462)[a]	53,127 (52,629)[b]	44,743 (45,130)[a]
Parents' Time			
Mother Feminine Tasks	18.26 (5.38)[ab]	17.18 (5.09)[a]	19.29 (4.92)[b]
Father Feminine Tasks	8.35 (5.26)[b]	9.73 (4.72)[a]	7.92 (5.32)[b]
Difference in Mother-Father Feminine Tasks	10.08 (8.06)[a]	7.58 (6.93)[b]	11.46 (6.73)[a]
Mother-Firstborns	6.06 (5.12)[a]	6.50 (5.42)[a]	6.65 (5.5)[a]
Mother-Secondborns	7.36 (5.24)[a]	8.35 (5.28)[a]	8.35 (5.27)[a]
Father-Firstborns	5.54 (5.18)[a]	5.95 (5.05)[ab]	7.58 (5.44)[b]
Father-Secondborns	7.37 (6.37)[a]	7.47 (4.55)[a]	6.40 (4.85)[a]

Note: Scores for time variables represent square root transformations of number of minutes.

[a, b, c] Scores with different subscripts are significantly different, $p < .05$;

Table 22.5 Distribution (and Cell Percentages) of Sibling Gender-Constellation by Family Types

	CLUSTER 1: TRADITIONAL	CLUSTER 2: EGALITARIAN	CLUSTER 3: DIVERGENT	TOTAL
Girl-Girl	22 (6.15%)	36 (10.06%)	30 (8.38%)	88
Girl-Boy	46 (12.85%)	30 (8.38%)	12 (3.35%)	88
Boy-Girl	42 (11.73%)	34 (9.50%)	14 (3.91%)	90
Boy-Boy	54 (15.08%)	26 (7.26%)	12 (3.35%)	92
Total	164	126	68	358

comparisons, these analyses revealed that parents differed from one another in both the traditional and the divergent groups such that fathers were less traditional than mothers in the traditional group, but more traditional than mothers in the divergent group. There were no differences between siblings in any of the groups. Finally, except for a father-second-born difference in the traditional cluster, the divergent cluster was the only family type in which parent–child differences were significant.

Conditions Underlying Family Patterns of Gender Role Attitudes

To identify the conditions under which different family patterns of gender role attitudes emerged, we conducted a series of mixed model ANOVAs and chi-squared analysis. Specifically, the analyses examined differences between the family clusters in terms of SES, parents' time spent on gendered household tasks, parents' time spent with children, and the sex constellation of the sibling dyad (see Tables 22.4 and 22.5).

Hypothesis 2(a) posited that parents in families characterized by more traditional gender role attitudes would have lower SES. A 3 (cluster) × 2 (parent) mixed model ANOVA revealed a significant effect of cluster on mothers' income, $F(2, 352) = 5.07$, $p < .01$, $\varepsilon = .15$, a trend-level effect of cluster on fathers' income, $F(2, 352) = 2.19$, $p < .11$, $\varepsilon = .08$, and a significant overall cluster effect, $F(2, 352) = 6.29$, $p < .01$, $\varepsilon = .17$. Tukey follow-up tests revealed that, consistent with our hypothesis, parents in both traditional and divergent families had significantly lower income than those in egalitarian families. Additionally, a 3 (cluster) × 2 (parent) mixed model ANOVA focusing on mothers' and fathers' education revealed a significant effect of cluster on mothers' education, $F(2, 355) = 13.01$, $p < .01$, $\varepsilon = .25$, father's education, $F(2, 355) = 13.08$, $p < .01$, $\varepsilon = .25$, and an overall between cluster effect, $F(2, 355) = 17.82$, $p < .01$ $\varepsilon = .29$. Consistent with our expectation, a Tukey follow-up test revealed that parents in both the traditional and divergent families had significantly lower levels of education than parents in egalitarian families. Given these findings and a significant correlation between parents' education and family income, $r = .51, p < .01$, we created a composite SES score, combining family income and both parents' education levels by standardizing each score and summing them. This SES index was used as a control variable in all remaining analyses.

Hypothesis 2(b) posited that parents in families characterized by more traditional gender role attitudes would have a more traditional division of household labor. A 3 (cluster) × 2 (parent) mixed model ANCOVA with parent as the within groups factor and SES as a control variable revealed a trend-level univariate cluster effect for mothers' participation in household tasks, $F(2, 336) = 2.51, p = .08, \varepsilon = .09$, a significant cluster effect for fathers' participation in household tasks, $F(2, 336) = 4.07, p < .01, \varepsilon = .13$, a significant overall parent effect, $F(2, 336) = 465.33, p < .01, \varepsilon = .85$, and a significant overall cluster × parent interaction, $F(2, 336) = 5.20, p < .01, \varepsilon = .16$. Tukey follow-up tests for the main effects for cluster showed that mothers in the divergent group spent more time on feminine household tasks than did mothers in the egalitarian group, and that fathers in the egalitarian group spent more time on feminine household tasks than fathers in both the traditional and divergent groups. The overall parent effect indicated that mothers generally spent more time on feminine household tasks than did fathers. However, consistent with our hypothesis, follow-up of the parent × cluster interaction indicated that mothers and fathers in the egalitarian group were more similar in time spent on feminine tasks as compared to the other groups.

Hypothesis 2(c) posited that fathers in families characterized by more traditional gender role attitudes would spend more time with their sons. Analyses of parents' time with children revealed no univariate cluster effect for mothers' time spent with children. However, a 3 (cluster) × 4 (gender constellation) × 2 (sibling) mixed model ANCOVA revealed a univariate cluster effect for older siblings' dyadic time with father, $F(2, 334) = 5.31, p < .01, \varepsilon = .16$, and a cluster × sibling interaction, $F(2, 334) = 4.75, p < .01, \varepsilon = .15$. A follow-up test of the univariate main effect showed that fathers spent significantly more time with their older children in the divergent group as compared to the traditional group. A Tukey follow-up test of the cluster × sibling interaction revealed that fathers in the divergent group spent more similar amounts of time with their two children compared to fathers in the traditional and egalitarian groups. Taken together, this pattern suggests that fathers in the divergent group were relatively more involved with their children.

Hypothesis 2(d) posited that families characterized by more egalitarian gender role attitudes would be more likely to have girl-girl sibling dyads than boy-boy or mixed-sex sibling dyads. A 3 (cluster) × 4 (gender constellation) chi-squared analysis, $\chi^2 (6) = 28.91, p < .01$, suggested that, in partial support of our expectation, the traditional family type included a preponderance of brother-brother pairs, whereas the divergent family type was made up largely of sister-sister

Table 22.6 Means (and Standard Deviations) of Family Conflict by Family Types

	CLUSTER 1: TRADITIONAL	CLUSTER 2: EGALITARIAN	CLUSTER 3: DIVERGENT
Parent-Child Conflict			
Mother-Firstborn	24.34 (6.29)[a]	22.98 (5.62)[a]	22.56 (5.72)[a]
Mother-Secondborn	25.71 (6.51)[a]	23.84 (6.50)[b]	24.46 (6.91)[ab]
Mother-Child	24.83 (4.69)[a]	23.27 (4.72)[b]	23.54 (4.77)[ab]
Father-Firstborn	23.11 (6.62)[a]	21.06 (5.77)[b]	21.05 (5.33)[ab]
Father-Secondborn	23.85 (6.74)[a]	21.42 (6.24)[b]	22.28 (6.88)[ab]
Father-Child	23.34 (5.11)[a]	21.21 (4.72)[b]	21.90 (4.83)[b]
Marital Conflict			
Mothers	19.66 (6.56)[a]	20.47 (6.06)[a]	20.27 (6.04)[a]
Fathers	18.36 (6.20)[a]	18.16 (5.66)[a]	18.37 (5.47)[a]
Sibling Conflict			
Firstborns	19.47 (7.27)[a]	18.41 (7.41)[a]	18.75 (7.49)[a]
Secondborns	19.70 (7.30)[a]	18.89 (7.81)[a]	18.78 (7.37)[a]

Note:
[a, b, c] Scores with different subscripts are significantly different, $p < .05$.

pairs. In addition, the egalitarian group had somewhat more sister-sister than brother-brother pairs. In contrast to our hypothesis, however, mixed sex dyads (sister-brother and brother-sister) appeared to be distributed equally across the family types (see Table 22.5).

Gender Role Attitudes and Family Conflicts

Hypothesis (3) posited that families characterized by incongruent gender role attitudes across family members would have higher levels of parent-child, marital, and sibling conflict compared to families characterized by congruent gender role attitudes across family members. A 3 (cluster) × 2 (parent) mixed model ANCOVA revealed no effects involving cluster for marital conflict. Similarly, a 3 (cluster) × 2 (sibling) mixed model ANCOVA revealed no effects involving cluster for sibling conflict. For parent-child conflict, however, a pair of 3 (cluster) × 4 (gender constellation) × 2 (sibling) mixed model ANOVAs revealed significant cluster effects for both mother- and father-child conflict, $F(2, 352) =$

3.90, $p < .01$, $\varepsilon = .13$, and $F(2, 352) = 6.15$, $p < .01$, $\varepsilon = .17$, respectively. Inconsistent with our hypothesis, Tukey follow-up tests revealed higher levels of mother-child conflict in the traditional group compared to the egalitarian group and higher levels of father-child conflict in the traditional group compared to the other two family types.

DISCUSSION

Although some researchers have begun to use person-oriented or pattern-analytic approaches to studying families (e.g., Crouter, McHale, & Tucker, 1999; Johnson, 2003), these approaches have traditionally been used to study individuals (Bergman, Magnusson, & El-Khouri, 2003). The current study demonstrates the utility of a pattern analytic approach for studying family systems. Our analyses revealed that families varied in their patterns of parents' and children's gender role attitudes. In the majority of families, there was congruence across four family members, in that all family members were either relatively more egalitarian or relatively more traditional as compared to individuals from other families. One group of families, however, showed an incongruent pattern in which both siblings displayed more egalitarian attitudes despite the more traditional views of their parents. This pattern is consistent with family systems notions about within-family variability. The emergence of a divergent pattern also suggests that, whereas social learning processes explain children's gender role attitude development in some families, different mechanisms may be at work in other families.

Our analyses revealed that between- and within-family comparisons provide somewhat different pictures of family attitude congruence and divergence: In both the divergent and traditional groups, mothers and fathers also differed in their attitudes, such that fathers in the divergent group were more traditional than their wives, and mothers in the traditional group were more traditional than their husbands. As we have suggested, most studies of gender attitudes focus on individuals or dyads. Our family-oriented approach reveals a more complex set of processes than has been found in prior work.

There were no instances in which two siblings differed from each other in their gender role attitudes. Social learning mechanisms may be functioning in these families such that younger siblings model the gender role attitudes of their older siblings (e.g., McHale et al., 2001). Future work exploring the relationships between siblings' gender role attitudes over time could provide further insight into the social learning processes that impact gender role development throughout adolescence.

Conditions Underlying Family Patterns

In exploring the conditions underlying these family patterns, the results were consistent with earlier studies in showing that parental education and income distinguished families with more traditional attitudes from those with more egalitarian attitudes (e.g., Bolzendahl & Myers, 2004). The divergent group was also characterized by lower education and income, as would be expected given parents' traditionality; however, in this family type, as noted, the attitudes of children were more egalitarian. Although the attitudes of parents in this group may have been grounded in socioeconomic factors, it appears that those of their children were not.

In addition to background characteristics, family patterns of gender role attitudes also differed in terms of parents' time use within the family. The divergent group exhibited a seemingly paradoxical pattern. On the one hand, parents in this group displayed a more traditional division of household labor; on the other hand, fathers appeared to be more involved with their children compared to fathers in other family types. Although the traditional division of household labor fits with the traditional gender attitudes of the parents in this group, the relatively high involvement in children on the part of fathers suggested less traditionality. High paternal involvement in the divergent group is particularly noteworthy, given that girl-girl sibling dyads were over-represented in this group and that fathers in this group reported the most traditional attitudes. Notably, although mothers in this group reported more traditional attitudes compared to other mothers, they were less traditional than their husbands. The findings illustrate the multidimensionality of gender: A person with traditional gender role attitudes does not necessarily exhibit gender-typed behaviors in all domains of life.

The findings also provide some insight into the basis for the incongruence between parents' and children's attitudes in the divergent families. When fathers differ in their attitudes and behaviors, their messages to their children about gender may be diluted. Despite the traditional attitudes of both parents, children in these families (daughters in particular) may notice the more egalitarian side of their fathers and react against their mother's traditional role in domestic labor. This highlights the complexity of socialization influences: both mothers' *and* fathers' attitudes *and* behaviors may be important in children' gender attitude development.

Our results revealed that family patterns of gender role attitudes were linked to the sex constellation of the sibling dyad. It was having not just one, but two girls, however, that increased families' chances of falling into the divergent group, and having not just one, but two boys that increased families' chances of falling into the traditional group. Although one cannot draw causal inferences from a correlational study like this one, it seems more sensible to conclude that the sex constellation of the dyad "caused" the family pattern of gender role attitudes rather than the other way around. Other researchers have pointed to the importance of considering the role of child effects in shaping the family environment and experiences (Bell & Chapman, 1986; Crouter & Booth, 2003; Russell & Russell, 1992), and yet there is a tendency in family and child development research to assume unidirectional effects from parents to children. McHale and Crouter (2003) have previously demonstrated the important role that the sex of children plays in shaping family dynamics. Other research examining parents' differential treatment of siblings suggests that the sex constellation of siblings may influence the levels and types of parents' behaviors toward each of their children (e.g., McHale, Updegraff, Jackson-Newsom, Tucker, & Crouter, 2000). Future researchers may gain new insights when moving beyond between- to within-family comparisons.

Particularly important was the finding that having not one, but two children of a particular sex distinguished between the family clusters. In the case of the divergent group in which sister-sister pairs were more common, girls may have found it easier to express attitudes that were inconsistent with parents' when they had support from their sisters. Similarly, the higher number of sister-sister pairs in the divergent group may explain mothers' less traditional attitudes relative to fathers, in the sense that having two daughters may encourage mothers to gravitate toward less traditional attitudes. In the traditional group, in contrast, the preponderance of boys in these families may have limited parents' exposure to and understanding of issues related to gender discrimination and equality that may arise when raising daughters.

Family Gender Role Attitudes and Family Conflict

Contrary to expectations, there was no evidence that the attitude incongruence of the divergent group had negative implications for parent-child relationships. Instead, there were higher levels of parent-child conflict in the traditional families. Importantly, this family type had an abundance of boy-boy pairs. One possible explanation of the high conflict, then, is that a high value placed on "masculinity" in these families could encourage more stereotypically masculine relationship behaviors, such as dominance, competition, and aggression (Maccoby, 1990; Thompson & Pleck, 1986). Furthermore, the traditional gender role attitudes of parents may be coupled with more authoritarian parenting styles that have implications for conflict with sons and daughters. Interestingly, mothers in this group were more traditional than fathers, and it is possible that this relative incongruence between parents' attitudes fueled conflict among parents and children.

Limitations and Future Directions

This investigation provides a contribution to understanding how families work as systems. Nonetheless, there remain some issues to be addressed in future research. First, this study was limited to a cross-sectional analysis. In order to fully understand the processes involved in the formation of family patterns of attitudes, longitudinal studies are vital. Although it may seem logical to conclude that the sex constellation of sibling dyads exerted an influence on family patterns of attitudes rather than the other way around, a longitudinal analysis exploring the development of gender role attitudes within the family could help to pinpoint the unique way in which parents and children impact the family system. Just as children's gender role attitudes may arise through developmental processes, patterns of family attitudes may ebb and flow. Similarly, longitudinal analyses are necessary to better understand what experiences and conditions precede the divergence of attitudes among family members and whether these differences have implications over the long-run.

A second limitation of our study pertains to the generalizability of the results. Although the participants reflected the demographic characteristics of the region in which they resided, the sample was fairly homogenous, both in terms of ethnicity and SES. Gender role orientations are not only multidimensional within family systems, but also across different family contexts. As such, these patterns of gender role attitudes may not be universal. The results of the cluster analysis should be replicated in other samples before drawing conclusions about the nature and correlates of family gender role attitude patterns.

Finally, the measure of parent-child conflict may be limited in its validity. Although the 11 domains assessed in the parent-child conflict scale certainly represent domains of family life that may trigger conflict, it is possible that these domains more closely represent household disciplinary or regulatory practices. Future studies could validate the findings in this study related to conflict by using alternative measures of parent-child conflict.

In conclusion, our findings highlight the importance of measuring the gender role attitudes of multiple family members. By examining family patterns of gender role attitudes rather than just focusing on individuals or single dyads, a deeper understanding of the processes involved in gender role attitude development, among both parents and children, can be gained. As this study demonstrates, gender role attitudes are connected to aspects of family life, including relationship quality and division of labor, and are shaped by the family context in which they are embedded.

ACKNOWLEDGMENTS

The authors are grateful to their undergraduate and graduate student, staff, and faculty collaborators, as well as the dedicated families who participated in this project. This work was funded by grants from the National Institute of Child Health and Human Development, R01-HD32336 and R01-HD29409, Ann C. Crouter and Susan M. McHale, Co-Principal Investigators.

REFERENCES

Acock AC. Parents and their children: The study of intergenerational influences. Sociology and Social Research. 1984; 68:151–171.

Allen WD, Olson DH. Five types of African-American marriages. Journal of Marriage and Family Therapy. 2001; 27:301–314.

Ansbacher, HL.; Ansbacher, RR. The individual psychology of Alfred Adler. Basic Books; New York: 1956.

Antill JK, Russell G, Goodnow JJ, Cotton S. Measures of children's sex typing in middle childhood. Australian Journal of Psychology. 1993; 45:25–33.

Antill JK, Cunningham JD, Cotton S. Gender-role attitudes in middle childhood: In what ways do parents influence their children? Australian Journal of Psychology. 2003; 55:148–153.

Atkinson J, Huston TL. Sex role orientation and division of labor early in marriage. Journal of Personality and Social Psychology. 1984; 46:330–345.

Atzaba-Poria N, Pike A. Are ethnic minority adolescents at risk for problem behaviour? Acculturation and intergenerational acculturation discrepancies in early adolescence. British Journal of Developmental Psychology. 2007; 25:527–541.

Bandura, A. Social Learning Theory. Prentice Hall; Englewood Cliffs, NJ: 1977.

Bell RQ, Chapman M. Child effects in studies using experimental or brief longitudinal approaches to socialization. Developmental Psychology. 1986; 22:595–603.

Benin MH, Agostinelli J. Husbands' and wives' satisfaction with the division of labor. Journal of Marriage and the Family. 1988; 50:349–361.

Bergman, LR.; Magnusson, D.; El-Khouri, BM. Studying individual development in an interindividual context: A person-oriented approach. Lawrence Erlbaum; Mahway, NJ: 2003.

Blair S. The sex-typing of children's household labor: Parental influence on daughters and sons' housework. Youth and Society. 1992; 24:178–203.

Blashfield, RK.; Aldenderfer, MS. The methods and problems of cluster analysis. In: Nesselroade, JR.; Cattell, RB., editors. Handbook of multivariate experimental psychology: Perspectives on individual differences. 2nd ed.. Plenum Press; New York: 1988. p. 447–473.

Bolzendahl CI, Myers DJ. Feminist attitudes and support for gender equality: Opinion change in women and men, 1974–1998. Social Forces. 2004; 83:759–790.

Burleson BR, Denton WH. A new look at similarity and attraction in marriage: Similarities in social-cognitive and communication skills as predictors of attraction and satisfaction. Communication Monographs. 1992; 59:268–287.

Braiker, HB.; Kelley, HH. Conflict in the development of close relationships. In: Burgess, R.; Huston, T., editors. Social exchange in developing relationships. Academic Press; New York: 1979. p. 135–168.

Brooks C, Bolzendahl C. The transformation of US gender role attitudes: Cohort replacement, social-structural change, and ideological learning. Social Science Research. 2004; 33:106–133.

Cassidy ML, Warren BO. Family employment status and gender role attitudes: A comparison of women and men college graduates. Gender & Society. 1996; 10:312–329.

Cook JL, Jones RM. Congruency of identity style in married couples. Journal of Family Issues. 2002; 23:912–926.

Collins WA, Russell G. Mother-child and father-child relationships in middle childhood and adolescence: A developmental analysis. Developmental Review. 1991; 11:99–136.

Cox MJ, Paley B. Families as systems. The Annual Review of Psychology. 1997; 48:243–267.

Crompton R, Lyonette C. The new gender essentialism—domestic and family `choices' and their relation to attitudes. The British Journal of Sociology. 2005; 56:601–620. [PubMed: 16309438]

Crouter, AC.; Booth, A. Children's influence on family dynamics: the neglected side of family relationships. Lawrence Erlbaum; Mahwah, New Jersey: 2003.

Crouter AC, McHale SM, Bartko WT. Gender as an organizing feature in parent-child relationships. Journal of Social Issues. 1993; 49:161–174.

Crouter AC, McHale SM, Tucker CJ. Does stress exacerbate parental differential treatment of siblings? A pattern-analytic approach. Journal of Family Psychology. 1999; 13:286–299.

Crouter AC, Whiteman SD, McHale SM, Osgood DW. Development of gender attitude traditionality across middle childhood and adolescence. Child Development. 2007; 78:911–926. [PubMed: 17517012]

Crow JF, Felsenstein J. The effect of assortative mating on the genetic composition of a population. Eugenics Quarterly. 1968; 15:85–91. [PubMed: 5702332]

Cunningham M. Parental influences on the gendered division of housework. American Sociological Review. 2001; 66:184–203.

Eccles JS. Understanding women's educational and occupational choices: Applying the Eccles et al. model of achievement-related choices. Psychology of Women Quarterly. 1994; 18:585–609.

Epstein E, Guttman R. Mate selection in man: evidence, theory, and outcome. Social Biology. 1984; 31:243–278. [PubMed: 6400148]

Ferree MM. Beyond separate spheres: Feminism and family research. Journal of Marriage and the Family. 1990; 52:866–884.

Fisher L, Ransom DC. An empirically derived typology of families: I. Relationships with adult health. Family Process. 1995; 34:161–182. [PubMed: 7589416]

Fowers BL, Olson DH. Four types of premarital couples: An empirical typology based on REPARE. Journal of Family Psychology. 1992; 6:10–21.

Fortin NM. Gender Role Attitudes and the Labour-market Outcomes of Women across OECD Countries. Oxford Review of Economic Policy. 2005; 21:416–438.

Harris KM, Morgan SP. Fathers, sons, and daughters: Differential paternal involvement in parenting. Journal of Marriage and the Family. 1991; 53:531–544.

Henry DB, Tolan PH, Gorman-Smith D. Cluster analysis in family psychology research. Journal of Family Psychology. 2005; 19:121–132. [PubMed: 15796658]

Ickes W. Traditional gender roles: Do they make, and then break, our relationships? Journal of Social Issues. 1993; 49:71–85.

Johnson VK. Linking changes in whole family functioning and children's externalizing behavior across the elementary school years. Journal of Family Psychology. 2003; 17:499–509. [PubMed: 14640800]

Kaslow F, Robison JA. Long-term satisfying marriages: Perceptions of contributing factors. American Journal of Family Therapy. 1996; 24:153–170.

Kulik L. The impact of social background on gender-role ideology. Journal of Family Issues. 2002; 23:53–73.

Lackey PN. Adult attitudes about assignments of household chores to male and female children. Sex Roles. 1989; 20:271–282.

Luo S, Klohnen EC. Assortative mating and marital quality in newlyweds: A couple-centered approach. Journal of Personality and Social Psychology. 2005; 88:304–326. [PubMed: 15841861]

Lye DN, Biblarz TJ. The effects of attitudes toward family life and gender roles on marital satisfaction. Journal of Family Issues. 1993; 14:157–188.

Lytton H, Romney DM. Parents' differential socialization of boys and girls: A meta-analysis. Psychological Bulletin. 1991; 109:267–296.

Maccoby EE. Gender and relationships. American Psychologist. 1990; 45:513–520. [PubMed: 2186679]

Maccoby, EE. The gender of child and parent as factors in family dynamics. In: Crouter, AC.; Both, A., editors. Children's influence on family dynamics: The neglected side of family relationships. Lawrence Erlbaum Associates; Mahwah, NJ, US: 2003. p. 191–206.

Martin CL, Ruble D. Children's search for gender cues: Cognitive perspectives on gender development. Current Directions in Psychological Science. 2004; 13:67–70.

Martin CL, Ruble DN, Szkrybalo J. Cognitive theories of early gender development. Psychological Bulletin. 2002; 128:903–933. [PubMed: 12405137]

McHale, SM.; Crouter, AC. How do children exert an impact on family life?. In: Crouter, AC.; Both, A., editors. Children's influence on family dynamics: The neglected side of family relationships. Lawrence Erlbaum Associates; Mahwah, NJ, US: 2003. p. 207–220.

McHale, SM.; Kim, J.; Whiteman, SD. Sibling relationships in childhood and adolescence. In: Noller, P.; Feeney, J., editors. Close Relationships. Psychology Press; 2006. p. 127–150.

McHale SM, Updegraff KA, Helms-Erikson H, Crouter AC. Sibling influences on gender development in middle childhood and early adolescence: A longitudinal study. Developmental Psychology. 2001; 37:115–125. [PubMed: 11206426]

McHale, Updegraff KA, Jackson-Newsom J, Tucker CJ, Crouter AC. When does parents' differential treatment have negative implications for siblings? Social Development. 2000; 2:149–172.

Minuchin, S. Families and family therapy. Harvard University Press; Cambridge, MA: 1974.

Raley S, Mattingly MJ, Bianchi SM. How Dual Are Dual Income Couples? Documentary Change from 1970 to 2001. Journal of Marriage and the Family. 2006; 68:11–28.

Risman BJ, Myers K. As the twig is bent: Children reared in feminist households. Qualitative Sociology. 1997; 20:229–252.

Ross CE, Mirowsky J, Huber J. Dividing work, sharing work, and in-between: Marriage patterns and depression. American Sociological Review. 1983; 48:809–823. [PubMed: 6666885]

Ruble, DN.; Martin, CL.; Berenbaum, S. Gender Development. In: Eisenberg, N., editor. Handbook of Child Psychology: Vol. 3. Social, Emotional, and Personality Development. 6th ed.. Wiley; New York: 2006. p. 858–932.

Russell A, Russell G. Child effects in socialization research: Some conceptual and data analysis issues. Social Development. 1992; 1:163–184.

Serbin LA, Powlishtak KK, Gulko J. The development of sex typing in middle childhood. Monographs of the Society for Research in Child Development. 1993; 58(2, Serial No. 232)

Spence, JT.; Helmreich, RL. Masculinity and femininity: Their psychological dimensions, correlates, and antecedents. University of Texas Press; Austin: 1972.

Stocker CM, McHale SM. The Nature and Family Correlates of Preadolescents' Perceptions of their Sibling Relationships. Journal of Social and Personal Relationships. 1992; 9:179–195.

Tenenbaum HR, Leaper C. Are parents' gender schemas related to their children's gender-related cognitions? A meta-analysis. Developmental Psychology. 2002; 38:615–630. [PubMed: 12090490]

Thompson EH, Pleck JH. The structure of male norms. American Behavioral Scientists. 1986; 29:531–543.

Thompson L, Walker AJ. Gender in families: Women and men in marriage, work, and parenthood. Journal of Marriage and the Family. 1989; 51:845–871.

Tsai-Chae AH, Nagata DK. Asian values and perceptions of intergenerational family conflict among Asian American students. Cultural Diversity and Ethnic Minority Psychology. 2008; 14:205–214. [PubMed: 18624585]

White LK, Brinkerhoff DB. The sexual division of labor: Evidence from childhood. Social Forces. 1981; 60:170–181.

Whiteman S, Loken E. Comparing analytic techniques to classify dyadic relationships: An example using siblings. Journal of Marriage and Family. 2006; 68:1370–1382.

Ying YW, Han MY. The longitudinal effect of intergenerational gap in acculturation on conflict and mental health in Southeast Asian American adolescents. American Journal of Orthopsychiatry. 2007; 77:61–66. [PubMed: 17352586]

Zuo J, Tang S. Breadwinner status and gender ideologies of men and women regarding family roles. Sociological Perspectives. 2000; 43:29–43.

SWALLOWED UP BY LIFE

By Jules O'Neal

D ays go by, weeks go by, and I am not sure where I am at; I feel swallowed up by life. What part of my life you ask? Is it my part time work that is new to me, teaching some college courses? Is it managing my son's special needs, school issues for him, finding more treatment for him and contemplating his fate? Is it worrying about my daughter who is a 13 year old with social skills problems, no friends, her own trauma, as well as being traumatized by her brother in her own home? Is it being a single parent? Is it trying to process the separation from my husband for almost 5 years? Is it trying to do regular tasks in life? Is it my inability to find balance and peace?

As I was walking out of class a few weeks ago heading to my car I couldn't even think about what to think about first as things in my head were swirling around. How will I ever write an essay in six weeks, what shall I write about, is it long enough, short enough, meaningful enough, well I have forty eight years of experience to draw from.

Remember the book I started to write on the day of my forty-fifth birthday which was called "Today I Turned 45" but I can't recall the password I used in Word, to protect my life in writing?

Stop, think, focus, prioritize and give my worries to God. Jesus is with me each step of the way, though I do not call on him often enough and wish I could practice being in His presence more regularly. But know he is there; likely carrying me as in the poem Footprints.

O'Neal, J. (2014). Swallowed up by life. In S. Torres, Jr. (Ed.), *Palabra: The Book of Living Essays* (pp. 166–175). Sacramento, CA: Petraglyph Publishing.

In reflecting, I would say balance is likely my most predominant struggle, losing myself amongst these many factors. I go to church regularly and I love the experience. I attend women's Bible study group usually weekly and I… A) get a break from my children, B) socialize, C) I can pray, think, and receive prayer and support, D) learn about what the Bible has to teach me and more importantly attempt to apply this knowledge to my life, E) I feel pampered by our wonderful group leader who presents me, and my sisters in Christ, with a peaceful, calm, and inviting environment. Why can't I keep this with me when I walk out the door?

Well let's see what have I done to not be swallowed up? I keep the radio and television turned off most days and I LOVE the silence. However, I am not so good with news worthy information and current events. I have a small but powerful support system of friends and family. One friend in particular would get the Purple Heart of Friendship if there were such an award. What I don't know is where I would be in life without her. I have other wonderful women too; my mother, step-mother and mother-in-law, sometimes my sisters (all 5 of them and after all they are my *sisters*), and my sisters-in-law, and my husband, all who rally around me, provide me different aspects of support for different aspects of my life. Oh yeah, I don't want to forget my two brothers, who have helped shape me and support me. What about ALL the people who have been in my life path both in a positive and negative manner? I must not leave out my father, father-in-law, and Nani (grandmother) who have passed from this earth, but who are loved and missed dearly.

Not having my contract renewed from my job, due to health reasons, from a highly stressful job with tons of vicarious trauma for the past eight years in addition to the previous fifteen; what a blessing for real. I realized I am also traumatized in my own home primarily by my son and his yelling, screaming, obsessive, deviant, erratic and impulsive behaviors each day, in which he is physically aggressive towards things, but not usually people, though at times, his sister may be at the receiving end.

So how do I keep doing life and not be swallowed up? Maybe it is my son's sense of humor, his creativity, his loving heart, beautiful smile, his unique perspectives and intelligence. Maybe it is my broken heart for my daughter's difficult life, and my guilt of not attending to her more. Maybe it is her intelligence, potential, strengths, beauty, smile, caring heart, and wittiness and the beautiful being and little girl I hear and see inside of her. Her radiance as she sleeps. Ahh, I can see some peace for her. Oh wait and my son is sleeping and he is peaceful too, THANK YOU JESUS … how they need these moments and how these moments provide me strength for life. Is it the fact that rarely, does a day go by, that they don't make me smile, laugh, or touch my heart in some manner?

Maybe it is my sense of humor, my sarcasm, the laughter of my friends and family as I recount incidents in my home daily that no one could make up even if they tried. Does my yelling get me through at times, as so sadly that is the best that I can do at some moments? God has equipped me well for this job of parenting, but sometimes I don't know how to do it alone. I think of Jesus as my co-parent, so He can bring some yin to my yang, the one I can ALWAYS turn to, like He is in the room with me. It truly takes a village to hold each child up. Hold my children up in front of me to see their strengths and weaknesses that I am blind too. Is it the love and support of my friends and family for me as a woman, mother, daughter, estranged wife, or sister?

I am unsure of the days that have gone by and forget what day it is, I feel scattered, and overwhelmed. I want to open my brain and heart to the world around me, but I am swallowed up by life. At times I feel self-involved, self-centered, selfish, demanding and entitled. At times I am angry, frustrated, fed up, and exhausted. Sometimes I feel like a conqueror, defender, advocate, protector, and champion.

My seven siblings alone could fill up the pages of my life and one reason why I feel swallowed up by life, and they can be the reason I stand proud to be a good listener, supporter, and encourager of life.

How does one achieve balance, acceptance, peace, and mindfulness? Yes, I am aware of the many books, resources, classes, techniques, and behaviors; but how does one begin to pick an area and begin to work on it, while being swallowed up by life?

Wait, my home is quiet, the kids are gone, I can eat what I want and not share. I can sit where I want, and move where I want, when I want. It is quiet; I do not feel swallowed up by life at this moment. Can I turn this moment into a few or several moments? Will my brain switch to the gigantic TO DO list in my head that I can't even put down on paper?

Ugh, I have to pack and move in two to three months. I have papers to grade, laundry, grocery shopping, phone calls, emails, text messages, cleaning, organizing, doctor appointments, babysitters, bank deposits, and preparation for classes, all to complete and attend too. Now preparing myself to pick up my children and spend almost every minute of the next 30 hours together!?!

Okay, that was just a quick sidebar into my mind, as my life *ATTEMPTS* to swallow me up, but it won't, I will not allow it, those around me will not stand for it, and others will dismiss it's power against me.

So as life tends to swallow parts of me up and at many times many, many parts of me up, I don't allow it. After all it is only life; my life, the **gift** that has been given to me for now, until I move on to eternal life. It is a season at a time, a day at a time. It is 48 years and hopefully many more to go.

Me versus life, me being my life, me being in my life, me being scared of life, me embracing and respecting life, and me loving life, this is my life. I will not be swallowed up today!

The Inspiration for the Essay

When asked to write this essay, after being extremely thrilled and honored to be part of this project, I began to ponder, contemplate, worry, and obsess on what to write about that was an important topic or something close to our hearts. As time continued to tick away, my anxiety rose, in addition to the stressors in my personal life. While sharing my woes with a dear friend I found myself texting that I was busy trying to not be "swallowed up by life," so I could focus on writing this essay. This phrase brought me to the place where I thought my life and stressors were of the utmost importance to me, at that time in my life, hence I spoke from my heart and released on the day I typed.

About the Author

Julie Ann (Jules) O'Neal has her Master of Social Work Degree, is a Licensed Clinical Social Worker, and a licensed School Social Worker in Illinois. She has practiced in the field of child welfare for over 20 years. Most of her work has focused on families, teens, and youth which has encompassed direct practice, supervision, management, consultation and private practice. She has done work with various facets of police social work, juvenile detention and juvenile corrections. She has extensive training experience in completing a variety of assessments, including children zero to three years of age. Other areas of specialization include working with children on the Autism Spectrum, trauma, attachment issues, adoption and special education. Jules taught English in Taiwan and continued her work in child welfare services while residing in the US Virgin Islands. Additionally, she is an adjunct professor with George Williams College of Social Work at Aurora University. She is married, has adopted two special needs children and has been a foster parent.

CAROL, ANNA, AND KHADIA: WORK WITH A THREE GENERATION BLACK FAMILY

By Veronique Faure

PURPOSE OF THE INTERVENTION

Anna (aged 16, Jamaican) has a child, Khadia (age 3). She became pregnant at the age of 12 by her step-brother Roy (also Jamaican), who was 17 at the time (see genogram, Figure 24.1). Both Anna and Roy were then living with Anna's mother Carol and their two half-sisters, Clare and Ginette. Roy's father had died five years earlier. Anna had become pregnant at the same time as her mother. Roy first admitted and then denied being Khadia's father. He was prosecuted and found guilty of four charges of unlawful sexual intercourse and sentenced to one year's imprisonment.

Carol was initially supportive to Anna. She decided on Roy's prosecution as a result of his denial that he was Khadia's father, which led to family and community feuds, and allegations that "Anna was probably sleeping with lots of boys". The relationship between Anna and Carol, however, deteriorated, leading to Anna and Khadia being accommodated with a friend.

This broke down after a few months and they were accommodated with a foster carer. This broke down after a year, leading to another placement, which recently also broke down. Anna and Khadia returned to live with Carol against their wishes, as social services did not have another placement to offer. The placements were considered to have broken

Faure, V. (2000). Carol, Anna and Khadia: Work with a three generation black family. In H. Martyn (Ed.), *Developing Reflective Practice: Making Sense of Social Work in a World of Change* (pp. 169-176). Bristol, UK: The Policy Press.

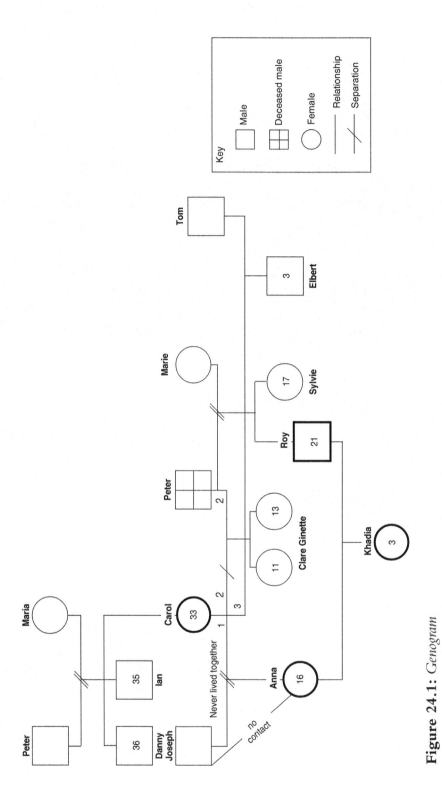

Figure 24.1: *Genogram*

down as a result of Anna falling out with the carers following arguments around Khadia's care, and the carers' feelings that Anna was failing to take responsibility for Khadia.

Anna and Khadia's social worker, Maxine (also Jamaican), became concerned that Khadia's needs for stability and consistency were not being met, and about the impact that placement breakdowns were having on her, as well as on Anna (who attends college full time.) Also, a new issue had come to Maxine's attention, in relation to Roy having recently resumed contact with Khadia. Contact was said to take place at the grandmother's house, supervised by Carol and Anna.

Due to pressure of other work, Maxine had had little time to allocate to Anna and Khadia, other than dealing with numerous practical issues and offering Anna support at times of breakdowns. She had been working with them for almost a year. She had tried to do work with Anna earlier around her experience and feelings about Roy and Khadia but without success, as Anna was unwilling to explore these issues. Her work with Carol had been mainly to do with seeking her cooperation in making care plans for Anna and Khadia.

Carol was adamant that she could not continue to look after Anna as they did not get on, but was prepared to look after Khadia as long as Anna was accommodated. Anna was happy with this plan. Maxine was also prepared to support the plan as she felt it met Khadia's needs for stability and consistency and Anna's need for space to finish her studies. In the light of Roy resuming contact with Khadia, however, she felt a child protection assessment needed to be carried out and requested a co-worker to do the assessment with her, as she felt she might fail to be objective in the assessment of risk due to her close relationship with the family.

ASSESSMENT

Both Anna and her mother Carol had been offered counselling together and separately at the earlier and later stages of social work involvement, but had declined. Anna and Carol both failed to see Anna and Roy's sexual relationship as child sex abuse (CSA). Both had said that Anna had consented to the sexual relationship which was 'not incestuous' as they were only step siblings. Roy's prosecution had been seen by both as a means to force Roy to take responsibility for his paternity.

Anna had been given the choice by her mother of terminating the pregnancy but decided not to, although her mother had made it clear that even if she offered Anna practical support, the baby would be Anna's responsibility. Anna accepted this. Maxine's assessment was that even if Anna had always taken some responsibility for Khadia's care, as she grew up she had started to resent it. This had lead to confusion of roles between her and her carers and to placement breakdowns.

Maxine gave Anna a lot of credit for pursuing her studies and for her educational achievements, and felt that Anna needed to be relieved of Khadia's care. Anna's emotional bond with Khadia was considered to be often very distant, although she could not be faulted for her physical care. Anna and her mother's relationship was also felt to be distant emotionally. Khadia and her grandmother's relationship was considered to be warm and close.

I felt very strongly that the issues in this case had been so numerous and complex over the years that the family, as well as the social workers involved, had colluded with not addressing the issue of CSA, which had remained unresolved. From file notes, it seemed no groundwork had been done about CSA and I believed this to be causal to Anna/Carol's and Anna/Khadia's poor relationships. Also, if Khadia was to remain in their care, they had to be aware of the risk presented by Roy, not only to Khadia, but also to Anna's sisters who were now much the same age that Anna was at the time of the abuse.

My starting point was that Anna and Roy's sexual relationship was undoubtedly a case of CSA, as Anna, aged 12, could not have consented to sex whatever her feelings for Roy; and that the relationship was incestuous, even if they were step siblings, as they had been brought up as siblings for eight years. I felt the basic groundwork needed to be done with the family before they could challenge their own beliefs about what constituted CSA. This included sharing findings from research by those who worked with perpetrators of CSA.

THEORETICAL BASE AND METHODS USED

I approached this work from a feminist perspective on CSA. MacLeod and Saraga (1987) describe the feminist premise about CSA as follows:

> Men, in learning to become men, learn they have a right to be sexually and emotionally serviced by women; they learn that their power can ensure that this happens, and that in order to feel like a man, they have to feel powerful. Within the family, women are relatively powerless in relation to men, and children even more so. (p 24)

While the feminist perspective does not preclude factors such as class, culture or race which may compound the problem, CSA is seen primarily as a problem of gender (the majority of abusers are men), and of how society views male sexuality and dominance (the abuse occurs in 'ordinary' families, not just deviant ones). There are other hypotheses which may be compatible with this analysis, including the concept of abuse as "compensation for perceived lack and loss of power" (Finkelhor, 1984, quoted in VACSG, 1990, p 19) or as "an expression of frustration or anger" (Hartman, 1979, quoted in VACSG, 1990, p 19).

From studies on male perpetrators (for example Wyre, 1987) we learn how the emotionally vulnerable child in the family may be engaged in a trusting relationship, 'groomed' by a process of seduction, of entrapment and isolation, resulting in the child feeling confused and possibly believing (s)he consented to, encouraged and is responsible for the abuse.

It seemed essential in our work with this family that both Anna and Carol understood this process, to break the myth of Anna's consent. The power differentials in Anna and Roy's relationship had to be acknowledged, not only in terms of gender but also of age. It is well established that a majority of sex offenders begin their abusive career in adolescence, and this had to be borne in mind while raising Carol and Anna's awareness of the possibility of Roy re-offending and presenting a risk to Khadia and Anna's sisters.

Maxine and I intended to extend the family work to Anna's sisters at a later stage, as their views and understanding seemed essential in preventing any reoccurrence of abuse within this family.

PROCESS OF THE WORK

There were two stages to our work. The first involved a great deal of preparation for our intervention. The second was the actual work with the family, which failed as far as family work is concerned, as the relationship and communication between Carol and Anna completely broke down after our third session.

Preparation

Maxine acknowledged having little practice, experience and knowledge of CSA and felt overwhelmed by the complexity of the issues involved in this case. Although I had worked on a number of CSA cases, done a lot of reading and attended a one-year course at the Portman and Tavistock Clinic (Child Sexual Abuse within the Family: An Inter-Agency Approach, 1991–92), I was by no means an expert on CSA and felt equally anxious at the number of issues to be borne in mind, even if I felt more confident in addressing them. Over a few weeks, I collected a number of articles and books which I had found particularly helpful in understanding the dynamics involved in CSA and shared them with Maxine.

I believed it was important that Maxine felt equally empowered in understanding issues of CSA so that she could fully participate in the work. As a white worker I was anxious not to be oppressive in my joint work with a black colleague and a black family. Maxine's sensitivity to the family's experience of alienation from their past encounters with white workers was a real asset to my developing understanding of anti-discriminatory practice.

Intervention

We met on three occasions with Carol and Anna (at Carol's home). Carol quickly engaged in our work but Anna often remained quiet and silent. We started by dealing with the 'here and now', that is, our child protection concerns about Roy's contact with the family and the risk he might present to children. This was initially dismissed by Carol as she accounted for what she believed had happened between Anna and Roy as 'two teenagers exploring their sexuality'. Maxine and I were able to counteract her beliefs by raising the power differentials in age, gender and sexual maturity between Anna and Roy, leading to power imbalance, and how this, we believed, had been abused by Roy.

Anna stated her very strong, although confused, feelings for Roy and felt she did consent to the sexual relationship. We explored this further, until Anna acknowledged that she felt driven to the sexual relationship and was actually never asked by Roy if this was alright with her. She became very tearful at this point and agreed that if she was not asked, she could not consent.

We worked with Carol's initial stated anger at Roy for what she saw as abuse of *her* trust (she had left him in charge at home while she attended an evening course, which is when the abuse took place). It became clear that Roy had assumed a parental/paternal role in the family as he grew up after his father's death.

As the work carried on we encouraged Anna to become aware also of her anger towards Roy, which she had suppressed because of her guilt about his prison sentence and current inability to find a job because of this. Quite unexpectedly Carol started disclosing issues that were unknown to Maxine and previous social workers: her own history of sexual abuse by her father at the age of 10, the matrimonial violence suffered by her mother who escaped to America a few months after Carol's disclosure of abuse, and her care history as a result (Anna had knowledge of all of this).

Carol talked about how she had learnt to become detached and unemotional and acknowledged the impact this had had on her relationship with Anna. Anna in turn acknowledged the same process and impact on her relationship with Khadia. Carol's suppressed feelings of guilt became evident to Maxine and me as she talked about how determined she had been to ensure that her children would never go through the same experience of CSA, leading to her rationalisation that Anna and Roy's sexual relationship had nothing to do with CSA.

The day before our fourth session, Anna presented herself as homeless at the office. Her mother had 'chucked her out' after an argument about Anna coming home very late.

Khadia was with her, despite Carol offering to keep her. They were accommodated in a hotel with social work support as no other placement was available.

The work currently being done with Anna and Carol, separately as they are not now talking, is around stabilising Khadia's situation, although Anna is now certain that she wants to continue looking after Khadia herself. There is uncertainty still as to whether the family work could be resumed at a later stage.

EVALUATION OF THE INTERVENTION

We aimed to work in a way which confronted the family's denial and minimisation of CSA while not being inappropriately oppressive to either Carol or Anna, and in a way which we hoped would validate their feelings of confusion, anger and guilt. Although I believed we partly succeeded in raising their awareness as to what truly happened in their family, denial and minimisation had served a purpose. There had been 'coping/defence mechanisms' which had allowed the family to survive and continue to function, at least in their ability to offer each other practical support.

I feel, however, that Maxine and I failed to evaluate the seriousness, in terms of impact and implications, that shaking a family's belief system would have on the dynamics of individual relationships (not just Carol and Anna's, but also theirs in relation to Khadia, Roy, the extended family and the community). I also question the timing of our intervention. This work needed to have been done earlier, not at a time of crisis when both Anna and Khadia's situations were unsettled. This met the agency's need to carry out a risk assessment at that particular time, which was probably not a safe time for the family, and I fear that it might have further damaged Carol and Anna's relationship.

In Maxine's continued work with Anna, however, what she feels we might have achieved is to have empowered and enabled Anna to feel strong enough to think about confronting her mother and Roy, and stand more independently and confidently in the assessment and decisions she is making about what has happened and what should happen next.

Anna, for instance, has decided that she wants to carry on addressing some of the issues we raised and is seeking counselling. She says she does not want to avoid confronting the issues any more as she wants to be prepared for dealing with Khadia who, as she grows up, will ask questions and need explanations about her parentage.

The work is not concluded. There is no final resolution of any of the issues that still need addressing (in terms of child protection and Khadia's need for consistent parenting and stability), and this is ongoing. What I feel emerged from our work, as practitioners and not as experts, is a true reflection of our striving to come to grips with the various perspectives, theories and skills which we judged to be helpful in working with this family, and effective in enabling them to confront some of their difficulties.

🙟 Section 3 🙝

Critical and Creative Thinking Resources

USE OF THESE LEARNING ACTIVITIES AND RESOURCES

The activities and resources provided in this section are aimed at supporting the learner as they apply critical and creative thinking. Our hope is that faculty who might adopt the book will find these useful as assignments and/or in-class activities. Many of these activities were created by us and others have been modified from sources utilized in our teaching. A recent learning tool, the Evidence-Based Self-Assessment (EBSA), is a learner-centered tool that we have created and now use in all of our classes; therefore, we wanted to also include it here. We would appreciate any feedback on your use of any of these resources, and do ask that if you use or adapt any of our material to please request permission first.

ANALYZING THE LOGIC/ REASONING OF AN ARTICLE

When completing this assignment, it is expected that the student will answer the questions delineated below on a separate sheet of paper. Students should not try to write a paper but rather address each question completely. One-word or short-phrase answers are not acceptable. Thoughts should be more developed than that.

1. The main purpose of this article is _____.

    (State as accurately as possible the author's purpose for writing the article.)

2. The key question that the author is addressing is _____.

    (Figure out the key question in the mind of the author when the article was written.)

3. The most important information in this article is _____.

    (Figure out the facts, experiences, and data the author is using to support their conclusion(s).)

4. The main inferences/conclusions in this article are _____.

    (Identify the key conclusions the author comes to and presents in the article.)

5. The key concept(s) we need to understand in this article is (are) _____. By these concepts the author means _____. (Figure out the most important ideas you would have to understand in order to appreciate the author's line of reasoning.)

6. The main assumption(s) underlying the author's thinking is (are) _____. (Figure out what the author is taking for granted and that might be questioned.)

7. a) If we take this line of reasoning seriously, the implications are _____.
    (What consequences are likely to follow if people take the author's line of reasoning seriously?)

8. b) If we fail to take this line of reasoning seriously, the implications are
    _____. (What consequences are likely to follow if people ignore the author's reasoning?)

9. The main point(s) of view presented in this article is (are) _____.

    (What is the author looking at, and how are they seeing it?)

(Adapted from Paul and Elder, 2009, p. 11)

ARTICLE CRITIQUE AND INTERVIEW ASSIGNMENT: TOP FIVE READS IN YOUR PROFESSION

This assignment is designed to give students an opportunity to identify and critique what they consider to be some of the most important readings in their profession. You are to identify the current five must-read articles in your field. An important resource is an instructor or program director. You should interview them to learn or compare notes with them on what the current five most important articles are in your field. Your paper will include an annotation for all five (see "How to Annotate") but a critique of only one. The article you critique will need to include the components listed.

Assignment Requirements and Instructions
Cover Page

The paper should have a separate cover page with your name, the course name and number, the term and year, and the instructor's name. The paper itself should be two to three typewritten, double-spaced, and numbered pages, using a 12-point font and 1-inch margins. Students are required to use the heading and numbering system provided.

I. **Bibliographic Citation**
   Use APA style to format the article citations (see General APA Format Guide). Also, identify by name and title the instructor or program director you interviewed as part of this assignment.

II. **Summary**
   Before addressing this article specifically, explain how it is a "top read" in your profession or discipline. Next, write a summary of the main points of the article. Include in this section the author's goals and hypothesis. The hypothesis consists of the point and purpose of the article.

III. **Methodology**

Briefly discuss how the author(s) gathered data (casework, participant observation, surveys, random observations, etc.).

IV. **Data**

What are the actual findings, conclusions, or results? Be selective and cite the more representative ones, particularly those relating to the author's goals and hypothesis.

V. **Analysis**

Having identified the actual findings, what is their overall significance? How do they support the goals of the author? Be selective and cite the ones most relative to the hypothesis.

VI. **Personal Reaction**

Identify aspects of the article that were particularly enjoyable and/or informative to you. Again, be sure to cite evidence to support your statements. You may want to include here why the person you interviewed in your field thought this particular article was a must-read in your field and whether you agree or disagree.

(Created by Debra Welkley and Santos Torres Jr.)

A TOOL FOR ASSESSING THE CREDIBILITY OF INFORMATION FOUND ON THE INTERNET

Website name: _____

Subject: _____ Author: _____ Date of Access: _____

URL: _____

Sponsoring organization: _____ Date on website: _____

Domain name: _____ .com   _____ .edu   _____ .gov   _____ .org   _____ other

Criterion #1 — Credibility

1. Does the site display the name or logo of the institution or organization responsible for the webpage? _____ Yes   _____ No
2. Is there a source of works cited?   _____ Yes   _____ No
3. Do you recognize the author(s) or institution as an expert in the subject? _____ Yes _____ No   Why/why not? _____
4. Based on this information, the website is   _____ Credible _____ Not Credible

Criterion #2 — Bias

1. What does the domain name tell you about the website?
2. Is there a hidden message? Explain.
3. What is the purpose of the website?
4. Based on this information, the website is _____ Credible _____ Not Credible

Criterion #3 — Accuracy

1. Are the grammar and the spelling correct? _____ Yes _____ No
2. Is the information consistent with information from other sources and your previous knowledge? _____ Yes _____ No
3. Based on this information, the website is _____ Credible _____ Not Credible

Criterion #4 — Currency

1. Is the information up to date? _____ Yes _____ No
2. When was the information last revised?
3. Based on this information, the website is _____ Credible _____ Not Credible

Criterion #5 — Usefulness

1. Are there links to other websites related to the topic? _____ Yes _____ No
2. Is the information presented easy to understand? _____ Yes _____ No
3. Is the website easy to navigate? _____ Yes _____ No
4. Based on this information, the website is _____ Credible _____ Not Credible
5. Based on your overall observations, is this a worthwhile website for your research needs? _____ Yes _____ No

(Adapted from Diestler, 2009, pp. 197–200)

BOOK CRITIQUE

Students are given a list of six or seven books from which they choose one to read and then write this book critique. This critique has been used as the major paper which students submit at the end of the course and then share during a roundtable discussion.

I. **Bibliographic Reference**
Cite the book in APA format.

II. **Author's Background**
Provide an overview of the author's background. What makes them an expert relative to the material they write about, what are their credentials, etc.?

III. **Primary Issue Explored**
Identify the social issue primarily discussed by the author. Indicate what leads you to this understanding. Can you frame it in the form of a question and/or did the author do that for you? Be sure to refer to specific information and pages where applicable.

IV. **Author's Conclusion/Premise**
Indicate what the author's overall premise is in the book. This may be a bit challenging, as we will have been dealing with articles throughout the semester. Be sure to indicate what leads you to identifying this as the author's premise. Be sure to include citations where appropriate.

V. **Development of Reasoning**
Identify how the author develops his or her reasons. This will require that you indicate what reasons the author points to in order to support his or her premise. This section is where you will provide facts, examples, reasons, sub-reasons, research, experiments, opinions, etc., that are provided by the author. Remember, try to keep this focused on what the author provides. Be sure to give specific examples and cite appropriately.

VI. **Assessment and Evaluation**
How well do you think the reasons and information presented by the author support his/or her conclusion? Be specific in your discussion. Be sure to apply critical thinking skills we have been working with throughout the semester regarding

clarity, validity, quality, fallacy identification (if there are any), etc. Be sure to provide support for your analysis and cite where appropriate.

VII. **Personal Reaction**

Identify and state your position relative to the issue discussed by the author. Do you agree or disagree with his/her premise? Why? Be sure to support your position clearly and logically. Discuss what the opposing side says in response to this argument and evidence and then rebut it to further support your position. Also address any fallacies in the opposing arguments.

VIII. **Personal Application**

How can you apply and/or use the information you gained from this book? How do you intend to use this information in your professional and/or personal life in the future? Be specific.

(Created by Debra Welkley and Santos Torres, Jr.)

CRITICAL AND CREATIVE THINKING – INTERACTIVE READING FORM (IRF)

This form was created to aid readers when identifying the important parts of an article and to then assess the article by applying their critical and creative thinking skills.

Name: _____ Date: _____

1. **Citation of the article (in APA format):**

2. **Briefly state the primary issue discussed in the article.**

3. **Identify the conclusion/premise. Specifically identify it with a page number and the quotation itself, then indicate how/why you believe this to be the conclusion.** (As you provide your rationale, incorporate information provided in article 1.)

4. **Are there any key concepts? If so, what are they?** (Keep in mind what a *key concept* is. It is not a key or main point, but a word or abstract idea presented by the author.)

5. **Identify at least three main reasons (and their evidence, examples, and support) that the author(s) uses in an attempt to support the identified conclusion statement.**

6. **Evaluate and assess the reasons (as well as the key concepts, facts, and examples) provided as to how they relate to and/or support the conclusion.** (Your discussion here should be specific. Apply the critical thinking skills discussed in the course, such as clarity, validity, quality, fallacy identification, etc., where applicable. Examine the *standards of reasoning* handout found in the text to use in your evaluation. Be sure to explain.)

7. **What is YOUR overall view/opinion of the article? How do the pieces fit together? What biases of yours were impacted? Be sure to explain.**

8. **Generate at least two questions based on your reading of this article.**

(Created by Debra Welkley)

CRITICAL AND CREATIVE THINKING: INVENTORY

On a scale of 1 to 10, rate yourself on the following when you examine information presented (e.g., in an article, the news, or a lecture). Circling "1" is very low and circling "10" is very high. There is no right or wrong, just your self-assessment.

1. Ability to be fair minded:
   1-----2-----3-----4-----5-----6-----7-----8-----9-----10

2. Ability and/or tendency to ask questions:
   1-----2-----3-----4-----5-----6-----7-----8-----9-----10

3. Confidence in identifying the important points in an article:
   1-----2-----3-----4-----5-----6-----7-----8-----9-----10

4. Understanding of the research process:
   1-----2-----3-----4-----5-----6-----7-----8-----9-----10

5. Ability to assess data presented by an author:
   1-----2-----3-----4-----5-----6-----7-----8-----9-----10

6. Consideration of language used:
   1-----2-----3-----4-----5-----6-----7-----8-----9-----10

7. Awareness of own biases:
   1-----2-----3-----4-----5-----6-----7-----8-----9-----10

8. Comfortability with being incorrect:
   1-----2-----3-----4-----5-----6-----7-----8-----9-----10

9. Initiative to look deeper:
   1-----2-----3-----4-----5-----6-----7-----8-----9-----10

10. Ability to articulate your position clearly and with rational support:
    1-----2-----3-----4-----5-----6-----7-----8-----9-----10

After completing the inventory, add up your points and write the total here: _____. Now take a few minutes to notate areas in which you believe you can improve your skills and what this rating means to you as you think about your critical thinking abilities.

(Created by Debra L. Welkley)

CRITICAL AND CREATIVE THINKING JOURNAL

Throughout the semester students could be asked to write Critical and Creative Thinking Journal entries. The questions posed for possible entries are provided below (some mirror questions posed previously in the book).

Students are asked to incorporate class discussion and other course reading material as they respond to the listed questions. Most importantly, they should continually be thinking and expanding how they can demonstrate critical and creative thinking skills as they respond to questions for these entries.

Critical and Creative Thinking Journal 1—Respond to the following having read the first three chapters of this text:

1. What are your strongest critical and creative thinking skills?
2. In what ways do you think you can improve your critical and creative thinking skills? How will you do that during this semester?
3. What questions can you develop that would help broaden your understanding of the information covered thus far in the course?
4. Anything else you believe would be important to reflect on as you integrate your critical and creative thinking skills.

Critical and Creative Thinking Journal 2—Respond to the following after reading the article found in the textbook, "Why Sexist Language Matters", by Sherryl Kleinman (found in the *Gender* subsection in Section 2):

1. What do you believe is the overall point in Kleinman's article and how well does she support her position?
2. What is your reaction to Kleinman's position? Do you agree or disagree?
3. What questions are you left to consider after reading this article and reflecting on critical and creative thinking skills?
4. Anything else you believe would be important to reflect on as you integrate your critical and creative thinking skills.

Critical and Creative Thinking Journal 3—Respond to the following after reading the three articles found in the section *Research: Thinking about the Hard Stuff* (the first set of articles in Section 2):

1. Have you ever found that you have fallen into "statistical traps"?
2. In what ways do you believe your critical and creative thinking skills were strengthened by exposure to the information contained in these articles?
3. How can critical and creative thinking help you when considering the quality and value in quantitative and qualitative research?

Critical and Creative Thinking Journal 4—Respond to the following after reading the section *Gender: Women and Children First*:

1. Having read the section *Gender: Women and Children First*, what are your thoughts about gender equality in society today?
2. What critical and creative thinking techniques do you think would be helpful in assessing Nichols's (2011) statement that "disrupting the work-play binary [will] open up new ways of orienting to education and social participation"?

Critical and Creative Thinking Journal 5—Respond to the following after reading all of the articles in *Race and Immigration: Confusion and Illusion* found in Section 2 of the text:

1. What did you find most interesting or informative in the information presented in these articles (you may or may not agree with the author, but it can still be interesting or informative)?
2. Using this subset of articles as a starting point, what do you think the dialogue regarding race, ethnicity, immigration, and culture will be like in a hundred years from now?
3. In what ways do you think political, social, cultural, and economic factors contributed to the construction of our modern conception of race? What impact do you think our current conceptualization of race is having on our society?
4. After reading these articles, are there questions you can develop to help broaden your understanding of race and immigration?

Critical and Creative Thinking Journal 6—Respond to the following after reading the articles found in *Family: Sorting Out the Pushes and Pulls* in Section 2 of the text:

1. After reading the section *Family: Sorting Out the Pushes and Pulls*, what are some ways you can apply Bernacki's attributes for "thinking outside the box" (addressed at the beginning of Chapter 3 of this book) in terms of your family or upbringing?
2. What connections can one draw between the articles by O'Neal and Marks, Bun, and McHale?
3. Anything else you believe would be important to reflect on as you integrate your critical and creative thinking skills.

(Created by Debra Welkley and Santos Torres, Jr.)

CRITICAL THINKING: ELEMENTS AND STANDARDS

ELEMENTS OF CRITICAL THINKING/REASONING/READING	STANDARDS OF CRITICAL THINKING/REASONING/READING
These do not need to be addressed in a linear fashion; they are dynamic to the process.	These should be applied to the elements to check the **quality** of the reasoning.
• **Purpose**—What is my purpose? What is the author's purpose? • **Questions**—What questions do I want to explore or raise? What questions are being addressed? What are the key questions raised by the author? • **Information**—What information/data am I using to come to a conclusion? What information do I need to settle the question? What information/data/evidence does the author present? • **Inferences/Conclusions**—How did I reach this conclusion? Is there another way to interpret the information? What key conclusions is the author coming to? Are those conclusions justified? • **Concepts (Key Concepts)**—What important or instrumental concepts guide my reasoning? What important or instrumental concepts guide the author's reasoning? Are these concepts defined or explained? • **Assumptions**—What am I taking for granted with my reasoning, conclusion, etc.? What assumptions led me to my conclusion? What is the author taking for granted? Are there underlying assumptions in the author's conclusion? How are these demonstrated in the evidence? • **Implications/Consequences**—If someone accepted my position on this issue, what would be the implications? What am I suggesting? What is the author suggesting one should accept if one sees the reasoning in the author's position? • **Points of View**—From what point of view am I looking at this issue? Is there another point of view to consider? What is the author's point of view? Were other points of view considered by the author?	• **Clarity**—Is the author clear, or is further explanation necessary? • **Accuracy**—Are the statements or claims of the author true, or should they be questioned? • **Relevance**—Does the author support his or her views with relevant reasons and evidence (meaning, is there a rational relationship)? • **Depth**—Do the author's answers address the complexities in the questions at issue? Does the author's reasoning lead to significant and far-reaching implications? • **Logic**—Does the author's reasoning make sense? Do the conclusions follow from the information given? • **Breadth**—Does the author approach the issue(s) from multiple viewpoints (where relevant) or is the reasoning too narrowminded? Are opposing viewpoints considered?

(Adapted from Paul & Elder, 2004)

EVIDENCE-BASED
SELF-ASSESSMENT RUBRIC

(You may want to highlight or change the font color for the area(s) you select)

Areas	Not Complete Omitted	Low "I consider my work/participation/preparation as unsatisfactory in some regard."	Average "I consider my work/participation/preparation as meeting expectations as identified in the syllabus."	Above Average "I consider my work/participation/preparation as *exceeding* requirements and *going above and beyond* what is expected."
Task Completion		I complete assigned work. Yet, my work reflects a very basic understanding of an assignment(s) and barely meets the minimum expectations.	I complete assigned work. My work demonstrates a clear understanding of the directions and meets the identified expectations. However, I did not move much beyond this level.	I complete assigned work and demonstrate a clear understanding of the assignment(s). However, it moves beyond the basic instructions and demonstrates my ability to apply concepts and connect different elements of the course together even though that might not have been stated in the instructions.
Preparation		I read but do not reflect on the readings prior to class. After preparing an assignment, I submit it without ensuring the work is written clearly and is corrected for grammatical errors. I seldom prepare questions to ensure I understand assignments and the material. I attend group meetings most of the time, but do not prepare information or work for that particular meeting; I wait to do it when we are together.	I read and quickly reflect on the readings prior to class. After preparing an assignment, I review it once before submitting to see if there are any errors that glare at me. From time to time I prepare questions, but not always. I attend group meetings and prepare based on what we all said we would do the time prior.	I read, review, and reflect on the material covered prior to class. I think of questions to ask and bring notes from my reading and reflection. After preparing an assignment, I review it for writing errors and clarity several times and may have someone else proof it as well. I attend group meetings and prepare what was agreed upon the time prior but also consider what we need to do next to contribute that to the group when we get together.

Participation		I attend class but do not ask questions. I am sometimes responsive when the instructor asks questions. When participating in small group discussions, I talk as little as possible so I can listen to everyone else. In my assigned, small group, I attend the meetings but do not provide much information. I wait to be assigned aspects of the project. I do not post often to the online discussions but I read some of my peers' comments.	I attend class and sometimes ask questions. I am responsive when the instructor poses questions. When participating in small group discussions, I talk and listen to everyone in the group. In my assigned, small group, I attend and readily contribute to the group process. I post on time to the online discussions and respond to my peers on a consistent basis.	I attend class and pose questions that add to the lecture or class discussion. I am responsive when the instructor poses questions and am able to connect concepts presently covered with ones already covered. When participating in small group discussions, I readily contribute and encourage others to contribute, and listen attentively. In my assigned, small group, I attend and readily contribute to the group process. My contributions move the group work forward in ways that go beyond the expected level of participation. I post on time to the online discussions and respond to peers in ways that help to support our learning and move the conversation forward.

NAME THAT FALLACY

Divide the class up into teams of three (3) to five people. At the beginning of the class, ask for two volunteers (they will act as the timekeeper, scorekeeper, and referees if there is a **challenge** invoked). The team with the most points at the end of class will be the winning team.

The overall objective of this activity is to familiarize students with the form of various fallacies so that they will be able to identify their use in articles, speeches, books, and arguments given in other situations.

Game Rules and Scoring

Objective: To accumulate points by correctly identifying/naming fallacies.

1. The instructor will read a fallacy example and each team will have a turn. The first team will have **30 seconds** to identify the **type of fallacy** demonstrated by the example.
2. If the team answers correctly, they will receive **one point** and the next team will have a turn.
3. If the team answers incorrectly, the next team will have **15 seconds** to answer, and if correct, will receive a **half point**.
4. If the second team is incorrect, there will be an opportunity for all teams to bid to answer and receive **one fourth of a point**. The instructor will count to three and the first team to have **their spokesperson raise their** will be called upon to immediately provide the correct answer. If the answer is incorrect, the instructor will give the correct answer and the question is "dead." (Each team has been given a colored index card for this part of the game.)
5. The next round begins.

Challenging a Fallacy Example: If a team provides an incorrect answer to an example but wants to support the correctness of their response, they can invoke a challenge, but only after all steps above have occurred **and before the next round**.

Within five seconds of invoking the challenge, the team spokesperson will then need to provide a rationale for why they believe their fallacy identification is correct relative to the example given and not the one on the card. The **referees** will hear this challenge and decide together whether to agree with the challenging team. When a team invokes a challenge and the **referees** agree with the validity of their challenge, the team will then receive **one point**; however, if the referees disagree with the validity of their challenge, the challenging team will lose **one half point**.

Reward

Once a team obtains three points, they can have some candy.

The team with the most points wins the *Name That Fallacy* game!

THINKING CRITICALLY ABOUT MOVIES

In order to think critically about movies, it is important to understand their basic elements, which are the same as those in short stories, novels, and plays.

Characters
Identify the characters by name. How are they presented?

> **Note:** During the class session prior to playing the game, introduce the fallacies and have students generate examples that demonstrate the different fallacies. Use those for the game. After several semesters of using this game, I (Debra Welkley), now have a stack of questions to choose from and am able to substitute with new and more current examples.

Setting
Notate the elements of setting: time, place, and circumstances in which the story takes place.

Plot
This is the sequence of events in the story. The essential element in a movie plot is conflict. The conflict may be external or merely within the characters' minds. However, this is what they struggle to resolve.

Theme
The theme of a movie is the message or lesson offered. Generally, not stated directly, yet dialogue in the movie may contain statements that clearly imply it.

(Adapted from Ruggiero, 2012, p. 176)

WEBSITES AND RECOMMENDED VIDEOS

Websites

These can be used in the classroom as part of an assignment or assigned to students to complement the content covered in the course and expand students' critical and creative thinking.

Six Critical Thinking Skills You Need to Master Now: Grant Tilus outlines and describes six core critical thinking skills. Application exercises are provided for each of these identified skills.
http://www.rasmussen.edu/student-life/blogs/main/critical-thinking-skills-you-need-to-master-now/

Al Jazeera: Focusing "on people and events that affect people's lives," this media network brings "topics to light that often go underreported, listening to all sides of the story and giving a 'voice to the voiceless'."
http://www.aljazeera.com/

Creative Thinking Skills: Information found at Skills You Need assists thinkers with their creative thinking skills and how they are complementary but different from critical thinking skills.
https://www.skillsyouneed.com/ps/creative-thinking.html
https://www.skillsyouneed.com/ps/understanding-creative-thinking.html

Critical and Creative Thinking: This University of Michigan website provides information on how these ideas interrelate, along with possible class activities.
http://www.umich.edu/~elements/probsolv/strategy/crit-n-creat.htm

Foundation for Critical Thinking: The work of the Foundation is to integrate its research and theoretical developments, and to create events and resources designed to help educators improve their instruction.
http://www.criticalthinking.org/

Study Guides and Strategies: A resource that is learner centered and provides various study guides and strategies relative to creative thinking, critical thinking, problem solving, time management, stress management, research, reading, and more.
http://www.studygs.net/creative.htm

The Daily Show: An American late-night satirical television program.
http://thedailyshow.cc.com/

The Onion: An American digital media company and news satire organization.
http://www.theonion.com/

Thinker Academy: A website that gives information on critical thinking specifically targeting for teens with the overall purpose being to "advance the science of thinking and learning for education."
https://thinkeracademy.com/critical-thinking-skills/

Recommended Videos

These can be used in the classroom, as part of an assignment, etc.

Absolute Truth—What is Truth? "Randall Niles looks at Unchanging Truths in a Changing World. Absolute Truth is defined as inflexible reality: fixed, invariable, unalterable facts. For example, it is a fixed, invariable, unalterable fact that there are absolutely no square circles and there are absolutely no round squares." (YouTube) The speaker challenges the listener to consider what is true and whether or not there are any absolute truths.
http://www.youtube.com/watch?v=ZgUiVfeRFDA&feature=youtu.be

Danger of the Single Story "Novelist Chimamanda Adichie tells the story of how she found her authentic cultural voice—and warns that if we hear only a single story about another person or country, we risk a critical misunderstanding." (TedTalks)
http://www.ted.com/talks/chimamanda_adichie_the_danger_of_a_single_story

On Being Wrong "Most of us will do anything to avoid being wrong. But what if we're wrong about that? 'Wrongologist' Kathryn Schulz makes a compelling case for not just admitting but embracing our fallibility." (TedTalks)
http://www.ted.com/talks/kathryn_schulz_on_being_wrong

Race: The Power of an Illusion (Part 1) "This episode shows that despite what we've always believed, the world's peoples simply don't come bundled into distinct biological groups. We begin by following a dozen students, including Black athletes and Asian string players, who sequence and compare their own DNA to see who is more genetically similar. The results surprise the students and the viewer, when they discover their closest genetic matches are as likely to be with people from other 'races' as their own.

Much of the program is devoted to understanding why. We look at several scientific discoveries that illustrate why humans cannot be subdivided into races and how there isn't a single characteristic, trait—or even one gene—that can be used to distinguish all members of one race from all members of another." (PBS.org)

What do we do with all this big data? "Does a set of data make you feel more comfortable? More successful? Then your interpretation of it is likely wrong. In a surprisingly moving talk, Susan Etlinger explains why, as we receive more and more data, we need to deepen our critical thinking skills. Because it's hard to move beyond counting things to really understanding them." TedTalks)
http://www.ted.com/talks/susan_etlinger_what_do_we_do_with_all_this_big_data

WHAT IS CRITICAL THINKING?

Break into groups of five. Give the groups the instructions once they have completed each step. Before they get started, have them identify a "notetaker." The notetaker should fold a sheet of paper lengthwise. The first column (left side of the paper) will be the first step and the second column (right side of the paper) will be the second step.

First: Brainstorm and generate a list of names of as many *people* (real and/or fictional) as possible who you would say are *critical thinkers*. If others in the group don't know who a person is, explain, but everyone does not need to agree. You are generating a list.

Second Look at your list and generate another list of the *characteristics* that were/are part of what makes the people on your list *critical thinker*.

Third Group those characteristics to the extent that you can. ***Remember*** to group the characteristics, **not** the thinkers, on the other side of the page.

Fourth: As a group, you need to develop (and agree on) a definition for critical thinking. Your definition should start out with:

"Critical thinking is … "

Final Process: Now have a spokesperson from each group share their definition. Also, process the activity with the class and have them discuss the characteristics that are important to critical thinking.

(Modified over the last two decades from an unknown original source.)

Glossary

Accuracy — free from error or defect; consistent with a particular standard or rule

Analysis — careful study of something; detailed examination

Assumptions — something taken for granted; a thing that is accepted as true or certain without proof

Bias — concentration on or interest in one particular area or subject; if unacknowledged, may create a distortion of the information

Clarity — quality of being easily understood; clearness of thought

Conclusion statement — response to the identified issue; author's position

Connotation — idea or feeling that a word or phrase carries or holds; contextual meaning

Critical thinking elements — eight basic structures that are present in all thinking (purpose/goal, question at issue/problem to be solved, information, inferences, concepts, assumptions, implications/consequences, point of view)

Critical thinking intellectual traits — seven or eight identified characteristics that critical thinkers should be invested in cultivating and perfecting (fair-mindedness, faith in reason, intellectual perseverance, intellectual integrity, intellectual empathy, intellectual courage, intellectual humility)

Critical thinking standards — set of specific items that one should review and uncover when engaging in critical thinking (clarity, breadth, depth, accuracy, logic, precision, significance, fairness, relevance)

Cultural lens — way of viewing a situation or the world that has been influenced by one's background, experiences, prior knowledge, etc.

Deductive analysis — top-down logic; reasoning from one or more general statements to reach or end up at a logically certain conclusion; moves from the general to the specific

Denotation — literal or primary meaning of a word; dictionary definition

Depth — provides or demonstrates complexity and moves beyond the surface of information

Elements of an argument/Structure of an argument —

Ethnocentrism — judging another's values, beliefs, and behaviors based on one's own cultural viewpoint

Evaluation — determine the significance or worth of the reasoning provided and the included evidence

Evidence — available facts or information that can be used to support a broad reason or conclusion

Fair-mindedness — impartial, honest, open way or manner of thinking or consideration

Fallacy — mistaken belief, error in reasoning, reasoning trap

Hypothesis — proposed explanation based on available evidence that needs further investigation

Identification — the act of discovering or pinpointing facts, parts of an argument, evidence, etc.

Inductive analysis — aims to generate theory; reasoning that considers specific pieces of information to generate a general statement or idea; moves from the specific to the general

Issue — specific dimension of a topic explored

Key concept — abstract idea or term that is particularly important in an argument; defining or explaining such terms provides clarity in the argument

Point of view — a particular outlook or manner of consideration

Population — the group of people the researcher seek knowledge about

Quality — the degree of excellence something has

Reasoning — the process of forming a conclusion

Reasons — evidence or support provided for a conclusion

Reflective thinking — personal consideration of one's own learning

Relevance — connection to the matter being addressed

Research design — a systematic plan or set of steps to study a problem or dimension of society

Sample — a segment of the population the researcher seeks knowledge about

Soundness — set of reasoning statements that not only fits a deductive or logical form but is also "true"

Symbols — signs with meaning

Topic — subject or topic of discussion

Truth — quality or state of being "real" or factual

Validity — set of reasoning statements that fits a deductive or logical form

Values — one's judgment of what is important, good, appropriate, etc.

Credits: Readings for Application

Research: Thinking About the Hard Stuff

Schuman, H. (2002). Sense and nonsense about surveys. *Contexts, 1*(2), 40-47.

Bracey, G. W. (2006). *How to avoid statistical traps. Educational Leadership, 63*(8), 78-82.

Weiss, R. S. (2008). In their own words: Making the most of qualitative interviews. In J. Goodwin & J. M. Jasper (Eds.), *The Contexts Reader* (pp. 498-506). W. W. Norton & Company, Inc.

Gender: Women and Children First

Kleinman, S. (2002). Why sexist language matters. *Qualitative Sociology, 25*(2), 299-304.

Couture, K. A., & Johnson, K. R. (2011). The persistent disadvantage facing mothers working in gender-neutral occupations. *Journal of Applied Management and Entrepreneurship, 16*(1), 53-65.

Nichols, S. (2011). Girls and boys, work and play: gendered meanings and participation in early childhood education. In B. J. Irby & G. H. Brown (Eds.), *Gender and Early Learning Environments* (pp. 29-46). Information Age Publishing.

Rochlin, M. (1972). *The heterosexual questionnaire.*

Education: Equalizer or Replicator

Haimson, L., & Ravitch, D. (2013). Unequal schools. *The Nation*, 41-43.

Young, C., Austin, S., & Growe, R. (2013). Defining parental involvement: Perception of school administrators. *Education, 133*(3), 291-297.

Kahlenberg, R. D. (2010). 10 myths about legacy preferences in college admissions. *Chronicle of Higher Education*.

Race and Immigration: Confusion and Illusion

Lee, E. K. O., Blythe, B., & Goforth, K. (2009). Teaching note: Can you call it racism? An educational case study and role-play approach. *Journal of Social Work Education, 45*(1), 123-129.

Moylan, A. (2014). The one who left. In S. Torres, Jr. (Ed.), *Palabra: The Book of Living Essays* (pp. 88-109). Sacramento, CA: Petraglyph Publishing.

Bowie, S. (2014). In search of country: how chasing the American dream can become a nightmare. In S. Torres, Jr. (Ed.), *Palabra: The Book of Living Essays* (pp. 250-263). Sacramento, CA: Petraglyph Publishing.

Cole, J. (2012, August 9). Top ten differences between white terrorists and others. Retrieved from http://www.juancole.com/2012/08/top-ten-differences-between-white-terrorists-and-others.html.

Inequality: A Burden Shared by All

Neuman, S. B. (2013). The American dream: slipping away?. *Educational Leadership, 70*(8), 18-22.

Garcia, M., & McDowell, T. (2010). Mapping social capital: A critical contextual approach for working with low-status families. *Journal of marital and family therapy, 36*(1), 96-107.

Cherlin, A. (2008). Should the government promote marriage. In J. Goodwin & J. M. Jasper (Eds.), *The Contexts Reader* (pp. 55-61). W. W. Norton & Company, Inc.

Family: Sorting Out the Pushes and Pulls

Marks, J. L., Lam, C. B., & McHale, S. M. (2009). Family patterns of gender role attitudes. *Sex roles, 61*(3-4), 221-234.

O'Neal, J. (2014). Swallowed up by life. In S. Torres, Jr. (Ed.), *Palabra: The Book of Living Essays* (pp. 166-175). Sacramento, CA: Petraglyph Publishing.

Faure, V. (2000). Carol, Anna and Khadia: Work with a three generation black family. In H. Martyn (Ed.), *Developing Reflective Practice: Making Sense of Social Work in a World of Change* (pp. 169-176). Bristol, UK: The Policy Press.

References

Adler, J. (2009). What's race got to do with it? Newsweek. Retrieved from _____

Anonymous (n.d.) *Why English is hard to learn.* In R. Nordquist, *Plural forms of English nouns: The lighter side of English plurals.* Retrieved from http://grammar.about. com/od/basicsentencegrammar/a/Engpluralspoem.htm

Bassham, G., Irwin, W., Nardone, H., & Wallace, J. M. (2011). *Critical thinking: A student's introduction* (4th Edition). New York, NY: McGraw-Hill.

Bernacki, E. (2002). *Exactly what is "thinking outside the box"?* Retrieved from http://www.canadaone.com/ ezine/april02/out_of_the_box thinking.html

Browne, M. N., & Keeley, S. M. (2010). *Asking the right questions: A guide to critical thinking* (9th Edition). Upper Saddle River, NJ: Pearson Prentice Hall.

Chapman, G., Cleese, J., Idle, E., Gilliam, T., Jones, T., & Palin, M. (Writers), & Gilliam, T., & Jones, T. (Directors). (1975). *Monty Python and the Holy Grail* (Motion Picture). United States: Twentieth Century Fox.

Cooper, S., & Patton, R. (2007). *Writing logically, thinking critically* (5th Edition). Upper Saddle River, NJ: Pearson.

Diestler, S. (2009). *Becoming a critical thinker: A user-friendly manual* (5th Edition). Upper Saddle River, NJ: Pearson.

Hartigan, J., Jr. (2010). What does race have to do with it? Making sense of our 'national conversation' [The Chronicle of Higher Education website].
Retrieved from https://sacct.csus.edu/bbcswebdav/pid-2482331-dt-content-rid-10097644_1/ courses/2173-SOC801-34069/What%20Does%20Race%20Have%20to%20Do%20With%20It_% 20-%20The%20Chronicle%20Review%20-%20The%20Chronicle%20of%20Hig.pdf?target=blank

McKay, T. (2000). *Reasons, explanations, and decisions: Guidelines for critical thinking.* Cengage.

Nosich, G. M. (2005). *Learning to think things through: A guide to critical thinking across the curriculum* (2nd Edition). Upper Saddle River, NJ: Pearson Prentice Hall.

Notar, C. E., & Padgett, S. (2010). Is "think outside the box" 21st century code for imagination, innovation, creativity, critical thinking, intuition? *College Student Journal, 44*(2), 294–298.

Paul, R., & Elder, L. (2004 & 2009). *The miniature guide to critical thinking: Concepts & tools.* Sonoma, CA: Foundation for Critical Thinking.

Paul, R., & Elder, L. (2014). *Valuable intellectual traits [Foundation for Critical Thinking website].* Retrieved from http://www.criticalthinking.org/pages/valuable-intellectual-traits/528Sweet, C., Blythe, H., & Carpenter, R. (2013). Teaching creative thinking and more. *NEA Higher Education Advocate, 30*(4), 6–9.

Quality Matters. (n.d.). QM rubrics and standards. Retrieved from https://www.qualitymatters.org/qa-resources/rubric-standards

Sagan, C., Druyan, A., & Soter, S. (Writers), & Malone, A. (Director). (1980). Persistence of memory [Television series episode]. In Carl Sagan Production (Producer), *Cosmos.*

Thinking like a genius—Problem solving: Creative solutions (n.d.). *Study Guides and Strategies.* Retrieved from http://www.studygs.net/genius.htm

University of Rhode Island. (2014). Mentor-from-the-middle. *Student Learning, Outcomes Assessment and Accreditation.* Retrieved from http://web.uri.edu/assessment/mentor-from-the-middle

CPSIA information can be obtained
at www.ICGtesting.com
Printed in the USA
BVOW09s2338180118
505693BV00002B/19/P